Fulfilling the Pledge

Fulfilling the Pledge

Securing Industrial Democracy for American Workers in a Digital Economy

Roger C. Hartley

The MIT Press
Cambridge, Massachusetts
London, England

The MIT Press would like to thank the anonymous peer reviewers who provided comments on drafts of this book. The generous work of academic experts is essential for establishing the authority and quality of our publications. We acknowledge with gratitude the contributions of these otherwise uncredited readers.

This book was set in Stone Serif and Stone Sans by Westchester Publishing Services. Printed and bound in the United States of America.

Library of Congress Cataloging-in-Publication Data

Names: Hartley, Roger C., author.
Title: Fulfilling the pledge : securing industrial democracy for American workers in a digital economy / Roger C. Hartley.
Description: Cambridge, Massachusetts : The MIT Press, [2024] | Includes bibliographical references and index.
Identifiers: LCCN 2022061533 (print) | LCCN 2022061534 (ebook) | ISBN 9780262547130 (paperback) | ISBN 9780262377355 (epub) | ISBN 9780262377348 (pdf)
Subjects: LCSH: Collective bargaining—United States. | Labor unions—United States. | Industrial relations—United States. | Labor laws and legislation—United States.
Classification: LCC HD6508 .H295 2024 (print) | LCC HD6508 (ebook) | DDC 331.890973—dc23/eng/20230112
LC record available at https://lccn.loc.gov/2022061533
LC ebook record available at https://lccn.loc.gov/2022061534

10 9 8 7 6 5 4 3 2 1

To Clinton Bamberger and Florian Bartosic

Contents

Preface

The title *Fulfilling the Pledge* tries to capture the theme of this book—namely, that as a nation, we have yet to fulfill the pledge made in the 1935 National Labor Relations Act (NLRA) to fulsomely support workers' efforts to bring industrial democracy to their workplaces. Efforts to keep that pledge during these early decades of the twenty-first century have confronted a dilemma. Workers need the protection of collective workplace representation, perhaps now more than ever. But the digital workplace is reshaping the hierarchical post–World War II industrial systems that for decades deployed collective bargaining to provide workers a voice. The structural changes that increasingly define the modern workplace invite one to ponder the future efficacy of collective bargaining. Does it remain realistic, or even desirable, for our labor relations legal regime to continue a policy that government will assist workers in large numbers to achieve through collective bargaining an effective voice in setting their conditions of employment? And, if so, what course of action is best calculated to secure industrial democracy for American workers in a digital economy?

There is a certain irony that these questions are becoming prominent now, since 2022 marked the milestone seventy-fifth anniversary of the 1947 Labor Management Relations Act (Taft-Hartley Act), the Republican-majority eightieth Congress's bold effort to weaken the pro-union 1935 NLRA.[1] Taft-Hartley's platinum anniversary should provide Americans no cause for jubilee. The seventy-five-year reign of the Taft-Hartley legal regime has witnessed an unprecedented contraction in the number of union-represented workers in the US, resulting in millions of American working people today attempting to cope with the hazards of a globalizing and deindustrializing economy with no access to the economic leveling potential of collective workplace representation.

This confluence of the Taft-Hartley Act's anniversary and the contemporary absence of the economic booster of collective power for most American workers calls for sober reflection. On the one hand, the Taft-Hartley Act added significant restrictions on workers and their representatives—changes that were calculated to assist employers in resisting unionization. But Taft-Hartley also confirmed the pledge, first made in the 1935 NLRA, that industrial democracy would remain a mainstay, a cardinal goal, of our national labor policy.[2] In 1947, Congress reaffirmed that "[i]t is hereby declared to be the policy of the United States [to encourage] the practice and procedure of collective bargaining and [protect] the exercise by workers of full freedom of association [and] self-organization." Yet seventy-five years after national labor policy renewed its pledge to "encourage and protect" workers' aspirations for industrial democracy, workplace representation remains beyond the reach of many millions who desire it.[3]

This book clarifies why collective bargaining can continue to prosper in our emerging digital economy and, thus, why it is not too late to redeem the pledge to support American workers' aspirations for a meaningful voice in setting their conditions of employment. The book also makes the case for why it is in the national interest for the American public to rally in support of a return to a robust system of workplace collective representation, which can be made possible only through labor law reform.

Introduction

National Labor-Management Relations Policy in Shambles

As we move beyond the seventy-fifth anniversary of the 1947 Taft-Hartley amendments to the National Labor Relations Act (NLRA), we find that American labor relations law is in shambles. Congress has been unable to enact labor law reform and, due to the US Senate's filibuster rules, enacting comprehensive labor law reform will continue to be a challenge.[1] Without legislative reform, we seem stuck, saddled with widely divergent views regarding our national labor policies and the role of the federal government in labor-management relations. Vacillation in our labor laws, tilting in either a pro-worker or a probusiness manner, has become the norm, with the meaning of our labor laws increasingly determined by which party won the most recent presidential election.[2]

This book addresses the disarray in contemporary American private-sector labor relations law in the context of the digital economy in which contemporary labor law must operate. The chapters that follow confront the fundamental question of whether the pledge of meaningful access to industrial democracy for American workers, first made in 1935 with enactment of the NLRA and later confirmed in the 1947 Taft-Hartley amendments, has become (and perhaps always was) just "an old dog that won't hunt"—a colloquial expression common in the Ozarks and elsewhere that refers to anything, especially a plan or idea, that won't work or is destined to fail. "It looks good on paper, but that dog won't hunt."[3]

A Vote for Optimism

The thesis of this book is optimism. To be sure, the NLRA's 1935 pledge to American workers to provide an effective means to secure collective empowerment and economic democracy remains unfulfilled.[4] But it is not too late to keep this pledge.[5] Legislative reform *can* reinvigorate the law in ways that provide workers who desire union representation the ability to obtain it far more readily than is currently possible. In this respect, I dissent from those who argue that in this digital age, "we need to scrap the National Labor Relations Act and start over from a clean slate."[6] The NLRA needs to be reformed, not scrapped. Moreover, such legislative reform is politically feasible if a sufficiently broad-based public constituency for reform can be assembled. And finally, such a constituency can be assembled if Americans are patiently and carefully shown why support for labor law reform is in the national interest. The challenge is to demonstrate in a convincing way that by reinvigorating the practice and procedure of collective bargaining, labor law reform holds the great promise of providing "America's working people . . . an inclusive and broadly shared economic prosperity [as] promised by the New Deal."[7] Political rhetoric will not suffice. Rather, it will be necessary to clarify, in ways that people can understand, exactly why and how American society will benefit from a rising public clamor for legislative labor law reform.[8] What are the pathways for building such a constituency for reform?

In order of priority: the first step is determining whether there is a substantial demand for union representation. If labor union representation is declining because American workers have turned away from unions and do not want them, why waste time and energy on labor law reform? However, what if the evidence substantiates (as it does) that workers in large numbers desire union representation but are unable to obtain it? That places the problem of declining union density in a far different light. Assembling the facts with respect to nonunion workers' unsatisfied desire for union representation is job one.

Second, even if workers desire union representation but are unable to obtain it, so what? Why should we care? Lots of people have desires that they are unable to achieve. How, if at all, is the inability to obtain union representation different from other unsatisfied desires? Persons of good will and possessing a reasonably open mind need to be carefully shown the societal costs associated with a declining union movement—costs borne by all of us, including those who are never likely to want or need union representation themselves. In other words, what do unions do that is of such great social value that a diminished labor union movement seriously weakens us as a society? Congress of Industrial Organizations (CIO) president

Walter Reuther understood the linkage between labor law reform and average Americans' understanding of unions' contribution to the public good when he maintained that "labor law reform would eventually come when the public realized and began to appreciate the role labor had played in pressing for progressive legislation."[9] The economist Joel Rogers has made a similar point, reasoning that "even to get discussion . . . going, reform must come to be seen as something in the general interest of the society. Its agent must be seen as the agent of the general will."[10] And, there is so much that unions do to contribute to a healthy economy and a just society. While the important societal role of unions may be self-evident to some, most Americans don't have a clue. For comprehensive labor law reform to become a reality, it is necessary to stimulate public awareness about how unions serve the economic and political interest of the US.

Finally, if the evidence substantiates that there is an unsatisfied demand for union representation, and if the inability to obtain union representation imposes unacceptable levels of societal cost, then what is the cause? Why clamor for labor law reform unless the decline in the rate of union representation can be linked to the current labor relations rules that structure workers' ability to organize and negotiate a collective bargaining agreement? Americans are a pragmatic people. Before they will agree to support labor law reform, they demand to be shown, and convinced, *exactly* how the current legal rules impede the fulfillment of the promise of industrial democracy—how they deprive millions of workers of a realistic ability to obtain a meaningful voice at the workplace through union representation, and how labor law reform is likely to make a difference. The following chapters carefully assemble the harvest of available empirical evidence that documents the negative impact of our current labor laws on workers' ability to freely choose union representation and obtain rights under a negotiated collective bargaining agreement. What follows demonstrates how relatively modest labor law reforms can reverse the decades-long contribution of the current NLRA provisions in facilitating the quest by many employers to remain, or become, union free through a combination of overtly illegal conduct and supposedly "lawful" intimidation. My claim is not that the law is the entire reason for the decline of collective bargaining at the American workplace, but rather that it is enough of the problem to warrant labor law reform.

In short, this book makes the case that our current labor relations scheme contributes significantly to an unmet demand by American workers for union representation and collective bargaining, and the continuation of this unmet demand harms us all. How activists might deploy the clarity that this book provides to organize a mass movement demanding labor law reform is beyond the scope of this text, and frankly beyond my expertise as a labor law professor and former labor law practitioner.

But there is reason for optimism. The Taft-Hartley Act's platinum anniversary has become a time of renewal on a broad scale as the economic inequality and other problems confronting workers increasingly have moved from the periphery of the public debate to the center. Through grassroots activism, workers are mobilizing and worker engagement is rising at levels not seen in decades. It may be, as has been suggested, that "the [COVID-19] pandemic has served to magnify all sorts of American deficiencies and pathologies," focused new attention on the lives and challenges of working people, and unleashed bottled-up grievances.[11] For example, private-sector union members are authorizing strikes at a rate rarely seen in postindustrial America, the beginning, perhaps, of "a moment with the flavor of 1945, the beginning of a period of massive strikes."[12] In addition, while the level of unemployment assistance during the pandemic was remarkable, "at least 9 million Americans thrown out of work by the pandemic . . . didn't receive any unemployment benefits." Accordingly, in 2021, tens of thousands of jobless mobilized, lobbying for an overhaul of the nation's unemployment assistance system.[13] The COVID-related mass walkouts at Amazon distribution centers, the first-ever unionization of an Amazon warehouse when workers at the company's Staten Island fulfillment center voted to unionize, teacher strikes in West Virginia, Colorado, Kentucky, Oklahoma, and Arizona, strikes at Tyson and other meat-processing plants, and the "Fight for $15" minimum-wage protests by restaurant servers and other low-wage workers all point to an increasing level of organizing intensity against the "prevailing regime of low-wages, minimal benefits, and a lack of rights and dignity at work."[14] "Walkouts are becoming a tactic in the non-unionized U.S. video game sector" as employees "protest years of alleged abuse at [software] studio[s]."[15] The high point of corporate insensitivity may have occurred two weeks before Christmas in 2021. The chief executive of Better.com, Vishal Garg, impersonally gathered 900 nonunion employees *on a Zoom call* and announced that they were all fired, effective immediately. Along with a one-month severance, the company provided each of them a trophy, a certificate, and a company T-shirt. The resulting outrage and backlash were swift and powerful—so much so that the corporate board called for an immediate investigation of its leadership and culture and announced that Garg was being forced to "take time off."[16]

With the economy recovering following the worst of the pandemic and the demand for workers increasing, "some workers have begun to reconsider their options, looking beyond low-paying, poor-quality jobs that put their health at risk."[17] It has been suggested that the contemporary "configuration of crisis and mobilization targeting the country's largest firms recalls the 1930s, though . . . without legal or other institutional changes at the federal level, [so that] translating this activity into growth in union density or coverage will be difficult."[18] Fair enough. But this much is clear: to transform this energy and activism into a coalition that can bring about change that makes union representation and collective bargaining realistic aspirations for working people, it is useful to articulate to willing listeners a straightforward explanation of what responsible labor law reform looks like and why labor law reform that responds to the realities of the modern workplace ought to be a national priority. This book is my best effort to make that case.[19]

I The Unsatisfied Demand for Union Representation and the Costs of a Declining Union Movement

1 What Do Workers Want?

If workers do not desire union representation and the system of collective bargaining that unions provide, then there is no point in investing the political capital necessary to reform the rules for obtaining union representation. Two data sets might lead one (erroneously, as it turns out) to conclude that American workers lack a strong interest in union representation. The first is the current rates of union membership and union representation at the workplace and the steady decrease in those percentages over the past fifty years. The second data set is the steady decline in union-organizing activity, as evidenced by the dwindling number of National Labor Relations Board (NLRB) union representation elections conducted and the declining number of employees who participate in these elections. A necessary starting point is a close examination of this data.

The Decrease over Time in Rates of Union Membership and Union Representation

In 2021, fourteen million wage and salary workers in the US economy were members of labor unions. That total represented 10.3 percent of all US wage and salary workers, full time and part time (the union density rate).[1] The union density rate among *private-sector employees* in 2021 was 6.1 percent, a slight decrease from 2020. See table 1.1 for more details.

Unions have a greater impact on the work lives of US workers than is evidenced by union membership alone because more workers than just union members are represented by unions. The reason is that unions represent all employees, members and nonmembers, in the bargaining units where they hold representational rights. In 2021, altogether, approximately 15.8 million

Table 1.1

Union affiliation of employed wage and salary workers, 2019–2020 annual averages

2020					2021				
	Members of Unions		Represented by Unions			Members of Unions		Represented by Unions	
Total Employed	Total	Percent of Employed	Total	Percent of Employed	Total Employed	Total	Percent of Employed	Total	Percent of Employed
All Sectors of the Economy									
132,174	14,253	10.8	15,939	12.1	136,393	14,012	10.3	15,802	11.6
Private Sector									
111,542	7,080	6.3	8,018	7.2	115,767	7,030	6.1	8,055	7.0

Note: Numbers are in thousands.

Source: Bureau of Labor Statistics: Union Membership (updated January 20, 2022)

wage and salary workers (11.6 percent) were represented by labor unions. And in the private sector, 8.1 million wage and salary workers (7.0 percent) were union represented (see table 1.1). In short, the decline in the union density rate needs to be kept in perspective. Union density is declining, but in the private sector, as well as overall, there remain millions of workers today who have chosen to become and remain union members, and even more who are represented by unions. With this extensive level of demand, it simply is unsustainable to argue that, as a general proposition, American workers have turned away from unions and show little interest in union representation. However, as can be seen in table 1.2, there is no denying that union density and the number of private-sector workers covered by collective bargaining agreements, while currently substantial, have been dropping gradually but relentlessly for decades. For example, table 1.2 shows union density among nonagricultural private-sector employees from 1973 to 2021. That union density level was 24.6 percent in 1973, 16.8 percent in 1983, 11.3 percent in 1993, 8.3 percent in 2003, and 6.8 percent in 2013, and by 2021 it had fallen to 6.1 percent. Between 1977 and 2021, total private-sector nonagricultural employment rose from 64.7 million to 114.7 million, an *increase* of 77 percent. Meanwhile, during this same period of rising levels of private-sector employment, the number of private-sector nonagricultural employees covered by collective bargaining agreements dropped from 15.37 million to 8.01 million, a decline of 48 percent.[2]

It should be noted—and this will become increasingly important as these statistics are more carefully evaluated in later chapters—that the decline over time in union density has not been uniform. The number of nonagricultural, private-sector union members held steady at roughly between 14.5 and 15 million from 1973 to the end of the 1970s, but beginning in the early 1980s, the rate of union membership began a precipitous decline that has continued to the present. See table 1.2 for more details. This rapid decline in union density coincides with increasingly aggressive, no-holds-barred, illegal (and sometimes legal) union avoidance campaigns by employers. We'll discuss this point more later in this book.

The challenge is to determine the causes of the declining union density and collective bargaining contract coverage rates shown in tables 1.1 and 1.2. Just in the past five years, for example, there has been a decrease of roughly 400,000 in the number of nonagricultural, private-sector employees covered by collective bargaining agreements (from about 8.4 million in

Table 1.2
Union membership and contract coverage—private-sector, nonagricultural workers, 1973–2020[3]

Year	Employment	Union Members	Covered by Contract	% Members	% Covered by Contract
1973	60,643.3	14,900.0	—	24.6	—
1974	61,632.5	14,671.0	—	23.8	—
1975	59,879.4	13,135.0	—	21.9	—
1976	62,539.9	13,585.8	—	21.7	—
1977	64,718.4	14,299.0	15,374.3	22.1	23.8
1978	68,154.6	14,388.9	15,622.5	21.1	22.9
1979	69,854.8	15,077.6	16,477.7	21.6	23.6
1980	70,013.3	14,285.5	15,475.7	20.4	22.1
1981	72,931.2	13,925.1	15,147.3	19.1	20.8
1982	—	—	—	—	—
1983	71,224.8	11,933.3	13,369.0	16.8	18.8
1984	74,930.6	11,647.3	12,942.6	15.5	17.3
1985	77,044.0	11,226.8	12,409.1	14.6	16.1
1986	79,090.9	11,051.4	12,165.3	14.0	15.4
1987	80,993.0	10,825.6	11,850.3	13.4	14.6
1988	82,740.5	10,674.0	11,723.0	12.9	14.2
1989	84,504.4	10,520.0	11,555.6	12.4	13.7
1990	84,610.1	10,227.0	11,336.2	12.1	13.4
1991	83,294.2	9,908.8	10,907.4	11.9	13.1
1992	84,038.6	9,703.4	10,659.9	11.5	12.7
1993	84,977.5	9,556.7	10,453.4	11.2	12.3
1994	88,169.0	9,618.3	10,611.7	10.9	12.0
1995	90,121.0	9,400.0	10,318.2	10.4	11.4
1996	92,058.9	9,385.0	10,293.4	10.2	11.2
1997	94,705.2	9,327.0	10,215.1	9.8	10.8
1998	96,589.6	9,279.7	10,072.9	9.6	10.4
1999	98,304.4	9,376.0	10,167.5	9.5	10.3
2000	99,988.8	9,109.7	9,923.7	9.1	9.9
2001	99,921.8	9,113.6	9,869.4	9.1	9.9
2002	98,830.7	8,612.4	9,325.4	8.7	9.4
2003	101,788.9	8,440.6	9,250.1	8.3	9.1
2004	102,753.1	8,188.4	8,936.6	8.0	8.7

Year	Employment	Union Members	Covered by Contract	% Members	% Covered by Contract
2005	104,679.8	8,237.2	8,941.1	7.9	8.5
2006	106,995.1	7,964.8	8,669.5	7.4	8.1
2007	107,844.0	8,100.1	8,854.3	7.5	8.2
2008	107,178.1	8,243.3	9,057.8	7.7	8.5
2009	102,479.0	7,424.3	8,218.3	7.2	8.0
2010	102,134.4	7,082.0	7,871.2	6.9	7.7
2011	103,828.6	7,190.6	7,953.6	6.9	7.7
2012	106,238.1	7,015.8	7,825.3	6.6	7.4
2013	107,851.6	7,304.1	8,112.8	6.8	7.5
2014	110,254.9	7,345.1	8,203.5	6.7	7.4
2015	112,119.6	7,539.7	8,390.9	6.7	7.5
2016	114,357.3	7,422.4	8,415.5	6.5	7.4
2017	115,855.9	7,579.3	8,467.2	6.5	7.3
2018	117,915.8	7,555.4	8,485.3	6.4	7.2
2019	119,632.8	7,492.0	8,536.0	6.3	7.1
2020	110,489.6	7,068.0	8,004.1	6.4	7.2
2021	114,700.6	6,989.1	8,011.8	6.1	7.0

Note: Numbers are in thousands. Also, no figures were given for 1982 in the data.
Source: Barry T. Hirsch and David A. Macpherson, "Union Membership and Coverage Database from the Current Population Survey," *Industrial and Labor Relations Review,* 56, no. 2, January 2003, 349–354, last updated February 2022 at unionstats.com

2016 to 8 million in 2021). But do these reductions in union membership and contract coverage reflect a drop in demand for union representation or are other causes at work?

The Historic Drop in Union Success in NLRB-Conducted Representation Elections

One might conclude (again erroneously) that NLRB representation election data substantiate a drop in the demand for union representation, as evidenced by the reduction in the number of representation elections that the NLRB conducts annually and the number of workers voting for union representation today compared to earlier periods (see table 1.3).

Table 1.3
Union-initiated (RC) representation elections (one union)—cases closed by fiscal year (FY)

	No of Elections	No. of Elections Won by Union	Percent Won by Union	Total Employees Eligible to Vote	Total Valid Votes For	Total Valid Votes Against	Percent Voting
FY 2011	1,297	926	71.40	88,659	40,481	27,203	76.34
FY 2012	1,202	781	65.00	83,153	38,714	29,159	81.62
FY 2013	1,238	780	63.00	73,873	33,072	27,475	81.96
FY 2014	1,260	857	68.00	85,530	39,969	27,701	79.12
FY 2015	1,490	1028	69.00	91,874	45,124	29,886	81.64
FY 2016	1,299	935	72.00	73,982	36,716	22,878	80.55
FY 2017	1,193	847	71.00	79,750	37,631	26,806	80.80
FY 2018	1,055	728	69.00	73,109	33,889	22,224	76.75
FY 2019	1,059	741	70.00	64,812	31,290	21,225	81.03
FY 2020	827	538	65.00	51,127	26,423	14,630	80.30
FY 2021	840	513	61.00	48,037	20,453	12,664	69.00

Source: *NLRB Annual Election Reports* (2011–2021)[4]

Particularly striking is that the number of union-initiated elections (RC elections) in FY 2020 (October 2019 to September 2020) dropped to below 1,000 for the first time since the enactment of the National Labor Relations Act (NLRA) in the late 1930s.[5] NLRB FY 2021 representation election data also are grim for unions, as table 1.3 shows.

But some caution with respect to FY 2020 and FY 2021 NLRB election data is warranted, as these two fiscal years most likely are outliers for several reasons. First, they cover periods during which the COVID-19 pandemic was at its zenith, so organizing inevitably suffered. Moreover, Peter Robb was the NLRB general counsel during FY 2020 and part of FY 2021. It has been persuasively argued that "Robb's mission in accepting the General Counsel job wasn't just to reverse Obama Board decisions and create pro-management precedent. It was to destroy the agency as we currently know it."[6] That would have been in keeping with the attitude of President Donald Trump's administration toward the NLRB. The agency reportedly lost over a quarter of its field staff during the Robb years as a result of a policy of "refusing to hire the manpower necessary to enforce federal labor law across the country."

Moreover, during the period between 2017 and 2020, the NLRB reportedly lost 10 percent of its *entire full-time staff* (both regional offices and in Washington). Robb offered buyouts to experienced staff, refused to hire replacements for those lost to attrition, and left many regional offices with a critical depletion in key leadership positions. None of this was due to lack of funds. Indeed, the inspector general investigated why Robb and the leadership of the Trump NLRB failed to spend millions of dollars, a decision that a former NLRB member who now represents management has described as "not good for employers, unions, and individual employees who come before the agency."[7]

In addition to creating a staffing crisis aggravated by the refusal to spend congressionally appropriated funds, the Trump-appointed Republican NLRB suspended all representation elections for a period of time in the spring of 2020, thereby creating another obstacle that thwarted workers' ability to obtain union representation during FY 2020. During the early months of 2020, "more workers petitioned for union representation elections . . . than they had [during a comparable period] during any year since 2016."[8] The stated justification for this nationwide suspension of NLRB-conducted representation elections was a response to safety concerns created by the COVID-19 pandemic, but the NLRB did not need to suspend these elections. Over 100 elections were suspended, including in scenarios when all the parties were prepared to proceed by mail ballot. Instead of requiring employees to vote at the work site, the NLRB could have conducted safe, efficient elections during FY 2020 through the use of mail ballots. It has been estimated that the suspended representation elections affected 17,000 workers seeking to unionize.[9] The House Committee on Education and Labor has concluded that even after the nationwide suspension of NLRB representation elections was lifted, the NLRB continued to suspend individual elections "in order to consider limiting the use of mail ballots."[10] Had there been no pandemic and no suspension of NLRB representation elections, or if the NLRB had been more generous in permitting voting by mail, the union-organizing momentum that was documented during the early months of 2020 might well have continued and resulted in a resurgence of union election victories in FY 2020.

Setting aside FY 2020 and FY 2021 as outliers, table 1.3 shows that from FY 2011 to FY 2019, unions won approximately 70 percent of RC representation elections—representation elections that unions initiate. This was a dramatically higher win rate compared, for example, to 1990, when "win rates continued to hover below 50%."[11] Indeed, even as recently as the late 1990s, unions were winning less than half of the elections held.[12] So the more recent win rates of approximately 70 percent represent progress. And table 1.3 also shows that between 2011 and 2019, more than 335,000 nonunion workers voted to unionize in RC elections, an average over those nine years of more than 37,000 nonunion workers annually choosing unions in these elections. The progress in the win rate and the impressive number of workers choosing unionization annually need to be kept in perspective, however. It is estimated that unions would need to add 300,000 new members annually "merely to keep up with the growth of the labor force and compensate for the thousands of union jobs lost each year as a result of layoffs and plant closings."[13] The essential fact, however, is that NLRB election statistics do not substantiate any generalized lack of demand for union representation among American workers.

Moreover, NLRB election statistics substantially understate the scale and success of union organizing. Increasingly, unions are obtaining representational rights through voluntary recognition, often as a result of neutrality agreements. By one estimate, in the mid-1990s and later years, "as many as 40–50% of newly organized workers were organized outside of the NLRB system, i.e., by 'card check' or voluntary recognition by employers."[14] Professor Benjamin Sachs reports:[15]

> In 2004, for example, UNITE and HERE—the garment and hotel workers' unions—reported that 85% of their new members were organized through private agreements with employers. Between 1998 and 2002, SEIU organized more than 100,000 private-sector members through such compacts (while adding only 82,000 members through NLRB elections), and in 2006 the union relied on private agreements in 100% of its campaigns to organize janitors and security guards. Similarly, the United Auto Workers reports utilizing private agreements for a majority of its recent organizing work.

The administration of Peter Robb manifested substantial legal hostility toward neutrality agreements.[16] That changed with the advent of the Biden administration, when guidance from the NLRB clarified that prerecognition neutrality agreements are lawful, insofar as they are in accordance with the framework set out in the Obama NLRB's decision in *Dana Corporation*.[17]

In short, a considerable amount of successful union organizing is not reflected in NLRB representation election statistics because many unions obtain representational rights following the negotiation of neutrality agreements that provide unions with voluntary recognition that avoids the need for an NLRB election. Unions can be expected to resume efforts to negotiate neutrality agreements now that the legal hostility toward them by Robb has abated and the Biden-appointed NLRB general counsel, Jennifer Abruzzo, has indicated that neutrality agreements will be permitted if they meet the *Dana Corporation* standard.[18]

Since there are many factors that can explain the recent decrease in the number of NLRB-conducted representation elections and the concomitant reduction in the number of employees voting for union representation, there is no basis to conclude that a reduced number of representation elections reflects any elemental lack of interest by workers in union representation.

The "Representation Gap": Workers' Unsatisfied Desire for Union Representation

Prior to 1980, little empirical work had systematically assessed the views of American workers toward unions. That began to change following the 1977 Quality of Employment Survey, conducted by the University of Michigan for the US Department of Labor.[19] In the 1977 Quality of Employment Survey, a large nationally representative sample of workers was asked questions regarding their attitudes toward unions. Specifically, (1) workers were asked their general beliefs about unions in general; (2) nonunion workers "were asked their voting preference if a union representation election were held where they work"; and (3) unionized respondents were asked to report their satisfaction with their unions.[20] These same questions were asked again in the 1995 Worker Representation and Participation Survey, conducted under the direction of Richard Freeman and Joel Rogers.[21] The inquiry of nonunion workers about whether they would prefer to be represented by a union if given the choice was particularly critical in 1995 to ascertain whether the labor movement's substantial loss of membership, which had taken hold by then, was the result of lost interest by workers in having a voice at their workplace through union representation. In 1977, and again in 1995, "the results were quite stable across the time periods of the two surveys. Approximately one-third of the nonunion, nonmanagerial workforce indicated that they would vote to unionize if given the opportunity."[22] Freeman and Rogers labeled this unsatisfied demand for collective bargaining representation among American workers as the "representation gap."[23]

In 2017, a new, nationally representative survey of 3,015 American workers updated the 1977 and the 1995 surveys by asking the same three questions, and in particular again asking nonunion employees their preference for union representation if it were made available to them where they worked. In this most recent survey, "[n]early 50% of non-union workers said that they would vote for a union . . . which points to continued interest in unions as a voice mechanism."[24] As Thomas Kochan et al. (2019) concluded, with respect to whether nonunion workers in the sample would vote for union representation if given the choice, "[t]he answer from our survey is yes, and considerably more so today than reported in the two prior surveys [because] [b]y 2017 that percentage had increased to almost half of respondents."[25]

These 2017 survey results demonstrating nonunion workers' substantial unsatisfied desire for union representation reinforces the validity of other findings, such as a 2005 survey, that found that 57 percent of workers would vote for a union if they had the chance to do so.[26] And, in 2022, in its *Report to the President*, the White House Task Force on Worker Organizing and Empowerment reported that as of 2018, 52 percent of nonunion workers (sixty million American workers) indicated that they would vote for a union at their job if given the chance. "Support for a union in their workplace rises to 74% for workers aged 18 to 24, 75% for Hispanic workers, 80% for Black workers, and 82% for Black women workers."[27]

Additional evidence of workers' affinity for union representation can be found in answers to the question in this 2017 survey addressed to unionized respondents who were asked to report their satisfaction with their unions. Kochan et al. reported that "a strong majority (83%) of currently unionized workers said that they would vote for a union again."[28] A 2022 Gallup poll reinforces Kochan's 2017 findings with respect to union-represented workers' satisfaction with the quality of their workplace representation. In that poll, 90 percent of union members rated their union membership as "important" to them, and 40 percent rated their union membership as "very important."[29]

The evidence is compelling: "A majority of US workers today still see unions as a desirable channel to exercise voice. . . . Thus, there continues to be a large unmet demand for union representation among American workers. . . . [D]espite the decline in union representation and the political and policy hurdles for organizing today, interest in joining a union has increased considerably."[30]

2 The "Representation Gap" and the Societal Costs of Low Union Density

As discussed in the previous chapter, the "representation gap"—the unsatisfied desire among nonunion workers for union representation—increased from 32 percent in 1977 to 48 percent in 2017 and to 52 percent by 2018. That 65 percent increase in the representation gap since 1977 represents millions of nonunion workers who would choose union representation if it were available to them. This burgeoning interest among workers in gaining a voice at the workplace by securing union representation is consistent with a parallel shift in the public approval of labor unions generally. For example, in 2020, the Gallup organization reported that 65 percent of Americans viewed labor unions favorably. By 2021, that favorable view of unions grew to 68 percent. Then, in 2022, union approval grew to 71 percent, the highest public approval rating for labor unions since 1965 (nearly sixty years ago).[1] At the advent of the modern US organized labor movement in 1936, Gallup recorded a 72 percent public approval of labor unions. That favorable view of unions topped out at 75 percent in 1953 and 1957. So the current 71 percent level of public approval of labor unions is approaching an all-time high. The low point of public support for labor unions "hovered around 50%" as recently as about ten years ago (2009 through 2012).[2]

Public support for unions remains politically polarized, and yet approval of labor unions has begun to cross party lines. Gallup's 2020 survey (as shown in table 2.1) showed that 83 percent of Democrats approve of unions, as do 64 percent of independents, but Republicans also report striking rates of union approval (45 percent). These levels of public support for unions are in stark contrast to the results just a decade ago, in 2009, when 66 percent of Democrats and 44 percent of independents, but only 29 percent of Republicans, viewed unions favorably.[3] Support for unions differs, to a statistically significant degree, between women and men and among different levels of

Table 2.1
Approval of American labor unions—2020

Percentage Stating Approval of Union by Gender, Age, Education, and Political Affiliation

	Approve	Disapprove	No Opinion
US Adults	65	30	5
Gender			
Men	63	33	3
Women	67	27	6
Age			
18–34	71	25	4
35–54	63	31	6
55 and older	63	33	4
Education			
College graduate	68	29	3
Some college	62	31	6
No college	65	31	4
Political Affiliation			
Democrat	83		
Independent	64		
Republican	45		

Source: Adapted from Economic Policy Institute, "Working People Want a Voice at Work," and Megan Brenan, "At 65%, Approval of Labor Unions in US Remains High," Gallup website

education (see table 2.1). But the most striking difference is the reported support for unions among young adults (ages eighteen to thirty-four), which is much higher (71 percent) than the overall rate of approval of unions.

This rising public approval of unions is also reflected in the strong public support for comprehensive labor law reform. A survey of 1,000 likely voters that was conducted in June 2021 found that 40 percent of Republicans support the Protecting the Right to Organize Act (PRO Act), along with 74 percent of Democrats and 58 percent of independents. Overall, the poll found that the PRO Act has the support of 59 percent of likely voters.[4]

In sum, many indicators substantiate a continuing optimism that labor law reform is achievable: the introduction of the PRO Act in Congress; its majority support in the House of Representatives and broad support in the Senate; the whole-hearted support of President Joe Biden's administration for labor law reform; the majority support of the PRO Act among likely voters; and the abovementioned evidence of an ever-increasing desire for union representation among American workers and the rising public support for labor unions generally. But how can this favorable context for reform be converted to vocal citizen demand for labor law reform?

The key to labor law reform is an enlightened public that understands how such reform will benefit American society—benefit everyone, including those not represented by a union. Working with a group at Harvard University to structure labor law reform proposals that can gain broad political support, Sharon Block (2020) has persuasively argued that "labor law [is] a dynamic intellectual field, poised on the brink of change." But she also cautions, "What it will take to move any labor law reform is a big political moment and a compelling narrative that reform will make meaningful changes in people's lives."[5] The leadership of the AFL-CIO has come to a similar conclusion—that the essential precondition for labor law reform is a widespread understanding of the linkage between labor law reform and its positive impact on the lives of everyday Americans.[6] Advocates of reform must work to build a national consensus that collective bargaining is essential for the economic and political health of American society—not just for those represented by a union at their workplaces, but also to the larger society, most of whose members will never be represented by a union. And the American public must come to understand that without labor law reform, the practice and procedure of collective bargaining increasingly will atrophy, sentencing millions of American workers to cope with a globalizing and deindustrializing economy on their own, without the economic booster of collective power at the workplace.

Americans can be excused if they are unsure of what unions do, how and why collective bargaining is socially beneficial, and therefore what assigned societal functions of unions justify their existence and earn their right to broad public support. Survey data show that a great number of Americans share an uncertainty regarding the nature of American unions, their role in society, and the societal contributions that a flourishing labor movement would be able to deliver. For example, a 2018 survey of nonunion members "found that 56% of respondents said joining a union would make their life better. But, when asked why they had not joined a union, 57% said they did not know or had never considered it."[7] Mounting evidence shows that "misperceptions abound, particularly among young professionals, about what the labor movement is and why it is relevant to them."[8] The success of labor law reform requires public education that informs a broad spectrum of people about what unions do, how the labor movement benefits us all, and specifically, how a robust collective bargaining process, made possible by a healthy labor movement, benefits both those represented by unions and the larger society.

Acknowledging Historical Ambivalence about Labor Unions

Persuading large segments of the public that a reenergized labor movement will make meaningful changes in people's lives and contribute to the public good requires surmounting the American public's historic ambivalence with respect to labor unions. It is a mistake to ignore this historic reality.

During the colonial period, most of Britain's American colonies initially made strikes and concerted action by workers illegal.[9] That negative attitude toward the collective activity of workers was manifested during the early decades of the nineteenth century in common-law criminal conspiracy cases.[10] In its most rigid form, the criminal conspiracy doctrine held that unions were themselves criminal organizations.[11] Even as later moderated, the rule made criminal any combination of employees to achieve either an unlawful object or to achieve a lawful object by means considered unlawful.[12]

The early criminal conspiracy cases reveal societal ambivalence concerning unions' societal role. This ambivalence is documented in the political and economic claims made by union proponents and the rhetoric of the judicial reaction to the criminal conspiracy litigation.

During the criminal conspiracy trials, workers and their allies advanced four related claims for privileging the assertion of group interests through worker combinations. First was the societal interest in *fractionalization of power*—namely, that unions are necessary to advance the collective interests of workers and to resist the demands of individuals, other groups, and society as a whole.[13] The political system, it was argued, encourages and relies upon pluralism, and "in view of the multitude of organizations existing in other walks of life, it is tyrannical to deny workers the right to combine."[14]

Second, was the *societal interest in industrial democracy*. The participation of workers in the government of the workplace helps free them from the emasculating and dehumanizing effects of work and is as important to freedom as is political democracy.[15]

The third claim supporting the case of a public interest in permitting worker combinations focused on the *permanent want resulting from the impotence of workers' bargaining power as individuals*. It is a mockery, proponents argued, to suggest that "a solitary poor workman shall resist a wealthy and powerful combination of masters." Only [a] combination [of workers] can assure "a contestation where one side endeavours to get as much wages for lawful labour as it can; the other, to get as much labour for as little money as it can."[16]

Finally, worker combinations claimed a *stabilizing role*. Adequate representation and compensation would attract skilled artisans to a community, thereby increasing the "stock of industry, population, and revenue"; conversely, repressive prosecutions deprive the law of "dignity and efficacy . . . and tend to make the law feared, but not respected."[17]

Early American law and culture largely refused to privilege workers' right to act in combination to advance their group interests.[18] In contrast to the arguments advanced by union proponents, the nineteenth-century courts perceived four competing sets of values supporting society's right, and need, to contain employee collective activity. The first was the employer's property right to manage and control his business; the second was the individual employee's right to sell his labor as he chooses and to associate or not associate as he chooses; the third was the need to control private groups (factions) that create a threat to political stability by gaining control through the power to withhold labor; and the fourth was the need to preserve the economic well-being of the nation by protecting commerce from the uncompetitive impediments of high wages and industrial instability in portions of the country, and by protecting the community from union monopoly power over wages and prices contrary to the natural forces of a free market.[19]

The criminal conspiracy cases thus introduced two recurring themes that permeate American labor law and policy debate to the present time. As Neal Chamberlain (1958) observed, even among those who might have agreed with the public interest claims justifying worker collective action, two questions remained: what should the power of the group be as it affected the individual, and what should be the role of the group as it affected society at large?

The transition from the nineteenth-century view that worker combinations are criminal to the eventual recognition that worker groups are legitimate and privileged to assert group interests was slow but inexorable. The emergence of business unionism and recognition of the need for unions as a countervailing force in a highly organized industrial economy both significantly influenced societal acceptance in the 1930s of the right of workers to engage in concerted activity for their mutual aid and protection and also have shaped attitudes with respect to unions' assigned societal role at present.

The Rise of Business Unionism

Union representation of workers through collective bargaining had coexisted with political action and the cooperative movements during the first three-quarters of the nineteenth century. Yet, by the end of the nineteenth century, "skilled craftsmen, finding they could improve their own conditions by trade union action, separated themselves from the unskilled whose bargaining power was weak and who consequently looked to politics and social reform for amelioration."[20] Many national unions soon developed, and by the end of the century, 120 were in existence.[21] The new union movement, "centering in the American Federation of Labor, was based upon the conviction that it was preferable to eschew long-range reforms and concentrate upon immediate gains. It thus committed itself to an acceptance of the wage system . . . and sought only to improve the lot of its members within that system."[22]

With business unionism came the predominance of collective bargaining as the preferred strategy. The labor agreement "led the way from an industrial system that alternatively was either despotism or anarchy to a constitutional form of government in industry."[23] While distrustful of government regulation, the national unions undertook political action when their freedom of economic action was threatened. Thus, by the beginning of the twentieth century, the American Federation of Labor (AFL) and its state federations routinely introduced legislation protecting the legal status of unions, and in 1906, the AFL began seeking to influence federal elections. Political action had also become an essential part of unionism.[24]

Thus, by the beginning of the twentieth century, the unions had begun to mature. As Summers (1979) describes, "Workers were to achieve a voice by forming strong independent trade unions, the economic strength of which would compel employers to listen."[25] Yet unions' societal role as representatives of workers' collective voice could not mature fully until the unions' social value was more fully and widely understood and honed to a point of public acceptance. This had not yet happened.

Recognition of Unions as an Essential Countervailing Force

Societal acceptance of labor unions rose as American society recognized the need for unions as a countervailing force to emerging corporate power. By the end of the nineteenth century, according to Dulles (1963), "[t]he corporation became the accepted form of business organization . . . and a complacent government and complacent courts, wedded to the economic doctrine of laissez faire, gave free rein to policies that rapidly created a concentration of economic wealth and power that the country had never before known."[26] During this period, rule-making and administration were considered the exclusive prerogatives of management. Summers (1979) continues, "Insistence by workers for a voice in management decisions was a violation of property rights and the moral order."[27] Labor law reinforced this moral order and maintained the social structure through new doctrines barring the assertion of both individual and collective employee rights.

One of these doctrines was the employment at will doctrine. By the end of the nineteenth century, the dominant American rule was that a general or indefinite hiring is prima facie a hiring at will. While the doctrine has been significantly eroded in many jurisdictions, it remains the common law rule in many states.[28] As an often-quoted Tennessee decision states, absent agreement to the contrary, an employer may discharge an employee "for good cause, for no cause, or even for cause morally wrong, without being thereby guilty of a legal wrong."[29] Accordingly, employers are free to discharge a worker without notice or cause, regardless of years of satisfactory performance.[30] The doctrine creates a legal barrier to individual employee rights at the workplace, deprives workers of even a limited measure of job security, and highlights the need for collective action as a countervailing force to corporate power.

Abandoned as individuals by law, employees increasingly relied on collective action to advance group interests. Here also, however, the courts reinforced the "moral order" that decision-making was the prerogative of management.[31] For example, departing from the English rule, the American courts granted employer requests to have employee-concerted activity enjoined if either the means or the object were found not "justified."[32] The

Sherman Antitrust Act[33] was applied by the Supreme Court in 1908 to regulate worker collective activity.[34] The court in 1921 found that a secondary boycott was an enjoinable restraint of trade in *Duplex Printing Co. v. Deering*,[35] even though Congress seemingly had exempted unions from the antitrust laws in § 6 of the Clayton Act and forbidden such injunctions in § 20.[36] Four years later, the Supreme Court held that a strike intended to prevent the movement of products in interstate commerce creates an actionable restraint of trade.[37] Finally, the US Constitution was used by the Supreme Court in *Adair v. United States*[38] in 1908 to rebuff legislative efforts to protect employee-concerted activity. Blumrosen (1959), synthesizing the reasoning of these cases, has suggested that they reflect the "constitutional blindness" of the Court toward the group interests of employees.[39] The dismantling of this negative legal environment in which unions operated required a reawakened public understanding that unions are a positive force that ought to be encouraged.

Recognition of Unions' Economic and Democratic Functions

The 1930s saw a startling shift in the attitudes toward unions. The Norris-LaGuardia Act,[40] enacted in 1932, remedied the major abuses of the labor injunction in federal courts.[41] The National Labor Relations Act (NLRA; also known as the Wagner Act)[42] was enacted in 1935. Moreover, the Supreme Court, in *Thornhill v. Alabama* (1940),[43] recognized picketing as a form of speech protected by the First Amendment to be applicable to the states through the Fourteenth Amendment. Finally, the Court held that, subject to certain exceptions, unions are substantially exempted from the antitrust laws when they engage in self-help activities.[44]

Two reasons stand out to explain this legal revolution. First, by the 1930s, there developed "a changing approach to the question of the relationship between the individual and the group with increasing acceptance of the group as the agent representative of the individual, not depriving him of liberty but guaranteeing him liberty, making his liberty real."[45]

In addition to this democratic function of representing workers' interests, both at their places of employment and within the wider society, there arose increased public awareness, due to the Great Depression of the 1930s and its concomitant economic dislocations, that only "through the organized efforts of employees to secure a fairer distribution of income [could] purchasing power . . . be sustained and the economy kept on an even keel. . . . [T]he labor union had a role to play in society . . . protective in a sense of the community welfare, of its economic prosperity."[46] In sum, by the 1930s, public opinion coalesced that unions were a necessary countervailing force to perform both democratic and economic functions.[47]

Yet society continued to manifest a fundamental ambivalence over the place of labor in a capitalistic system. According to Irving Bernstein (1969), in the period between World War I and the transformation of labor policy in the 1930s, "[e]mployers did not know whether to clutch workers to their breasts as partners in a great cooperative adventure in production or to keep them at arm's length as potential, if not present, enemies."[48] Many business leaders, endorsing the "American Plan," launched a direct and hostile attack on the union movement. Others, seeking an alternative to independent, "outside" unions, opted for various forms of "welfare capitalism"—company unions, industrial relations departments, and various types of nonunion employee representation plans.[49] While motivated to avoid outside unions, and though essentially paternalistic, these welfare capitalism plans can be seen now as a rudimentary movement in the direction of industrial democracy—providing workers at least a modicum of voice at the workplace. More fundamentally, the experiments in welfare capitalism reflected an enduring shift in social attitude. The individual in a complex industrial society is helpless, and accordingly, the group interest must be recognized. Labor unions had not yet become heir to this changing social attitude, but, in Bernstein's words, "employers who might later seek to turn the clock back would meet resistance not just from the labor movement but also from an enlightened public opinion."[50]

The welfare capitalism movement died with the Great Depression. As job standards began to erode, the basic flaw of welfare capitalism became more evident: it did not create a shop government that gave workers the means to protect their group interest at a time of serious social and economic dislocation. By the spring of 1934, it had become clear that federal legislation was needed.[51]

The Wagner Act was introduced, and a great debate over it occurred in the spring of 1935 before the Senate Labor Committee. A review of proponents' arguments, the statement of purpose in the act itself, and subsequent judicial statements concerning the purpose of the act show that four arguments prevailed in moving social policy.[52] These arguments were not novel; they were the twentieth-century endorsement of the four core nineteenth-century arguments advanced by union proponents during the criminal conspiracy trials.

Fractionalization of Power

Proponents argued that the Great Depression had been caused, in part, by an unbalanced economy, and economic stability required a more equitable income distribution. Private ordering through collective bargaining was chosen as the preferred equalizing mechanism. Proponents maintained that it produced a better national wage policy than did centralized wage determination by government, it shortened the reach of government, and it was needed as a balance in the economy against the "integration of wealth and power."[53]

Industrial Democracy

Senator Robert F. Wagner believed that workers' dignity is secured only when workers can express their group interest through freely chosen representatives. In 1932, he argued, "We can raise a race of men who are commercially as well as politically free. . . . To me the organization of labor holds forth far greater possibilities than shorter hours and better wages. Organization plants in the heart of every worker a sense of power and individuality, a feeling of freedom and security, which are the characteristics of the kind of men Divine Providence intended us to be."[54]

Subsequently, urging the adoption of the Wagner Act, he stated, "[D]emocracy in industry must be based on the same principles as democracy in government. Majority rule, with all its imperfections is the best guarantee of workers' rights, just as it is the surest guarantee of political liberty that mankind has yet discovered."[55] Wagner and others, seeing the increase of company unions as a threat to genuine industrial democracy, argued that only through majority rule, exclusive representation, and government-supervised elections could the promise of industrial democracy be fulfilled.[56]

Impotence of Individual Bargaining Power

By the 1930s, the impotence of individual bargaining power had begun to be recognized more fully.[57] Testimony before the Senate Labor Committee in 1935 noted that this impotence was exacerbated by the rule in this country stating that a worker's contract might be changed without notice at the will of the employer.[58] Accordingly, in its Statement of Findings and Policies, the Wagner Act explicitly recognized the "inequality of bargaining power between employees who do not possess full freedom of association or actual liberty of contract, and employers who are organized in the corporate and other forms of ownership association."[59] As the Supreme Court subsequently made plain, the Wagner Act was intended "to supersede the terms of separate agreements of employees with terms which reflect the strength and bargaining power and serve the welfare of the group."[60]

Stabilizing Function of Unions

Societal acceptance of collective bargaining and labor unionism was finally understood as promoting both industrial and political stability. The Wagner Act's Statement of Findings and Policies stated that the denial of the right of employees to organize and the refusal by employers to accept the practice and procedure of collective bargaining were leading causes of strikes and other forms of industrial strife or unrest.[61] Accepting this view, the Supreme Court in *NLRB v. Jones & Laughlin Steel Corporation* took judicial notice that the refusal to negotiate has been one of the most prolific causes of strife, and therefore the right to self-organization is an "essential condition of industrial peace."[62] Moreover, testimony before the Senate Labor Committee advanced the view that unions promote political stability because "organized labor in this country is our chief bulwark against Communism and other revolutionary movements."[63] When workers can express and redress their grievances, they have no inducement to overthrow the social order.

In short, unions' contemporary societal role is rooted in this history of the American labor movement. That history includes the uncontestable fact that American unions have always operated in a society that has been ambivalent concerning condoning the power that unions employ. Yet, by the 1930s, without resolving this ambivalence, public opinion approved business unionism and collective bargaining as acceptable means for workers to assert their group interest, along with political action and reform *within the existing order*. The legitimacy of labor unions and their privilege to assert group interests evolved from a gradual recognition that in a complex and highly integrated industrial society, unions are a necessary countervailing force performing for workers and society *both economic and democratic functions*.

The historical ambivalence toward unions has never fully abated, but it coexists with the competing view that unions are an appropriate and legitimate means for workers to assert group interests. These contrasting views of unions' place in American society often pull in divergent directions in terms of unions' ability to maintain a strongly positive public opinion of them. This understanding can be broadened and deepened by tracing subsequent developments that refine national labor policy, and by canvassing contemporary attitudes of unions' societal role.

Providing Unions with the Power to Perform Their Societal Functions

Labor union membership (exclusive of Canadian membership) tripled between 1933 and 1941, reflecting an expression by workers of "a surprisingly strong and militant desire to form and join unions."[64] Company unions and nonunion employee representation plans faded in the face of statutory prohibitions and a revitalized labor union movement.[65] By 1940, the sectors of the economy with the heaviest concentration of blue-collar workers—mining, construction, transportation, and manufacturing—became highly unionized as both the AFL and the Congress of Industrial Organizations (CIO) organized industrial workers.[66] Business unionism continued as the dominant model, but political action and reform efforts by labor intensified "to bring about those conditions in our economic and social life that would enable the system of free enterprise to operate successfully with the largest possible degree of social justice," according to Dulles (1963).[67]

Strong resistance to unions by business also continued, beginning from the day that Congress enacted the Wagner Act. The 1937 report of the La Follette Civil Liberties Committee documented an undeniable pattern of employer financed "labor espionage," violence, and campaigns to organize community opposition to unions.[68] The American Liberty League organized an extraordinary campaign to marshal legal opinion opposing the constitutionality of the Wagner Act. Many employers justified noncompliance with the Wagner Act based on its asserted unconstitutionality.[69] After the Supreme Court's 1937 decision holding that the act was constitutional,[70] employer groups maintained a strategy of opposition. Discrimination against employees for engaging in union activities was rampant;[71] the National Labor Relations Board (NLRB) was denounced as "public enemy number one"; pressure was mounted to restrict the Board's jurisdiction; and a litigation strategy seeking to contain both unions and the scope of protections afforded by the

Wagner Act was initiated. Moreover, proposals to amend the act were soon introduced.[72]

The World War II period had a great impact on labor union structure, labor-management relations law, collective bargaining, and Americans' view of unions. First, the War Labor Board (WLB) of World War II, created in the wake of the Depression and operated under emergency conditions, gave the reforms of the 1920s and 1930s much of their current shape. For example, the WLB gave impetus to the use of seniority to determine things such as order of layoff and assignment of job openings and adoption of the need to satisfy a "just cause" standard for discipline of workers. The grievance-arbitration machinery, found today in nearly all collective bargaining agreements, developed with the support of the WLB. These innovations provided benefits for workers and gave management much-needed stability and labor peace to take advantage of expanding markets.[73] The WLB also encouraged union security agreements. Recognizing unions' agreement not to strike during the war, the WLB granted unions maintenance of membership clauses in labor agreements, requiring employees who were members of the union to remain members for the term of the contract and to pay dues, often via checkoff provisions.[74] It refused to order closed shop or union shop clauses, but it "would approve the continuation of such clauses if they previously existed in collective bargaining agreements"; and by 1944, half of all collective bargaining agreements, covering about 6.5 million workers, contained these more effective forms of union security.[75]

World War II also profoundly influenced how Americans viewed labor and "the images created tended to carry over *after* the war."[76] The labor unrest during the last two years of World War II and in the years immediately following the end of hostilities galvanized political opposition to union power.[77] Accordingly, in 1947, Congress overrode President Harry S. Truman's veto to enact the Taft-Hartley Act.[78]

Taft-Hartley is significant both for what it did and what it did not do. On the one hand, the act can be seen as a reaffirmation of the national commitment to the practice and procedure of collective bargaining. There was no turning back from the view that workers had a right to a voice at the workplace, and the best hope to secure that voice remained with the organized group. Yet, instead of just protecting the group, labor law also placed controls on workers' collective action in the interest of dissenting individuals, other groups, and society-at-large. One of the most important changes was the introduction of the legal right to refrain from participating in concerted activities and the prohibition on unions restraining or coercing individuals who choose to exercise this right.[79] Agreements requiring union membership as a condition of hiring (the closed shop) were made unlawful. Agreements requiring union "membership" as a condition of continued employment (the union shop) were permitted but subjected to complex restrictions, including the right of states to prohibit such agreements,[80] the requirement that none could be initiated without majority vote of the affected employees, and the right of employees to revoke such agreements by majority vote.[81] Provisions permitting employees to rescind a union's bargaining authority through an NLRB-conducted election were added as well.[82]

The Taft-Hartley legislation supported the appropriateness of small bargaining units to protect groups of workers who believe that their interests conflict with the interests of those in a larger bargaining unit.[83] In short, protecting the assertion of group interests through legislation also entailed a commitment by government to mediate, through legislation, certain social conflicts thereby created.[84]

Following a mostly unsuccessful effort to repeal or amend Taft-Hartley, by 1954 the labor movement concentrated on preventing the enactment of bills that would greatly expand the Taft-Hartley controls.[85] In 1957, the Senate created a special committee, the McClellan Committee, to study improper practices among some unions and employer groups. The McClellan Committee hearings, Wellington (1968) states, "revealed extensive corruption in a small number of unions, but the hearings also resulted in a renewal of interest in unions and their appropriate role in society."[86] Following these hearings in 1959, Congress enacted the Labor Management Reporting and Disclosure Act (better known as the Landrum-Griffin Act), which provided for certain democratic procedures in union government. The arguments successfully advanced to the Congress urging enactment of these protections demonstrate that, as in 1935, unions were understood to serve the dual economic and democratic societal functions that had been articulated by unionists over 150 years earlier during the criminal conspiracy trials.

As Senator John L. McClellan stated to the Senate, strong unions serve a vital economic function, for "the individual worker in an industrial economy has little or no power, when he stands alone, to deal effectively with his corporate employer."[87] Moreover, unions add self-government to industry because only through the group and collective bargaining does the worker have an effective voice. The *Report of the Senate Committee on Labor and Public Welfare* also recognized that national labor policy had assigned unions a "vast responsibility" for the economic welfare of the workers that they represent. This function fractionalizes power by countering other private and public power.[88] Senator McClellan's statements confirmed the expanding understanding that national labor policy justifies protecting the assertion of group interests because the group serves both economic and democratic functions. Without the group, the individual would have no effective voice at the workplace and would be subject to the tyranny of superiors.[89]

National labor policy had taken a giant step in a remarkably short time. Although still ambivalent, Congress and the American public had finally settled on a somewhat abstract view of unions' assigned societal functions. Not surprisingly, this did not end the debate. Canvassing the functions that unions presently perform, and how others—the general public, union members, union and business leaders, and the academic community—view unions' societal role will clarify the contours of unions' contemporary societal functions.

Unions' Role in Suppressing the Inequality of Income Distribution

It is widely accepted that collective bargaining has historically been the unions' primary function. Collective bargaining is described by Hertel-Fernandez, Kimball, and Kochan (2020) as the "lynchpin of conventional US unions."[90] Among other things, collective bargaining includes attempting to advance the economic welfare of bargaining unit members by improving wages and benefits. Kochan's early study of data obtained from a nationally representative sample of 1,500 workers found that over 85 percent agreed that a primary benefit gained by a strong union movement was improvement of wages and benefits.[91] In 2019, Kochan and colleagues updated and expanded the inquiry of worker attitudes by examining responses from a nationally representative sample of 3,915 American workers drawn from a survey conducted by the National Opinion Research Corporation.[92] These more recent survey results confirm earlier findings. A majority of US workers today (including 80 percent of those currently represented by unions) view unions as a desirable channel "to exercise voice on the full spectrum of issues affecting how they work, how they are personally treated, [and] their compensation and working conditions"[93] Additional evidence that workers view unions primarily as a source of security at the workplace can be found in a representative survey of more than 4,000 employed American workers, showing that they are most willing to join unions and support unions financially when the union possesses legal authority to negotiate with employers over wages, benefits, and working conditions.[94]

Globalization and technological advances have changed the labor market and, to some degree, have affected workers' preferences for labor representation. For example, some leading academics have called for changes to our national labor policy to make room for alternative labor organizations that would provide workers alternative workplace governance systems commonly found in Western Europe, such as "enterprise-wide joint worker-management committees or councils" (often referred to as "works councils") and formal representation on corporate boards of directors.[95] The most recent survey evidence shows that workers value the voice provided through informal, workplace-level participation opportunities on the shop floor to improve the productivity and quality of work life, but not as a substitute for or an alternative to the ability to improve their conditions of employment through collective bargaining. Survey data show that what workers "most value," and are willing to financially support, is workplace representation by organizations that have the legal right to demand "traditional, employer-centered model of private-sector union representation emphasizing formal collective bargaining at the level of the workplace or enterprise. . . . These results suggest a significant disadvantage . . . of alt-labor organizations that do not formally bargain with employers."[96]

It should not be surprising that potential union members have made clear that collective bargaining should be the primary function of their workplace representative. There is convincing evidence of the long-run relationship between unionization, collective bargaining, and workers' economic welfare. This can be found in the vast literature that has investigated the presence and causes of substantial and continuing growth in wage and earnings inequality in the US. That body of evidence shows that "U.S. income inequality has varied inversely with union density over the past hundred years."[97]

Chad Stone and his coauthors have been tracking the inequality in income distribution for many years. In 2020, they reported their most current findings:[98] From the end of World War II until roughly the early 1970s, the American economy experienced substantial economic growth that generated a "broadly shared prosperity. . . . Up and down the income ladder [rapidly growing incomes benefited Americans] at roughly the same rate." Income disparities existed, but the "gap between those high up the income ladder and those on the middle and lower rungs—while substantial—did not change much during this period." This changed beginning in the 1970s, when there developed what Lane Windham has described as "the birth of a new economic divide"[99] and others have termed the dawn of "the new gilded age."[100] Stone et al. (2020) describe this economic divide as follows:[101]

> Beginning in the 1970s, economic growth slowed and the income gap widened. Income growth for households in the middle and lower parts of the distribution slowed sharply, while incomes at the top continued to grow strongly.
>
> The concentration of income at the very top of the distribution rose to levels last seen nearly a century ago, during the "Roaring Twenties."
>
> Wealth—the value of a household's property and financial assets, minus the value of its debts—is much more highly concentrated than income. The best survey data show that the share of wealth held by the top 1 percent rose from 30 percent in 1989 to 39 percent in 2016, while the share held by the bottom 90 percent fell from 33 percent to 23 percent.

By 2021, the high earners were "winning a[n even] bigger piece of the economic pie. . . . [T]he share of income going to the top 10 percent of the earners rose to more than 45 percent in recent years, up from about 30 percent in the 1970s."[102] "The wealthiest one percent of Americans takes home nearly a quarter of our national income and owns forty percent of the nation's wealth."[103] American workers' real wages have stagnated while executive pay has soared.[104]

Technological change, globalization, and tax policy account for some of this wage and earnings inequality, as does stagnation in the real value of the minimum wage. But after the late 1980s, especially among males, studies have shown that the decline in unionization accounts for a significant portion of the growth of wage inequality.[105] Recent research has confirmed that the decline in unionization continues to account for much of the ongoing growth in wage and earning inequality.[106] One of the most convincing examinations of the long-run relationship between unionization and workers' economic gains is the 2018 work of Henry S. Farber and his coauthors.[107] Farber et al. (2018) considered a longer time period than other studies (from 1936–2014). They examined what is referred to the "90–10 gap"—the difference in wages and earnings between those in the top ninetieth percentile and those in the lowest tenth percentile, and found that increased levels of unionization accounted for 46 percent of the decline in the 90–10 gap (reduction in income inequality) between 1936 and 1968, and decreased unionization accounted for 16 percent of its increase (expanding income inequality) between 1968 and 2014. The more recent study by Fortin et al. (2021) states that their findings of the contribution of degree of unionization to changes in income inequality "echo those of Farber et al. (2018)."[108]

In addition to increasing the 90–10 wage gap, declining unionization swelled the inequality between high-wage earners and middle-wage earners—referred to as the "90–50 wage gap" (the gap between earners at the ninetieth percentile of the wage distribution and the fiftieth percentile). Between 1979 and 2017, the 90–50 wage gap grew substantially and de-unionization accounted for one-third of that growth in the wage inequality between high- and middle-wage earners. Mishel (2021) reports, "De-unionization has this result because it depressed the wages of middle-wage earners but had little impact on high-wage earners at the 90th percentile."[109]

High rates of unionization have the direct effect of compressing (i.e., reducing) wage and earnings inequality, as Farber et al. (2018) found had occurred until 1968. The explanation is straightforward: being represented by a union results in workers earning higher wages and benefits. Unionized workers benefit from what is referred to as the "union wage premium," the percent difference between the wages of unionized workers and those of nonunionized workers. Depending on individual, job, and market characteristics, the union wage premium is in the range of 10 percent to 30 percent above the wage of nonunion workers.[110] Unions also promote pay equity: through the principle of "equal pay for equal work," unions reduce gender, race, disability, and age discrimination in pay.[111] As the rate of union representation declines, the number of workers benefiting from the union wage premium and pay equity also shrinks. Wages and earnings fall as fewer and fewer workers enjoy the economic benefits of union-negotiated collective bargaining agreements.

For the "typical" average worker, declining unionization and the associated erosion of collective bargaining from 1979 to 2017 translated into a reduction in the median hourly wage by $1.56, the equivalent of $3,250 annually for a full-time, full-year worker. It is estimated that de-unionization during this same period lowered the male median hourly wage by $2.49, the equivalent of $5,171 for a full-time, full-year male worker.

Nonunion workers also suffer from declining rates of unionization. This is because of what is referred to as the "spillover effect"—the benefit that nonunion workers gain from the unionization of other workers and the erosion of this beneficial effect for nonunion workers as fewer workers are represented by unions.[112]

Until recently, "[w]ith few exceptions, existing studies of the impact of de-unionization on wage inequality ignore[d] possible spillover effects. . . . However, it has long been recognized that union power, as measured by the unionization rate . . . may also influence wage setting in the nonunion sector."[113] This is because many nonunion employers follow the lead of unionized industrial leaders, hoping that paying wages to their nonunionized employees that approach the union wage rate will discourage workers from supporting unionization. Labor economists and sociologists refer to this as the "threat effect" of unionization.[114]

It is now well established that widespread collective bargaining has a spillover effect on nonunion wages—it increases, and in some circumstances equalizes, wages for all workers.[115] For example, had private-sector union density in 2013 remained at its 1979 level, "weekly wages of nonunion men in the private sector would have been 5% higher, equivalent to an additional $2,704 in earnings for year-round workers." Among those same workers, but without a college education, "wages would be 8% higher, or $3,016 more per year."[116] In short, as Farber and his coauthors (2018) have concluded, "a large union income premium made midcentury unions a powerful force for equalizing the income distribution. . . . [U]nions were a major force in the Great Compression [compressing wage inequality at midcentury], above and beyond what can be accounted for by [just] the direct effect of unions on union members. We . . . find that . . . unions affect . . . the income distribution beyond what can explained by their effects on union members alone."[117]

In short, labor economists and labor sociologists have provided the data for those willing to examine it. The decline in unionization is economically harmful to American society. The American middle class has stagnated and is in the process of collapsing. The economic prospects of American working people are precarious. Today, many workers survive economically "by laboring all hours of the day, juggling part-time jobs, and barely scraping by on low wages and paltry benefits. The gap between the wealthy and the poor has become a chasm."[118] Productivity has been robust over the past forty years, but with a weakened labor movement and the collapse of collective bargaining in many sectors of the economy, wages no longer rise along with productivity: the two have been decoupled. The wealthy now expropriate what previously had been workers' share of increases in the nation's total income. For example, "[f]rom 1973 to 2011, the productivity of the U.S. worker rose 80.1 percent, but wages on the average worker rose only 4.2 percent, and hourly compensation—wages plus benefits—rose only 10 percent. So, while productivity was rising close to 3 percent a year, hourly wages of the average worker, adjusted for inflation, were essentially flat, the same in 2011 as in 1978. Three decades of getting nowhere." By contrast, corporate profits have trended upward: "In 2007, before the Great Recession, corporate profits garnered the largest share of national income since 1943, while the share of national income going to wages sank to its lowest level since 1929."[119] Even as productivity continues to rise, production and nonsupervisory employees today cannot expect to earn a paycheck in real dollars as good as—or certainly not much better than—what they could have earned in the early 1970s. In what economists refer to as "backwards mobility," vast numbers of Americans collectively have left the middle class and now have a negative net worth. For example, for a record 23 percent of Americans who have died over the past five years, their net worth was nothing—indeed, somewhere below zero.[120]

As Stone (2004) describes, "[T]he working poor now comprise the fastest growing portion of the workforce."[121] The gross inequality of income and wealth in the US—vast fortunes coinciding with mass economic insecurity—divides us into classes, spawns schisms and political cleavage, undermines our ideal of opportunity by locking many into a perpetual underclass, and threatens the moral authority of our social order. Both political liberals and conservative thinkers agree that "[t]he middle class is the key to greatness in this country" and the greatest danger to American democracy is the erosion of middle-class prosperity and devolution into separate classes divided by a "wealth chasm."[122] Polling data readily demonstrate that decades of "getting nowhere and slipping backward . . . has provoked popular discontent[, with] two-thirds of Americans . . . say[ing] they see 'strong' conflicts between rich and poor, and they see economics more divisive than race, age, or ethnic grouping."[123] In addition, the erosion of middle-class prosperity, caused by job loss, the lid paced on average wages and income, and economic backsliding, is "bad not only for individuals, but for the whole economy" since these conditions erode the robust consumer demand that is the main driving force of the US economy. Companies do not invest in new technology, new plants and equipment, or hire more employees. As a result, the economy "bog[s] down in long, painful 'jobless recoveries' as has happened several times over the past thirty years." As Hedrick Smith (2012) has cautioned, "[b]y sharing so little of their [productivity] gains with their U.S. employees [corporations] have put a crimp on middle-class spending, and without big consumer demand, the nation's economy can't move well." In short, "America's wealth gap is a drag on today's economy."[124]

It is too late in the day to attempt to explain the harsh realities of workers' precarious economic position as the unavoidable and inexorable consequences of globalization, technology, free trade, and other similar elements. The reality is that globalization and technology have generated trillions in corporate profits, creating vast fortunes for a privileged few. However, middle-class Americans got left out from sharing the bounty in significant measure, at least in part because of the declining union movement.[125] The terms with which average working Americans must face their economic fate are set by shrinking access to labor unions and an increased denial of the equalizing effects of collective bargaining. Accordingly, when dealing with their employers, workers are forced to face globalization, deindustrialization, and technological change individually, denied the collective negotiating leverage provided by union representation. De-unionization accounts for much of the peril visited upon American workers by the more precarious and unequal economy that we live in today. Paul Weiler, widely regarded as one of the leading academic authorities on US labor relations law, has thoroughly examined wage and income inequality. Upon sober reflection, Weiler (2001) has concluded that "a clear factor in the huge rise in inequality within the American labor market has been the decline in union representation."[126] It would be a sad day if average Americans give up on democracy because of lost confidence in the ability to affect policy because the balance of power has shifted so extensively from the middle class to the financial and business elites.

The argument is not that a revitalized labor movement will (or can) *alone* rebuild a robust American middle class that again shares more equally in the increases in national income that come with increased productivity. More modestly, the case here is that unions have been, and again can be, equalizing institutions that ensure that *more* of the gains in productivity translate into rising wages and benefits for workers. It is preferable that unions privatize economic redistribution, instead of that role being assigned to the state, as has been the case in most Western European countries in the post–World War II period.[127] Collective bargaining is good for the US. As Weiler says, it "serves as a valuable check and balance in the workings of the labor market."[128] Everyone who believes that the best political community is one that is formed around a large and economically robust middle class should support the reform efforts needed to preserve the equalizing effects of collective bargaining.

Unions' Role in Providing Job Security and Dignity at the Workplace

The union's collective bargaining function also includes efforts to enhance job security. Job security issues are fundamentally issues of job allocation: obtaining and maintaining employment. Job allocation strategies are premised on the concept that an existing job is a property interest that ought to be protected. Collective bargaining thus has traditionally used seniority to determine things such as layoffs, rates of pay, and promotions. In this way, seniority has served as a barrier against discrimination.[129]

Employee economic security also includes protection against capriciousness, error, or arbitrariness in the application of personnel policy. Accordingly, collective bargaining entails the negotiation of contract provisions that define rights and duties and provide for participation in the administration of these provisions through the grievance-arbitration procedures now incorporated into most union collective bargaining agreements.[130] The most important job security provision that unions negotiate is a "just cause" provision for discipline and discharge. Thereby, unions, as one observer has noted, "aid in extending the rule of law to industrial establishments."[131] This function of identifying and redressing work-related injustice is widely understood as a core of unions' historic societal contributions.[132]

Finally, the collective bargaining function includes efforts to modify the work environment to make work psychologically healthier. As higher educational levels have increased expectations, and as "a hierarchical, nonparticipatory and stifling workplace environment" has increased frustrations, collective bargaining agreements have begun to include job satisfaction reforms: worker teams participating in modifying job design, internal distribution of tasks, and production methods.[133] Twenty-first-century workers expect a voice in "the full spectrum of issues affecting how they work, how they are personally treated, their compensation and working conditions, the values their organization stands for, and the products or services they help produce or deliver."[134]

In short, collective bargaining provides workers with a means to participate in "industrial democracy,"[135] which one union leader explained as "the creation of industrial constitutions."[136] A union publication has stated that the concept of industrial democracy connotes the means for employees to realize aspirations for "intellectual equality" at the workplace.[137] Phillip Murray, a former president of the CIO, succinctly summarized this aspiration in 1940 as bringing "into play the heads as well as the hands of the workers."[138] It also has been summarized as "the re-creation of the individual as a person who is respected for what he does, who feels that he is being consulted in the determination of policy, and who is kept constantly informed of what is in fact policy."[139] However it is specifically described, the rationalizing principle is widely accepted: unions are the only true vehicle for workplace democracy—as Bronfenbrenner et al. (1998) describes it, "the only means through which workers gain an independent voice regarding their daily working conditions."[140] Through such participation, workers achieve the psychological benefits of increased status and dignity.[141]

Unions' Role in Representing Workers' Interests beyond the Workplace

Beyond the workplace, unions' democratic function is to fractionalize power within the society. This dimension of a union's societal role has two components. Unions participate in setting wage policy and thereby help avoid the necessity of centralized governmental regulation. In addition, acting as a power center, unions assert group interests against other groups and the government.

Through collective bargaining, unions decentralize economic decisions by participating in the process of private ordering. The Supreme Court's 1970 decision in *H. K. Porter Co. v. NLRB*[142] is instructive. The NLRB asserted that its statutory power included ordering an employer to adopt a substantive contract term as a remedy for its refusal to bargain in good faith. No section of the Wagner Act speaks specifically to the question, and yet the Court had little difficulty rejecting the Board's position. Relying on the legislative history of both the Wagner and Taft-Hartley acts, the Court stated:

> The object of [the Wagner Act] was not to allow governmental regulation of the terms and conditions of employment, but rather to ensure that employers and their employees could work together to establish mutually satisfactory conditions. . . .

> [I]t was never intended that the Government would . . . step in, become a party to the negotiations and impose its own views of a desirable settlement.[143]

The political theory underlying this commitment to private decision-making through collective bargaining has been well documented.[144] Summers (1965) explained that "allocation of power and control to the union . . . creates centres of power and instruments of control apart from the State, which then does not become unmanageable or dangerously large. Collective bargaining shortens the reach of central legal control by establishing a separate structure of industrial government as an alternative to suffocating statism."[145] Relying on what might be termed political pragmatism, Bok and Dunlop (1970) also understood the value in unions maintaining a viable separation between the government and units of economic power: "[Otherwise,] workers might easily demand government regulation as the only practical alternative to protect their interests."[146]

Others have viewed this decentralization of economic decisions as an "axiom" around which our political system is based[147] and an "essential of democracy."[148] Professor and former NLRB chair William Gould has been outspoken with respect to the benefits of collective bargaining as a means to promote private ordering and discourage direct state regulation of conditions of employment. Gould (1996) argues:[149]

> The absence of unions and collective bargaining means that the state through legislation or common-law litigation, is more directly involved in fashioning employment conditions than the parties themselves. . . . As collective bargaining recedes, it leaves a vacuum that nature inevitably abhors. Direct state legislation, which is a substitute, is frequently inferior to the expertise that can be brought to bear on employment conditions by labor and management.

Contemporary unions are also generally understood to serve what may broadly be termed as a political representation function by fractionalizing political power. Unions seek to stabilize workers' political power by operating as a counter-lobby to that of business and as a countervailing force to protect workers from the "tremendous state power inherent in a collectivist society."[150] According to Stone (2004), by "represent[ing] millions of [working people and other disadvantaged groups] who do not have any other access to the political process, [and whose] voice . . . would remain silent and unrepresented [, unions] are an essential element of a pluralistic democracy."[151]

The strategies are varied. Unions influence appointments to the local and national governments' inner councils and administrative agencies.

When representatives of labor are needed to serve on public boards or on government advisory agencies, organized labor designates them. As Leiserson (1959) put it, "Organized labor thus [influences interests] of working people outside the ranks of union organizations as well as those within."[152] Unions also directly and indirectly influence the election of state and local political candidates and lobby to influence legislation.[153]

A profound change has taken place during the last forty years in unions' interest in national politics.[154] Today, unions routinely endorse candidates and union members contribute large amounts of time and money to influence national elections.[155] Unions operate as a pressure group within a political party, seeking to influence the party's policies, mobilize voters, and increase their members' political knowledge both by providing information directly and by encouraging discussions of politics in the workplace.[156] An important reason for this political activity is increased awareness among union leaders that collective bargaining cannot end at the plant gate; its arena must extend into both domestic and international public policy, for union and management leaders alone cannot solve the economic problems affecting workers.[157] Tax policy, interest rate levels, spending priorities, and international trade policy are but a few examples of national concerns vitally affecting workers' economic lives. The importance of union political involvement can be understood in economic terms. "Collective bargaining efforts can have only a micro effect. The vexing problems of insecurity can be dealt with only through 'macro' techniques."[158] Justice Wiley Rutledge's classic conclusion in *United States v. CIO* (1948) seems to be increasingly appreciated. To say that unions have no legitimate role in politics, he stated, is to "ignore the obvious facts of political and economic life and of their increasing interrelationship in a modern society."[159]

Unions are viewed by some as "[i]deologically conservative and narrowly self-interested, . . . oriented toward the economic advancement of those in their particular union or trade rather than toward changes in the social system for the benefit of the wider society."[160] On the one hand, members expect the union to maximize their interests and not sacrifice them "to social purpose."[161] And, of course, strictly speaking, unions cannot "legitimately claim to speak for the totality of the interests of society."[162] But the record is clear: for decades, unions have been an integral part of a social reform movement in the US. Unions have been concerned with such things as eliminating slum conditions, providing medical care for the poor and the aged, and improving education.[163] Joining grassroots groups (sometimes too late), unions have engaged in civic activism in support of the civil rights and civil liberties movements, the environmental movement, the consumer movement, the women's movement, and voting rights. Moreover, organized labor has contributed to the enactment of legislation designed to improve the standards of the general working community, principally nonunion workers.[164] In addition to civil rights laws, examples include wage and hours laws, requiring advanced notice of plant closing and mass layoffs, workplace safety and health laws, Social Security, state workers' compensation laws, protection of federal employee whistleblowers who report employer wrongdoing, limitations on use of polygraph screening of employees and drug testing, the right to inspect personnel records, bans on sexual harassment and hostile work environment, and family and medical leave provisions.[165] Indeed, it has been estimated that "three-quarters of the issues that have occupied labor's legislative energies have had no special benefit for unions or union members; they are simply general social-welfare issues."[166] As recently as the federal government's response to the COVID-19 pandemic, unions lobbied for enactment of the Coronavirus Aid, Relief, and Economic Security (CARES) Act and the Families First Coronavirus Response (Families First) Act, each of which provides emergency paid sick leave and paid family and medical leave protection for both unionized and nonunion workers.[167]

This involvement in US political life is applauded, on the theory that unless unions "perform the expanded stewardship service of improving the life the worker leads after 5 o'clock," unions will be criticized justifiably for failing to address the concerns most frustrating to workers, thereby leaving these concerns unvoiced and unknown.[168] When the labor union movement weakens, unions lose political power and thus are less able to resist efforts by conservative legislators to roll back protective laws for workers and other progressive legislation.[169] According to Edsall (1984), "Without a strong labor movement, there is no broad-based institution in American society equipped to represent the interests of those in the working and lower-middle classes in the formulation of economic [and progressive social] policy."[170]

Public opinion surveys dating from the 1950s consistently have demonstrated strong support among union members and the public at large for unions' efforts to obtain general social welfare legislation.[171] A 1977 survey found 76 percent of the almost 1,500 adults surveyed believed that most unions had served a positive social role by working for such things as "national health insurance, higher unemployment compensation, better Social Security, minimum wage laws and other desirable social needs"; only 10 percent of the respondents disagreed and 14 percent were unsure.[172] In 2021, Kochan and his coauthors surveyed a large group of workers to uncover how, if at all, their willingness to join and financially support a union would be influenced by the union engaging in political activities. They discovered that a union's engaging in electoral politics marginally reduced workers' likelihood of joining a union:

> Compared to an organization that did nothing in politics, a labor organization that [the survey] described as campaigning for pro-worker politicians in elections was less likely [by 4%] to be selected by workers. . . . than non-active ones. *By comparison, there was no penalty for organizations that lobbied for pro-worker policies.*[173]

These findings create a paradoxical result since in the current political environment, unions need to participate in electoral politics to build and sustain the political influence required to protect workers' interests. Engaging in election campaigns does not rule out achieving broad-based worker support, but doing so might be unpopular among some workers whose support a union would desire during an organizing drive. Legislative lobbying is different: in terms of willingness to join a union, workers do not penalize unions for engaging in proworker legislative lobbying.

The Need for Grass-Roots Civic Activism

In sum, unions contribute enormously to contemporary American society by performing both economic and democratic functions. Unions serve a collective bargaining function that favorably influences the redistribution of income for all workers. Unionized employees obtain enhanced wages and benefits from the union wage premium, and those not represented by a union benefit from a spillover effect from unionization. Collective bargaining reduced income inequality when union density was high and collective bargaining was widespread. To reverse the collapse of the middle class caused by wage stagnation and unconscionable wage inequality, union density and collective bargaining need a revival.

Unions also are social institutions that provide workers status at the shop and in the wider community. In addition, unions contribute to democratic ordering by fractionalizing political power. Unions avoid the need for suffocating statism by participating in the private ordering of setting wage policy and conditions of employment. And, by representing the interests of American workers beyond the workplace, unions act as a political counterweight to the influence of corporations and the state. All these contributions to a healthy economy and democratic polity require a vibrant, growing, and influential labor union movement, one that is able to reverse the free-fall descent in union density experienced over the past several decades. It has been nearly forty-five years since the veteran labor reporter Abe Raskin (1979) prophetically warned of the harm to American democracy that results from the development of an "imperial status for corporate management operating on a global scale without any semblance of countervailing power in either government or labor."[174] Raskin's warning is no less applicable today.

The challenge is to achieve a rebirth of civic activism in support of unionism by average people at the grassroots level. For a modern political crusade modeled on the civil rights and environmental movements to develop, the starting point is a change in the climate of public understanding with respect to how unions beneficially affect the everyday lives of people and, concomitantly, how the loss of the equalizing effects of collective bargaining inflicts unacceptable societal costs. The mobilization of public opinion in these directions is necessary for legislative support of labor law reform.

To this point, part I of this book has made the case that more than 50 percent of nonunion workers have an unsatisfied desire for union representation and the benefits of collective bargaining, and this denial of access to collective bargaining adversely affects the daily lives of all of us in one way or another. The primary cause of this decline in workers' access to collective bargaining has been employer intimidation of various sorts and the ineffectiveness of our legal system to provide unions and workers with the legal tools to counter it successfully. That is shown next.

3 Causes: The Revolt of the Bosses

The "revolt of the bosses"[1] began in the early 1970s, as corporate leaders in the US orchestrated a political rebellion that pushed back against what they perceived as excessive government intervention and regulation in all areas of business—a regulatory environment that they argued was "hamstringing the free enterprise system and went far beyond any restrictions placed on their foreign competitors."[2] One commentator has described this rebellion as "one of the most remarkable campaigns in the pursuit of political power in recent history."[3] Rooted in the growing appeal of the anti-union and anti-government ideology of Arizona senator Barry Goldwater in the late 1960s, this business revolt strengthened and solidified—"came to life politically"—in 1971 by "leverag[ing] the enormous advantages of corporate money and organized business power."[4] The Chamber of Commerce initially led the anti-union/antigovernment mobilization, but corporate leaders soon added hundreds of Washington lobbyists. In addition, corporate money funded the founding of think tanks "to generate policy analysis from a business perspective."[5] In 1972, the chief executives of some of the leading US corporations founded the March Group, which later merged with other conservative organizations to form the Business Roundtable (BRT). Composed of "an exclusive fraternity of the nation's most powerful and prestigious business leaders [representing] two hundred of the largest corporations, [t]he BRT had great political power, wealth, organization, and influence with the mass media." Among the BRT's primary initial objectives was curbing the political influence of labor unions. Soon after its formation, the BRT invested considerable energy and money in 1973 into defeating labor law reform pending in Congress that was designed to strengthen labor law to make it more difficult for companies to intimidate workers who want to form unions.[6]

Early Efforts to Weaken Unions by the Labor Law Reform Group

But the less-often-told backstory of corporate America's decision to create a united front of employer resistance to unionization and collective bargaining predates by nearly a decade the formation of the BRT. In 1963, there developed a "drumbeat of discontent" and a growing conviction among some of the most virulently anti-union corporate leaders and their attorneys that "being competitive in domestic and international markets required getting or remaining free of unions." To do this, it would be necessary to organize a unified effort among business executives to develop proposed statutory amendments to the labor laws. These amendments, it was argued, would "increase the ability of employers to resist unionization or, if already organized, to [limit] what must be discussed during collective bargaining], while prohibiting unions from using certain economic weapons that could strengthen their bargaining positions." In addition, these business leaders concluded that it was necessary to constrain the ability of the National Labor Relations Board (NLRB) to develop remedies that would be effective in discouraging employers from violating workers' right to organize.[7] To achieve the goals of thwarting union organizing and weakening unions' ability to bargain effectively, a small, committed group of corporate leaders from some of the country's largest corporations (many unionized), and their management attorneys, formed the Labor Law Reform Group (LLRG), later known as the Labor Law Study Group (LLSG). By 1972, the LLSG was merged into the BRT.[8]

These efforts by the LLRG/LLSG to suppress union organizing and constrict the scope of collective bargaining have had lasting effects that continue to be felt today. By 1965, the LLSG had drafted a set of twenty-three proposals to amend the Taft-Hartley Act.[9] Although Richard Nixon was elected president in 1968, he never enthusiastically supported the LLSG's legislative agenda to amend the National Labor Relations Act (NLRA) to make it more employer friendly, because at that time, Nixon needed the political support of the AFL-CIO leadership to advance the administration's policies supporting the war in Vietnam. And then a Democratic Congress was elected in the Democratic sweep in the 1974 midterm elections, and the Democrat Jimmy Carter was elected president in 1976.[10]

The work of the LLRG/LLSG nevertheless had a long-lasting impact on unions' ability to organize because of their success in manipulating public opinion to view unions negatively.[11] These antiunion employer groups concluded that in addition to drafting statutory proposals to amend the labor laws, it was necessary to manipulate public opinion to create an anti-union "climate of understanding" among the American public. Accordingly, the LLRG, along with the many corporate leaders with whom it worked, funded a sophisticated, multimillion-dollar public relations (PR) campaign orchestrated by a leading New York PR firm to shape a favorable image of big business and promote anti-union public attitudes built around allegations of union abuse of power. Among other things, the PR firm developed "case-history stories" depicting the NLRB as pro-union, business as the underdog, and unions as abusive and impeding social and economic progress to the detriment of American society. These case studies were made available for publication and used by newspapers and magazines across the country. The PR firm drafted canned anti-union editorials that were printed by many newspapers, which published "virtually identical editorials critical of [the allegedly pro-union] NLRB."[12] School textbooks were manipulated to portray unions in an unfavorable light. The PR firm drafted anti-union story outlines and assembled data that it provided to authors who were regular contributors to publications read by "idea disseminators"—teachers, librarians, college students, academics, and commentators. Scripts were written and provided to radio commentators broadcasting from 5,000 radio stations, much of it calculated to manipulate public opinion to view unions negatively.

At this time, Congress held hearings on the work of the NLRB, and most of those who testified were business leaders who were active in the above-mentioned anti-union public opinion manipulation effort. Their testimony perpetuated the theme of unions' harm to society. It was considered critical that the involvement of the PR firm, the LLRG, and the BRT not be made public. For example, the PR arm of the BRT worked closely but clandestinely with the editor of *Readers' Digest* "on a series of three articles on abuses of union power in the construction industry." Later, the BRT paid *Readers' Digest* more than one million dollars to commission a series of "advertisements" proclaiming business's great value to society, the format of which was deliberately designed to make the paid-for published material look to readers "like any other article in the magazine." The "invisible hand" of the BRT and the LLRG that worked to manipulate public opinion finally surfaced when the president of the Chamber of Commerce, for the first time, openly confirmed to the labor editor of *The Los Angeles Times* "'that the nation's major corporations and almost every major employer association [had] joined forces in a . . . concerted effort to limit the strength of labor unions.'"[13] James Gross (1995) has described the cloaked efforts to undermine public confidence in the labor movement as an example of "the most powerful corporations and trade associations in the country [having] entered into a secret alliance to change the labor laws to suit their own interest, in great part by manipulating, controlling, and even misleading public opinion [regarding the societal value of labor unions] by use of sophisticated public relations techniques."[14] He concluded that this skillful use of image shaping "has help[ed] create the American public's impression of unions as a threat to the national economy, oppressors of the rights of individual workers, and enemies of the free enterprise system."[15]

In short, the record is clear: beginning in the mid-1960s, and particularly by the mid-1970s, large numbers of unionized and nonunion employers shared a conviction that maintaining the desired level of profitability in domestic and international markets required becoming (or remaining) free of unions. As a means to achieve that goal, powerful employer groups developed sophisticated PR campaigns to smear unions as asocial institutions. And, as part of an effort to aggressively counteract union-organizing tactics, corporate leaders partnered with certain law firms and consultants "skilled in 'union avoidance' who specialized in ways to keep unions out."[16]

But What about Globalization, Technological Developments, and Changes in the Labor Market?

Cynthia Estlund (2002) has written that in an effort to explain the decline in collective bargaining in the US, in addition to legal and illegal employer resistance, "[s]cholars have advanced several answers, not mutually exclusive but competing for emphasis: structural economic change, including deindustrialization and increasingly global and competitive product markets; a mismatch between the interests of both employees and employers and traditional adversarial unionism; and unions' own complacency and lack of commitment to organizing for several crucial decades."[17] To that list should be added "skill-based technological change": the advent of computerized technologies that place a premium on higher-skilled, more educated workers and a lower demand for less-skilled, undereducated workers—the worker population often represented by unions in mass production industries.[18]

All these structural forces, as well as neglect in organizing by some unions, need to be considered as possible agents contributing to the decline of unionization. As is shown in the following discussion, some decrease in union membership is explained by globalization and changes in international trade policy, both of which directly caused significant job loss in highly unionized industries due to the relocation of work to Mexico and low-pay countries in Asia. And some unions were slow to ramp up organizing among workers employed at skill-based firms that replaced much of America's mass-production manufacturing industry after it floundered. But the post-1970s extensive decline in unionization was not primarily caused either by moving American jobs offshore or by some unions being asleep at the switch as the economy became more digital. The crisis in union representation is primarily the result of corporate America's self-conscious determination to free itself of the constraints on managerial discretion imposed by collective bargaining. Corporate managers developed the view that labor unions and collective bargaining are incompatible with the new job structures that increasingly began to dominate American business at the dawn of the digital era, sometime after the mid-1980s. In other words, technology and globalization did not themselves account for the decline in collective bargaining, but they did cause profits to be squeezed, thereby motivating employers to cope by redesigning the workplace in ways that made traditional collective bargaining seem to corporate managers as out of step with new production methods. Accordingly, employers were motivated to double down on their opposition to unions. And labor relations law provided no real hinderance to this employer counterattack on unionism.

The Shift to a Digital Economy

Much has changed economically for American business, primarily in the past twenty-five or thirty years. Gone, or going, are the oligopolistic national product markets characterized by mass production, product uniformity, assembly line production, and relative immunity to foreign (and in many cases domestic) competition. An oligopolistic product market enables business to more readily pass cost increases on to consumers without dipping into profits, but oligopolistic product markets are becoming a thing of the past. In the now-receding system of industrial production that rose to dominance in the twentieth century, profits were relatively secure, and unions organized employers that had established what are referred to as "internal labor markets." This means that employers structured work around narrow job definitions and clearly defined hierarchical job ladders that encouraged long-term commitment to the firm by basing promotions on long-term progress along lines of progression within a job ladder created for each job classification. Employers invested in training employees to excel at competencies for a particular, firm-specific job and encouraged long-term relationships by rewarding longevity in order to discourage turnover and thus amortize those training costs. Compensation was increased through a formula that regularized increases (including cost-of-living increases). Through collective bargaining, employers assumed responsibility for providing social welfare—primarily vacations, health care, and pensions. Employers implicitly (or explicitly) agreed to promote from within and forgo lateral hiring. In collective bargaining agreements, employers typically agreed to a formalized use of seniority to determine important conditions of employment, such as job assignment, promotion into jobs vacated by more senior employees, order of layoffs, and levels of compensation. Plus, economic justice at the workplace was advanced by collective bargaining agreements containing a "for cause" clause that placed limitations on discipline, including employment termination, and promoted arbitration to adjudicate workplace disputes.[19]

Global competition, liberalized trade policy, and deregulation during the 1980s created a new, competitive environment. One effect was the loss of American jobs, especially in basic manufacturing and "union strongholds like automobile, steel., electrical appliance, and machine tool. . . . The heavily unionized manufacturing and transportation sectors [took] an enormous hit . . . producing layoffs that . . . decimated the ranks of major industrial unions like the [Auto Workers, Steelworkers, and Teamsters]."[20] Jobs were lost to foreign competitors as American businesses either folded or moved into new product lines. In addition, with the advent of the multinational corporation, many previously American-held, semiskilled manufacturing jobs were moved to what Edsall (1984) described as "so-called export platforms—assembly plants in low-wage, third world countries established by multinational corporations—where workers are paid less than the American minimum wage and where they are beyond the reach of the American trade union movement."[21] Public policy, such as trade policy and tax policy that permitted the offshore transfer of American jobs without penalty, were complicit in this decline of unionization.

Studies have consistently substantiated, however, that these changes in labor force structure and product markets have had at best a marginal impact on union decline. Goldfield and Bromsen (2013) report that "[a]lthough globalization has complicated union organizing, it does not account for the difficulties [in organizing the] many tens of millions of workers in 'landlocked' industries, including construction, trucking, mining, health care, and the public sector."[22] The highly competitive globalization of production and trade adversely affected union membership for reasons other than the offshore transfer of unionized American jobs. Windham (2017) says that "advances in shipping and distribution began to allow companies all over the globe to compete," with the result of slowing profits for American firms.[23] In what Katherine Stone (2004, 4) has called the system of "digital production," many American employers concluded that global competition and deregulation required them to adopt new ideas about how to structure (organize) the workplace and the production process. At these companies, management concluded that the digital workplace needed to become more flexible (i.e., less segmented). Accordingly, firms increasingly discarded the internal labor markets built around clearly defined, hierarchical job ladders; encouragement of a long-term attachment between the employee and the firm, with many employees qualifying for pensions by staying with one employer for the duration of their working lives; seniority determining the conditions of employment, such as job assignment, promotion, order of layoffs, and levels of compensation; implicit commitments by the employer to promote from within and forgo lateral hiring; and assurances of economic justice at the workplace through adoption of "for cause" standards for discipline and termination.

In the modern workplace, these firms increasingly "locate or operate as networks of firms that are located all over the globe."[24] Horizontal (lateral) mobility of employees engaged in the production process is a central tenet of the digital workplace—transfer and deployment of personnel within the firm (and among companies with whom the firm works in alliance). Accordingly, employees' careers increasingly are not bounded by working for a particular employer, but rather often develop through being assigned to work in joint ventures, outsourcing, "and other forms of network production that permit and sometimes even encourage mobility between related enterprises." Job definitions become "blurred" as employees are assigned to "cross-functional teams that cut across department lines for many projects [within one enterprise]." Or an employer may define a "job" as possession of a particular competency, and managers may deploy that competency by "assign[ing] workers to a broad range of tasks." In these and other ways, "horizontal mobility has become ubiquitous in the transfer and deployment of personnel." The key to understanding this commitment to lateral movement within, between, and among firms is that in the digital workplace, profits derive from human intellectual capital possessed by employees such as "skills, knowledge, information, know-how, . . . imagination, and capacity for learning and innovation." Even in relatively low-tech production processes, firms increasingly depend on this human intellectual capital and the creative use of computers to coordinate its productive deployment. Employers insist on managerial flexibility and autonomy to exploit this intellectual human capital wherever and however it is most profitable for the firm. Business leaders widely conclude that sharing decision-making with a labor union is anathema in a digital workplace.

In digital production, market conditions can shift swiftly, as can consumer demand. This requires that firms adopt flexible labor relations systems permitting increasing and decreasing levels of production on short notice. As Katherine Stone (2004) has explained:[25]

> [W]ork practices are being adjusted to production requirements. As firms find themselves in a more competitive environment through increased trade and global competition, they have to pay more attention to short-term cost reductions. In addition, the market for corporate control forces firm managers to be responsive to short-term changes in revenues and demand. Part of the responsiveness involves just-in-time production, just-in-time design, and just-in-time workers.

The digital workplace has produced a "profound transformation" of the mutual expectations of the employment relationship. For example, firm-level wage setting increasingly is determined by performance, particularly reward for an employee's initiative in developing new competencies that the employer can deploy to raise profits. This means that two employees with the same seniority working on the same task may be paid dramatically different rates of compensation, depending on a manager's subjective evaluation of their relative performance, productivity, and potential to contribute to the firm's profits in the future. Many employers expect employees to change jobs frequently, and they do. Employers make no explicit or implicit commitments of job security, either to retain an employee in his or her current job or to promote from within and forgo the advantages of lateral hiring to fill vacancies. As a result, according to Kalleberg (2011), "[m]any [employees] face the likelihood of frequent involuntary job loss throughout their working life." This is work without job security—"precarious employment systems," as they have been described.[26]

In what David Weil (2014) has called "the fissured workplace,"[27] more and more workers are being forced into low-wage jobs as employers shed the costs of providing health-care and retirement benefits by shrinking their full-time-worker labor force, often by splitting off certain core functions that previously had been managed internally. In their place, corporations hire a less expensive, contingent labor force—part-time and temporary workers, employees from an employee leasing agency, outside independent contractors, or on-call workers to perform tasks previously performed in house by the firm's regular full-time workforce.[28] Temporary employees, hired from a temp agency, may become what one scholar has termed "permatemps"—workers who remain employed with the same enterprise for years, performing tasks such as maintenance, custodial, legal services, or computer programming, which often are the same as what regular employees of the firm do, but they get no health-care or retirement benefits and are paid at a lower rate of compensation.[29] Temporary employees are vulnerable. They are easy to dispose of when no longer needed, so they serve as a "cushion for changes in product demand."[30] And termination for unsatisfactory performance is made easier when an employee is a temp, since no justification is required or expected for the removal of such an employee. Depending on the specifics of who controls their day-to-day work, temporary employees are likely to be considered employees of the temp agency, not employees of the lead firm where the temporary employee works. That becomes significant, as will be discussed later in this book, when unions attempt to organize an employer's employees, some of whom may be temporary employees leased from an intermediary temp agency and thus are not considered employees of the firm being organized. One recent study estimates that between 30 percent and 40 percent of the American workforce lack secure employment because they serve as contractors, temporary employees, or seasonal workers, or they have other contingent relationships.[31]

In short, since roughly the mid-1980s, employers increasingly have been reinventing the American workplace. Increasingly, employers have abandoned the labor relations system referred to as the internal labor market with its well-defined job classifications, fixed job ladders, predictable promotion and compensation arrangements, social welfare benefits, heavy reliance on seniority, application of "just cause" standards to limit arbitrary discipline, assurances of job security, and encouragement of long-term employment. In its stead, employers have sought to design what corporate managers deem a more effective and efficient workplace, with a structure considered necessary for profitability in an era of increased competition in the product market and technological change in production methods. Flexibility emerged as the gravamen of this revised approach to production.

In general, five changes define the new workplace: (1) withdrawal of implicit or explicit commitments to job security, wherein the most talented are recruited and the most productive remain employed—the rest are kept on as needed, but lateral hiring is used to fill vacancies and work may be assigned to temporary employees or outsourced to others; (2) a decentralized management that shifts responsible decision-making to groups of employees; (3) horizontal movement within and between firms as the norm; (4) compensation that is detached from longevity but instead is based on productivity with "steep performance incentives," and a reduction in health-care and retirement benefits, and (5) the elimination of "for cause" limitations on discipline or discharge, sometimes replaced by various forms of in-firm dispute resolution systems, occasionally with appeal to peer groups.

To be clear, millions of private-sector employees continue to work in traditional workplaces where the internal labor market continues and traditional collective bargaining thrives. As noted in chapter 1, as of 2020, more than eight million private-sector, nonagricultural employees currently are covered by collective bargaining agreements. Moreover, US government research shows that the highest concentrations of US workers who are not currently covered by a collective bargaining agreement work for large corporations in traditional employer-employee relationships where traditional collective bargaining would continue to be effective.[32]

Yet some traditional collective bargaining that focuses on the administration of the internal labor market would benefit from modifications that better respond to the new and evolving labor relations systems that increasingly are dominating the digital workplace. Rather than working in harmony with unions to design contract language suitable for the digital workplace, many US employers since the 1970s have opted for an assault on unionization and collective bargaining in a full-throttled effort to retain the utmost unilateral managerial control of the workplace.[33] As a result of the no-quarter-given attack on unions, employers have slashed wage obligations, reduced private welfare costs (medical and pension benefits), and retained the flexibility that they conclude they need to maximize corporate profits in an era of digital production. It is thus a grave mistake to conclude that the steep decline in union density in the US was no more than a natural process resulting from globalization and technological change. Globalization and technological change encouraged and motivated US employers to resist unionization, and thus reduce the number of workers who benefit from collective bargaining. So, to that degree, globalization and technological change are implicated indirectly in the decline of collective bargaining.[34] But the decline in unionization mostly resulted in the self-conscious decision by business leaders to rid the firm of unionization.

It is essential to appreciate, however, that collective bargaining is a flexible tool for adding economic justice to the workplace. Collective bargaining developed in the late nineteenth and early twentieth centuries to respond to the changing realities of mass production industry. There is no basis to conclude that collective bargaining cannot adjust to the realities of the digital workplace if given a chance. Corporate managers may insist on increased flexibility, but that is different from evidence that collective bargaining is incompatible with the digital workplace—that it cannot work. Labor unions are not obsolete in the era of the emerging digital workplace. Indeed, according to Stone (2004), "in the digital era, unions are more necessary than ever. They alone have the potential to enable workers to . . . ensure that the new workplace offers fairness, equity, and dignity."[35] The assault on American labor unions by US business has had the unfortunate effect of impeding opportunities to exploit and develop the creative potential of the collective bargaining process.

What remains to be considered is why corporate America has been able to be so successful in its efforts to deny union representation to the more than half of all nonunion workers who desire unionization and the benefits of collective bargaining. Why have workers and their unions been unable to effectively resist employer opposition? Much of the answer can be found in the current rules contained in our labor relations laws that create an uneven playing field. These rules provide employers who desire to resist unionization and collective bargaining a decided advantage. Taken up next is an examination of exactly how, as construed, the NLRA provides employers with this advantage. And we also need to evaluate whether it is realistic to conclude that by redressing the current imbalance, labor law reform can make a difference in the economic lives of workers.

Before embarking on that inquiry, however, it is useful to differentiate between two types of inequality built into our labor laws because the solution to each type of inequality is different. The first consists of the full range of the advantages that the law currently provides employers when resisting employees' attempts to gain union representation—obstacles to unions gaining representational status. The second type of inequality built into our labor laws is the advantages that the law provides employers during the collective bargaining process to resist agreeing to positions that a union advances during the collective bargaining negotiation process. For example, nearly half of all employees who choose unionization never obtain even a first collective bargaining agreement, and even fewer ever benefit from a second. The following chapters will evaluate how our current labor relations laws create each of these two types of inequalities, and how a reformed labor law regime would likely reverse the decline in the availability of meaningful collective bargaining for American workers.

II The Role of Contemporary Labor Relations Law in Creating Obstacles to Workers' Desire to Obtain Union Representation

4 The NLRA's Restrictions on Coverage: Constricting Eligibility for Legal Protection of the Right to Organize

Labor Law Reforms Needed[1]

Ensuring that employees are not misclassified as independent contractors and denied protections of the NLRA.

Ensuring that employees are not denied protections of the NLRA by being wrongly classified as supervisors.

Preventing the misclassification of workers.

Protecting employees who have multiple employers.

* * *

One way that the National Labor Relations Act (NLRA) facilitates employer resistance to the representational aspirations of millions of nonunion workers who want unionization and the benefits of collective bargaining is to constrict the supply of the potentially organized. The NLRA creates the right to "exercise [the] full freedom of association, self-organization, and designation of representatives of their own choosing for the purpose of negotiating the terms and conditions of their employment and other mutual aid or protection," but it extends that right only to "employees" as defined by the NLRA itself.[2] Tens of millions of workers do not qualify as NLRA "employees" because they fall within one of the several categories of workers that it excludes from coverage.[3] These exclusions from the definition of "employee" range from domestic workers and farm workers to tens of thousands of truck drivers and to charge nurses, who primarily perform normal patient-care nursing duties but incidentally also assign tasks to direct lower-skilled nurses, such as licensed practical nurses (LPNs). These millions of excluded workers are defenseless in the face of employer reprisals if they attempt to exercise associational choice by forming a union and demanding collective bargaining, by striking, or by otherwise joining with coworkers to protest objectionable conditions of employment. Constricting coverage of the NLRA also affects union strength: a union is in a better position to strike effectively when all (or nearly all) of those qualified to perform bargaining unit work are in the bargaining unit. In particular, the removal of workers with critical skills from the bargaining unit weakens the union's collective voice.[4]

Those who are not labor relations law specialists often miss the significance of the fact that the NLRA's protection of "concerted" employee activity is not restricted to unionized work places. The NLRA also protects nonunion employees from employer recriminations when they act in concert with other workers.[5] For example, one ruling found that "employees in nonunion workplaces have a right protected by the NLRA to request the presence of a coworker in an investigatory interview which the employee reasonably believes could result in disciplinary action[:] an employee's right to assistance emanates from § 7 of the NLRA, rather than from [an employee's right to union representation]."[6] And, by further example, employee-to-employee communications on a social network platform such as Facebook regarding the conditions of employment constitute concerted activity that the NLRA may also protect from employer retaliation.[7] However, these protections of concerted activity by nonunion workers apply only with respect to those who are "employees" within the meaning of the NLRA, not to those who are statutorily exempted from the definition of "employee."

As originally enacted in 1935, the NLRA excluded from its protections agricultural workers and domestic workers. Racial and gender discrimination "played a significant role in the [initial] exclusion[s]" because agriculture work and domestic service in private homes were sectors predominated by people of color and women. The enactment of New Deal legislation required excluding these groups of employees in order to gain the support of Southern members of Congress whose economies relied on the "exploitation of Black workers for agriculture, service, and domestic work."[8] The legacy of racism undergirding the NLRA's original exclusions continues to the present. The degraded working conditions for those excluded from NLRA's protections have disproportionately impacted immigrant workers, Black workers, other workers of color, and women workers and thereby have exacerbated racial and gender inequalities.[9]

For example, home care workers, those who assist elderly and disabled clients in their homes with basic activities such as dressing, bathing, toileting, and eating, are "one of the fastest growing sectors of the labor market," estimated to number in the range from 700,000 to nearly 1.5 million. "The great majority of home care workers are women and people of color, and most are able to secure only intermittent and part-time employment [with] the mean annual wage [of] $17,710, and [are rarely provided] health insurance, retirement, and related benefits."[10] A substantial and growing number of home care workers are employees of their elderly and disabled clients are thus are excluded from the NLRA's coverage because the Act excludes from its coverage any individual employed "in the domestic service of any family or person at his home." As Professor Benjamin Sachs (2007) explained, "these home care workers [have] little hope of [NLRA] coverage, leaving this large and growing sector of the labor force without protection from traditional labor law."[11]

The 1947 Taft-Hartley Act's amendments to the NLRA added two important additional exclusion categories: independent contractors and supervisors.[12] The exclusion of independent contractors also creates racial disparities. As Professor Sachs has demonstrated, "[t]he picture for [the estimated 1.8 million] home-based child care providers, who offer child care services in their own or their clients' homes, is much the same [as with home care workers]. An estimated] 94% of the child care workforce in the United States is female, more than 30% is African American and Latino, . . . the work is poorly compensated, [and as] with home care workers, home-based child care providers are without NLRA protection, primarily by virtue of the statute's exclusion of independent contractors."[13]

In addition to the racial disparities created by the independent contractor exclusion, the misclassification of an employee as an independent contractor is a wide-ranging and serious problem.[14] According to Compa (2000), "Congressional and administrative hearings have produced abundant evidence that many employers deliberately misclassify workers as independent contractors, confident that few workers will mount a challenge due to fear of lost income and the stress of legal action. One [early] study estimated that the number of misclassified workers [would] exceed five million by the year 2005."[15] Currently, the NLRA creates no disincentive to employers who find it advantageous to misidentify employees by, for example, falsely classifying NLRA-covered employees as independent contractors. In 2019, during President Donald Trump's administration, the National Labor Relations Board (NLRB) held that nothing in the NLRA prohibits employers from engaging in such misclassification, notwithstanding that misclassification falsely communicates to employees that they do not have rights under the NLRA and their organizing activities are futile.[16]

To address these deficiencies, NLRA reform is needed to (1) tighten the definitions of both "independent contractor" and "supervisor" and (2) ban misclassifying employees as either independent contractors or supervisors by making it an unfair labor practice to misrepresent to an employee that such employees are excluded from the definition of "employee" under § 2(3) of the NLRA.

Tightening the NLRA Definition of "Independent Contractor"

SuperShuttle International has developed proprietary software to administer a shared-ride shuttle van transportation system.[17] SuperShuttle Dallas–Fort Worth (DFW) maintains a license agreement with SuperShuttle International for the right to use the SuperShuttle trademark and its transportation and reservation/dispatch system in the Dallas–Fort Worth area. Before 2005, DFW hired drivers whom it designated as employees. During that period, these drivers earned hourly wages, and DFW assigned drivers to regularly scheduled shifts picking up customers in company-owned shuttle vans. In 2005, DFW restructured and classified its driver-employees as franchisees.

When the Amalgamated Transit Union filed a representation petition with the NLRB in an effort to unionize the DFW drivers, the company moved to dismiss the petition on the ground that the drivers were independent contractors and thus exempt from the protections of the NLRA.

The DFW reclassification effort, purporting to convert driver-employees into NLRA-exempt independent contractors, deployed a conversion structure used by other companies.[18] Following the reclassification of their drivers as independent contractors, DFW retained most of the indicia of control that are normal in an employer-employee relationship.[19] For example, the standard Unit Franchise Agreement (UFA) that DFW required each individual driver to sign was not subject to negotiation and could be unilaterally modified by DFW. By the terms of the UFA, drivers were required to state that they were nonemployee franchisees who operated independent businesses, and yet the UFA controlled many of the most important aspects of the drivers' work lives: for example, drivers were barred from engaging in *any* business activity that DFW deemed to conflict with their obligations under the UFA, which included a noncompete provision barring them from providing services for a DFW competitor and any involvement with another business that provided transportation services. The van that the drivers were required to purchase or lease must meet detailed specifications (make, model, color, size, age, and mechanical condition). DFW drivers must complete thirty-four hours of preliminary training and eighteen hours of on-the-job training. Among other things, this included training related to "disciplinary guidelines, dress standards, [and] customer service."[20] In addition, it entailed "training in [SuperShuttle's] brand standards and the operation of its communication systems—subjects that the UFA describes as 'unique to the SuperShuttle system.'"[21] Drivers who worked for DFW were required to use the Nextel cell-phone trip-generating system, which includes a pager, a two-way radio, and a global-positioning navigation system—all owned by DFW. Drivers were barred from using dispatch and reservation equipment outside the SuperShuttle system. Franchisees could use only equipment, signs, uniforms, and services approved by SuperShuttle.

With respect to compensation, DFW, not the drivers, set the fares and, as mentioned, drivers who wished to work for DFW had to do so exclusively for DFW and were barred from any involvement with another business that provided transportation services. DFW did not set drivers' work schedules, routes, or assignments, but the Nextel trip-generating system created job "bids." While drivers ostensibly were free to accept or decline a bid, testimony before the NLRB explained that drivers had been disciplined (i.e., fined) for declining bids.[22]

Moreover, DFW shifted to the franchisee-drivers most of the risk associated with a downturn of share-ride business at the airports because for the right to utilize the SuperShuttle trademarked name and its Nextel cell-phone dispatch and reservation apparatus, drivers paid DFW an initial $500 franchise fee (if providing transportation to and from both Dallas–Fort Worth and Love Field airports), paid DFW a flat weekly $575 fee for a Dallas–Fort Worth Airport franchise, and an additional $100 per-week contribution to reimburse DFW for its payment of certain driving-related fees. These weekly flat fees paid to DFW were required regardless of the amount of business that a franchisee generated in any given week.

Franchisees worked when and as much as they chose and were compensated by retaining the money they earned for completing the assignments that they selected. As a practical matter, the hefty weekly fixed payment paid by the drivers to DFW locked them in: they had to work a certain number of hours per week in order to earn sufficient money to make the obligatory weekly $675 payments to DTW. While the UFA permitted a driver to use a substitute or relief driver, such other driver must be approved by DFW, following successful completion of DFW's course of required training. At the time of the hearing before the NLRB, only one of eighty-eight drivers employed a relief driver.[23]

As is normal today among many companies, DFW's reclassification of employees resulted in workers "inhabit[ing] a gray area of independent contracting and traditional employment."[24] Lead companies reconfigure work so that it contains characteristics of independent contracting—for instance, franchisees at DFW worked when and as much as they chose, were compensated by retaining the money they earned for completing the assignments that they selected, provided their own vans, could employ relief drivers to operate their vans, and paid their own expenses. Meanwhile, the franchisor company maintains tight controls over the drivers that are typical of an employer's controls over its employees—for example, DFW prescribed limits on the apparel that workers could wear, the prices charged, equipment required to be used, training that must be satisfied, and through an obligatory noncompete agreement, banned *any* involvement with another business that provides transportation services. In other words, as Weil (2019) describes, franchisor firms attempt to have it both ways: they "benefit from work executed in strict compliance with central corporate objectives [and standards of performance] and [yet are] not . . . required to treat workers who do [the work] as [its] employees with the obligations that [the employer-employee] relationship holds."[25]

DRW successfully walked that line when it converted its employees to franchisees: the Trump NLRB ruled (2–1) that the DFW drivers were independent contractors and thus not entitled to the protection of the NLRA. Accordingly, the NLRB dismissed the union's representation petition.[26] The Board's reasoning is discussed later in this chapter.

According to the 2017 Contingent Worker Survey conducted by the US Bureau of Labor Statistics, 10.6 million workers are classified as independent contractors in the US—6.9 percent of total employment.[27] David Weil makes a convincing case that the Contingent Worker Survey actually understates the incidence of independent contracting in the US because "a growing body of evidence indicates that workers often incorrectly classify themselves as employees when they are not being treated that way by the organizations for whom they work." For example, these organizations often fail to comply with the minimum wage and overtime provisions of the Fair Labor Standards Act (FLSA), applicable only to "employees"; or they refuse to provide these workers the safety net of protective labor legislation such as workers' compensation and unemployment compensation insurance.[28] Weil conservatively estimates that the true incidence of employers treating workers as independent contractors could be nearly twice the 10.6 million (6.9 percent of total employment) estimated in the Contingent Worker Survey.[29]

Whatever the actual current number of workers being denied the legal status of an "employee" and instead being characterized as an independent contractor—10 million, 15 million, or 20 million—that figure is certain to rise significantly in the near future. The reason is that major companies have confronted increased pressure from investors (public and private) to improve financial performance and have responded to this pressure by "fissuring," as Weil (2019) has described the response by companies to these financial performance pressures.[30] Fissuring entails corporations splitting off certain core functions that previously had been managed internally.[31] Corporations engage in fissuring by "focusing their businesses on core competences—that is, activities that provide the greatest value to their consumers and [profit to their] investors—and by shedding less essential activities."[32] Accordingly, today a corporation (the "lead business") will routinely outsource its payroll, data entry, accounting, customer contact, labor relations, janitorial, maintenance, and security functions in various ways. For example, many hotels outsource the cleaning of rooms, restaurants do the same for the tasks performed by kitchen crews, and distribution centers (warehouses) do the same for the work on a loading dock.

Outsourcing by the lead business can occur in several ways. One is by contracting with a staffing agency (temp agency) to provide temporary workers to perform the outsourced functions under the supervision of the lead company's management. Another is by hiring a management company to come in, manage the outsourced function itself, and oversee leased employees who perform the outsourced functions. Outsourcing saves money: corporations benefit from the services of the temporary or leased workers, but they claim that they have no responsibility under labor laws to those who provide these services because they are the employees of the staffing agencies, not the lead corporations. Corporations make no contributions to Social Security or Medicare for these workers and claim no responsibility, for example, if workers performing outsourced work are not paid the minimum wage or properly compensated for working overtime, or if they claim employment discrimination or seek to recover under workers' compensation laws if they are injured on the job. Further, such outsourcing provides the lead companies with the argument that they need not recognize a union that seeks to represent workers performing outsourced functions because these workers are not the lead companies' employees. The question of whether a lead company and a company that provides the workers from outside are "joint employers" who must recognize a union representing the workers is discussed later in this chapter.

In addition to contracting with third-party staffing and management agencies to provide workers to perform outsourced functions, corporations that fissure split off certain core functions that previously had been managed internally by contracting those functions to subcontractors or franchisees. This was the model deployed by DFW. Cleaning companies, for example, may contract with the owners of office buildings, hotels, and other businesses such as grocery stores to perform janitorial services, but then they may "hire smaller businesses to provide workers for specific facilities or shifts."[33] In one case, a commercial office building owner in Seattle contracted with a large cleaning company. The cleaning company then turned around and franchised parts of the work to different groups of workers, mostly Central American and Asian immigrants. The cleaning company asserted that these franchisee workers were considered independent contractors who cannot claim the protections of the NLRA should they desire union representation to bargain with the cleaning company for better terms and conditions of employment. Moreover, the cleaning company/franchisor was able to disclaim all responsibility for payment of minimum wage and overtime, as well as Social Security, workers' compensation, and unemployment compensation because those performing the cleaning were not the cleaning company/franchisor's employees, as already discussed.[34]

In other examples, in 2000, 70 percent of guards and 45 percent of janitors were employed as contractors.[35] Since deregulation, tens of thousands of truck drivers have been reclassified as independent contractors. Typically, a trucking company may maintain a small office staff, but rather than employing drivers, the trucking company instead contracts with individual owner-operators to deliver goods from the nation's shipping ports to nearby warehouses for transfer to long-haul delivery trucks or to deliver products from a warehouse directly to an end user.[36] Classified as independent contractors exempt from labor law coverage, many drivers are not free to contract their services to the highest bidder because trucking companies require them to sign exclusive contracts that ban such contracting with others.[37] When companies shift employees to independent contractor status, workers are suddenly more vulnerable to costs that they did not face before. For example, truck drivers injured on the job previously had been covered by workers' compensation protection as employees. But as independent contractors, they must carry their own health insurance, a protection that many may forgo as too expensive or beyond their reach for other reasons. Meanwhile, trucking firms escape any obligation to maintain workers' compensation for injured drivers who have been reclassified as independent contractors.

At "'platform economy' companies," as Brishen Rogers (2016) has termed them, firms such as Uber, Lyft, TaskRabbit, Postmates, and Handy "provide online platforms that match consumers with workers for short-term tasks."[38] Platform economy companies deny that those workers who are matched with consumers, such as an Uber driver matched with a consumer requiring driving services, a plumber booked by Handy to repair a homeowner's burst pipe, or a SuperShuttle van driver picking up passengers at an airport—are employees of the platform company; rather, they are independent contractors. Amazon, for example, might use its own employees to deliver a package from an Amazon distribution center, or it might hire subcontractors to do this. Then, if the drivers attempt to unionize, Amazon can claim that they are independent contractors excluded from NLRA coverage. Or a package delivery company such as FedEx might conclude that the core competency that it controls is the application of specialized technology for routing packages most efficiently from one place to another, and it will outsource to subcontractors the actual delivery of the packages.[39]

Shifting work from a firm's employees to subcontractors (or franchisees) changes both the nature of employment and wage structures. With fissuring, wage setting devolves into a task of pricing the commodity of labor in the open market, resulting in depressed wages. For example, Amazon structured a package home delivery system named Amazon Flex. After being vetted by satisfactory completion of a multistep online course, individuals bid for deliveries using a proprietary app created by Amazon Flex. Using the worker's own vehicle, drivers must complete deliveries according to a tight schedule set by Amazon. Investment advisor A/B Bernstein analyzed the average earnings of a typical Flex driver, taking into consideration vehicle fuel, insurance, maintenance, amortization, tolls, and other related costs, and concluded that drivers received net earnings of $5.30 per hour. This is less than the US minimum wage of $7.25 per hour at the time of the survey and compares unfavorably with average hourly earnings of $23.10 for UPS drivers and $14.40 for FedEx drivers.[40] Workers generally suffer a wage penalty when work is moved from a firm's regular employees to subcontractors. For example, there is an estimated 15 percent decrease in earnings for janitors and 17 percent earnings decrease for guards following their reclassification from employees to independent contractors. In one large study of food service, cleaning, security, and logistics workers, the impact of subcontracting was a wage penalty of between 10 percent and 15 percent.[41]

In many ways, it is advantageous for companies to deploy reclassification models that blur the boundaries of what constitutes employment versus independent contracting because the ambiguity provides the lead companies with maximum control over workers performing outsourced functions, while at the same time providing creative opportunities for lead companies and their attorneys to assemble arguments that persuade business-oriented administrative agencies and courts that these workers are independent contractors who are ineligible to receive the benefits of protective labor legislation. Yet the workers excluded from coverage of labor and employment laws typically lack the bargaining power to protect themselves—and thus are the very workers who need legislative protection.

A recurring source of litigation before the NLRB entails a lead company refusing to recognize and bargain with the union chosen by its workers, claiming that the workers are independent contractors excluded from NLRA coverage. Currently, to determine whether a worker should be classified under the NLRA as an employee or an independent contractor, the NLRB and the courts apply the common-law agency test.[42] The Restatement (Second) of Agency contains a nonexhaustive ten-factor test that is not especially amenable to any sort of bright-line rule.[43] The factors that comprise the so-called common law right to control test were developed to establish vicarious liability in tort law, but they are not particularly useful for identifying which workers are so economically dependent on their employers that they need, and ought to be provided, the social and economic protections of New Deal and civil rights legislation.[44]

There is near-universal agreement, except among certain employer groups, that the nonexhaustive ten-factor common law test for distinguishing between employees and independent contractors is seriously flawed. It lacks predictability, and the common law's ambiguous factors invite manipulation that would permit a court or administrative agency to achieve any desired outcome, for reasons that remain unarticulated, in many cases. The fluidity of the common law factors, moreover, creates incentives for companies that fissure to misclassify employees as independent contractors in the hope (or perhaps expectation) that with quality professional guidance from experienced lawyers and careful planning, the corporations will be able to lower their wage costs and accountability under labor and employment laws because workers are misclassified as independent contractors while the companies retain their essential and traditional employee-employer control over the day-to-day activities of those who perform core outsourced functions.[45]

The indeterminate nature of the common law test for distinguishing employees from independent contractors has reached crisis proportions at the NLRB. The NLRB's independent contractor doctrine is in disarray.

In 2009, the D.C. Circuit Court of Appeals decided a case involving FedEx Home Delivery (*FedEx I*). That case constituted a major defeat for the NLRB.[46] In *FedEx I*, the D.C. Circuit, purporting to apply the common law factors, ruled that when attempting to "identify the essential quantum of independence that separates a contractor from an employee," control or lack of it by the lead company is critical but "'[c]ontrol' [does] not mean all kinds of controls, but only certain kinds [and] some controls were more equal than others." From these premises, the D.C. Circuit concluded: "Thus, while all the considerations at common law remain in play, an important *animating principle* by which to evaluate those factors in cases where some factors cut one way and some the other [which they always do] is whether the position *presents* the opportunities and risks inherent in entrepreneurialism."[47] This approach for defining "independent contractor" status that the D.C. Circuit adopted in *FedEx I* is calculated to increase the number of employees whom a corporation will be able to legally reclassify as independent contractors. Concomitantly, the approach to defining independent contractor approved by the D.C. Circuit will decrease the number of workers who are adjudged to be employees covered by the protections of the NLRA and other protective labor legislation. First, when entrepreneurial opportunity becomes the "animating principle" in the debate, what becomes secondary are the myriad of reserved controls and the extensive degree of supervision and oversight retained by the lead company to control the day-to-day activities of those doing outsourced work. Moreover, and critically, the inquiry as adopted by the D.C. Circuit is whether the scheme devised by the employer "*presents opportunities*" for profit, not whether the employees in fact have ever been able to benefit from such profit "opportunities." In the D.C. Circuit case of *FedEx I*, the record demonstrated that "contractors perform a function that is a regular and essential part of FedEx Home's normal operations, the delivery of packages, and that few have seized any of the alleged entrepreneurial opportunities." The court demurred, stating that "failure to take advantage of an opportunity is beside the point. [O]pportunities cannot be ignored unless they are the sort workers cannot realistically take, and even *one instance* of a driver using such an opportunity can be sufficient. . . . [I]t is the worker's retention of the right to engage in entrepreneurial activity rather than his regular exercise of that right that is most relevant for the purpose of determining whether he is an independent contractor."[48] In short, for the D.C. Circuit in *FedEx I*, the "animating principle" to determine "independent contractor" status is evidence of the worker's retention of some theoretical right to engage in entrepreneurial activity, not evidence that this theoretical opportunity has in fact ever benefited any of the workers. Any management labor lawyer who cannot devise a reclassification structure that meets that test ought to be fired.

Following this 2009 decision by the D.C. Circuit, the NLRB in 2014 attempted to reset the focus of the independent contractor inquiry and retreat from *FedEx I*, which had made entrepreneurial opportunity the litmus test. The Board in 2014 retained entrepreneurial opportunity as a factor to consider, but it also rejected making that factor the "animating principle." Instead, the Board in 2014 focused extensively on the control retained by the lead company. The Board held that entrepreneurial opportunity "represents [but] one aspect of a relevant factor that asks whether the evidence tends to show that the putative contractor is, in fact, rendering services *as part of an independent business*."[49] This focus on inquiring into the presence or absence of an "independent business" by the putative contractor inevitably shifted away from theoretical entrepreneurial opportunities for profit or loss that might be embedded within a corporation's reclassification scheme, but which few (if any) workers take advantage of. A focus on identifying if a worker in fact is "rendering services as part of an independent business" examines closely the common law factors of a corporation's reserved control over workers who are performing outsourced functions in order to exclude from the status of independent contractor workers who are economically dependent on the employer and need and will benefit from labor and employment law protections.

In 2016, the D.C. Circuit heard arguments on a challenge to the NLRB's 2014 *FedEx* opinion and denied enforcement (*FedEx II*).[50] In *FedEx II*, the court held that the D.C. Circuit's 2009 decision in *FedEx I* was the "law of the circuit," and the Board's 2014 decision had failed to make entrepreneurial opportunity the animating principle in an independent contractor analysis. Accordingly, the Board's 2014 decision was found to be inconsistent with the rule in the D.C. Circuit.

Two additional developments have added to the chaos that surrounds the NLRB's independent contractor rules and reinforce the need to provide a legislative solution. First, in *Alexander v. FedEx Ground Package System, Inc.*,[51] on facts highly similar to those in *FedEx I*, the Ninth Circuit Court of Appeals heard a claim by FedEx package delivery drivers who were asserting rights under state law for employment expenses and unpaid wages on the ground that the company had improperly classified them as independent contractors. Although *Alexander* was decided by applying California common law principles, those principles are not significantly dissimilar from the Restatement (Second) of Agency factors, and the Ninth Circuit found that the drivers were employees as a matter of law, reversing the lower court because it had improperly focused on entrepreneurial opportunity. The Ninth Circuit noted that the decision in *FedEx I* had placed primary emphasis on "entrepreneurial opportunity," but it ruled that under California common law, the focus needs to be on the degree that a company has reserved control over the workers' day-to-day activities—exactly what the NLRB had held in 2014 was the proper focus in NLRA cases.

The second development of significance is that in 2019, the Trump NLRB, in a 2–1 decision, reversed the 2014 NLRB *FedEx* decision. In *SuperShuttle DFW, Inc. (Amalgamated Transit Union, Local No. 1338)*,[52] the NLRB adopted the D.C. Circuit's rule in *FedEx I* that gives entrepreneurial opportunity heightened significance in determining "independent contractor" status. The majority in *SuperShuttle DFW* did not adopt from *FedEx I* the phrase that entrepreneurial opportunity is the "animating principle" to be considered. Instead, it held that, no matter how limited, "entrepreneurial opportunity . . . has always been at the *core of the common law test*."[53] In *SuperShuttle DFW*, the NLRB held that the drivers had entrepreneurial opportunities for increased profits because they owned their own vans, could work as many hours as they chose, could hire relief drivers (although at the time of trial at the NLRB, only one such driver was employed), and could sell their franchises. Relegated to subordinate significance was the evidence in the record that the drivers were not engaged in their own independent businesses and, in fact, their work was an integral part of the regular business of the employer, SuperShuttle, and was overwhelmingly controlled by SuperShuttle.[54]

In 2021, in *The Atlanta Opera, Inc.*,[55] the Biden NLRB issued an "Invitation to File Briefs" with respect to the following questions: (1) should the board adhere to the independent contractor standard in *SuperShuttle DFW, Inc.*, or (2) if not, what standard should replace it? Should the Board return to the standard in *FedEx Home Delivery (2014)*? Whatever the Biden NLRB decides, it is unworkable to continue to determine "independent contractor" status by which political party has won the most recent presidential election. Both workers and companies deserve a greater measure of predictability than is provided by the current state of the law. Plus, "the lack of predictability invites abuse and may enable employers to misclassify employees as independent contractors"[56]

Reform is needed both to enhance predictability and to provide a fair balance of the competing legitimate interests at stake. One approach is known as the "ABC test." As of 2020, the ABC test had been adopted by seventeen states (plus Puerto Rico and the Virgin Islands).[57] As articulated in the Protecting the Right to Organize Act (PRO Act), for example, the ABC test provides:

> The definition of "employee" under Section 2(3) of the NLRA is amended to clarify that an individual performing any service is an employee and not an independent contractor unless
>
> (A) the individual is free from the employer's control in connection with the performance of the service, both under the contract for the performance of service and in fact; and
>
> (B) the service is performed outside the usual course of the business of the employer; and
>
> (C) the individual is customarily engaged in an independently established trade, occupation, profession, or business of the same nature as that involved in the service performed.

The structure of the ABC test for identifying independent contractors is one of its most important features. It creates a rebuttable presumption that a worker is an "employee" and then sets forth a *conjunctive* three-part test to rebut that presumption. A worker is presumed to be an employee unless the hiring party that is asserting "independent contractor" status for him or her can carry the burden of showing that *each* of the factors in the test for defining an independent contractor is satisfied for that worker.[58]

Perhaps the most significant adoption of the ABC test was its 2020 codification into California law with passage of Assembly Bill 5 (known as AB 5).[59] Because the test creates a rebuttable presumption of employee status and avoids a totality-of-factors approach, its virtues are, among other things, (1) predictability, (2) ease of administration, and (3) reduction of disputes. The test has attracted broad-based support because its virtues benefit workers, employers, and enforcement agencies. In addition, Goldman and Weil (2021) argue that "[b]ecause it would be easier for enforcement agencies and private parties to challenge illegal business models, employers would have less incentive to misclassify workers than they do now."[60]

The first factor in the ABC test examines the worker's actual freedom from control by the employer, both under the terms of a contract for the performance of service and in fact. The control factor examines both actual and unexercised, but retained, control. Control in fact thus remains an important consideration. But the absence of employer control is not determinative of independent contractor status because the remaining two prongs (B and C) must also be met to classify a worker as an independent contractor. Sprague (2020) argues that "it is perhaps this shift away from the control factor that has caused platform-based enterprises . . . to consider . . . adoption of [the ABC test] to be an existential threat. For example, soon after the California legislature adopted the ABC test, California courts almost immediately began reevaluating employee-independent contractor classification for platform-based businesses [such as Uber and Lyft]."[61]

With the ABC test, courts are often able to avoid contentious and time-consuming litigation over employer control in independent contractor disputes because of the second conjunctive factor: whether the service is performed outside the usual course of the business of the employer. This inquiry is designed to deny independent contractor status to arrangements where the work performed is integral to the normal operations of the employer. For example, in litigation in California involving allegations that Uber and Lyft had misclassified drivers as independent contractors, the court was able to bypass the need to adjudicate the contentious issue of the degree of these companies' control over drivers (part A), as well as the need to determine whether the drivers were independently engaged in an established trade, occupation, or business (part C). Litigation was simplified because the court focused solely on part B of the ABC test: whether the service is performed outside the usual course of the business of the employer.[62]

Of course, disputes inevitably arise with respect to what constitutes an employer's usual course of business—especially in litigation involving a firm that has fissured, such as platform economy companies. For example, home delivery might be considered integral to the normal operations of FedEx unless a court is prepared to conclude that a highly fissured FedEx corporation is not a delivery company at all; rather, it is a technology company whose normal operations are limited to connecting persons who want packages delivered and those who desire to receive them. Is SuperShuttle DFW a ride-share company whose normal operations entail providing ground transportation to and from airports in the Dallas–Fort Worth area, or is it a software company that provides technology to drivers to assist them in connecting with customers who desire their ride-share services? In litigation in California involving Uber and Lyft, the companies argued that they were not transportation companies. Rather, they merely provided a "multi-sided platform" that served as a "matchmaker" to facilitate transactions between drivers and passengers. Rejecting this characterization, the California court concluded that Uber's and Lyft's "entire business [entails] transporting passengers for compensation," and thus when drivers transport customers for compensation, that work is an "integral part" of Uber's and Lyft's business.[63] The point is not that this second factor will eliminate all controversy, but rather that it will focus controversy where it matters—on those issues that are easiest to resolve and those considerations that will most likely uncover which workers are economically dependent on the employer and most need the protections of labor and employment laws.

The final part of the ABC test is whether the worker classified as an independent contractor is customarily engaged in an independently established trade, occupation, profession, or business of the same nature as that involved in the service performed. Evaluation of this third factor includes inquiry into any bona fide entrepreneurial opportunity for profit or loss based on managerial skill—not just on the person's willingness to work harder. In addition, this factor evaluates other indices of a truly independent business, such as the extent of relative investments of the employer and the worker and whether the work performed requires special skills and initiative.[64]

In short, the adoption of the ABC test offers a welcome solution to an issue that has plagued labor relations law for nearly seventy-five years and is becoming more contentious as companies increasingly engage in fissuring. By jettisoning the multifactor common law agency test, which was never developed to isolate those who are economically dependent on an employer, the ABC test will add predictability, reduce litigation, and increase the likelihood that the protections of workplace legislation will reach those workers for whom it was intended.

Tightening the NLRA Definition of "Supervisor"

The1947 Taft-Hartley amendments also denied supervisors the protections of the act by excluding them from the definition of "employee." The term "supervisor" is defined in § 2(11) of the NLRA.[65] Three preconditions must be proved for one to be a supervisor under the NLRA. First, one must have authority that is exercised "in the interest of the employer." That authority must consist of the power "to hire, transfer, suspend, lay off, recall, promote, discharge, *assign*, reward, [or] discipline other employees, *or responsibly to direct* [employees] or to adjust their grievances, or effectivity to recommend such action." Finally, "the exercise of such authority [must] not [be] of a merely routine or clerical nature, but require the use of independent judgment."[66]

To avoid employees being wrongly classified as supervisors, two changes to the NLRA are needed, each amending the definition of "supervisor" as set forth in § 2(11) of the NLRA. First, the definition of "supervisor" in § 2(11) needs to be clarified to require that in order to be classified as a supervisor, the individual's supervisory activities must be executed for a majority of the individual's work time. Second, the list of activities that are indicia of supervisory status needs to be amended by removing the putative supervisor's authority to "assign" or the "responsibly to direct" employees.[67]

A quick review of the history of the status of supervisors under the NLRA assists in understanding why these reforms are needed. The 1935 NLRA made no reference to supervisors. But well before the addition of the 1947 supervisor exclusion in the Taft-Hartley Act, the NLRB was required to define "supervisor" because the Board had concluded that when supervisors organized, they needed to be placed in bargaining units separate from nonsupervisors. Accordingly, prior to 1947, the Board had held that to be a supervisor, one needed to both direct the work of employees *and* "have the authority to hire, promote, discharge, discipline, or otherwise effect changes in the status of such employees."[68] Note that the indicia of the supervisor developed by the NLRB prior to 1947 did not include "assigning" employees. Neither was directing employees, alone, sufficient to establish one as a supervisor; one also must have the authority to "effect changes in the status of employees," such as the authority to hire, fire, promote, discipline, and other regulatory activities.[69]

The Taft-Hartley Act added "assign" and "responsibly to direct [employees]" to the authority over others that is independently sufficient to establish supervisory status. It is these 1947 additions that have caused considerable difficulty and that have unjustly excluded many workers from the protections of the act.

One major source of difficulty arises because the addition of "assign" and "responsibly to direct [employees]" creates an overlap between the definition of "supervisor" (an excluded category of worker) and "professional employee" (an included category of worker). Section 2(12) of the NLRA defines "professional employees" in a way that requires inquiry into whether work "involve[es] the consistent exercise of discretion and judgment in its performance." However, as others have pointed out, "most professionals (and many technical and other skilled employees) who also exercise independent judgment in their jobs routinely give assignments to [i.e., they "assign"] and direct other employees [i.e., they "responsibly direct"] in order to accomplish their professional duties."[70] For example, think of a lawyer who routinely assigns research projects to a law clerk and directs completion of the assignment. In the new digital economy, as was discussed in chapter 3, jobs increasingly entail work by professionals whose work "involve[s] the consistent exercise of discretion and judgment in its performance," and this work is performed by those who, for some portion of their workday, give routine assignments to and/or otherwise direct lower-skilled coworkers. But these professionals are not part of management in any realistic sense: they have no authority to affect the job status of coworkers, such as effectively recommending discipline. This overlap between the post-Taft-Hartley definition of "supervisor" and the protected status of professional employees threatens to sweep millions of professional employees into the classification of "supervisor." As Richardson (1994) points out, "Particularly as expert systems are used to take over more 'routine' problems, the number of non-supervisors who are members of the union or available to organize drops precipitously."[71] It is useful to recall that the Supreme Court has cautioned decision-makers to "take care to assure that exemptions from [the NLRA's] coverage are not so expansively interpreted as to deny protection to workers the Act was designed to reach [such as professional employees]"[72] The proposed clarification of the definition of "supervisor" discussed here responds to that admonition.

A second source of difficulty created by the 1947 addition of "assign" and "responsibly to direct [employees]" to the definition of "supervisor" is that these changes threaten to thwart Congress's intent that low-level, minor supervisors should not be exempted from the protections of the NLRA. Congress recognized that "certain employees with minor supervisory duties have [workplace] problems which may justify their inclusion in th[e] Act. [Congress] has therefore distinguished between straw bosses, leadmen, set-up men, and other minor supervisory employees, on the one hand, and the supervisor vested with such genuine management prerogatives as the right to hire or fire, discipline, or make effective recommendations with respect to such action."[73] Yet, other than carving out workers whose exercise of supervisory authority is "merely routine or clerical [in] nature," nothing in the language of § 2(11)'s definition of "supervisor" reflects Congress's intent not to classify as an excluded "supervisor" the "minor supervisory employees" whom Congress intended to include as NLRA-protected employees.

Litigation over the past twenty years with respect to nurses points out quite well the problems created by the Taft-Hartley Act changing § 2(11) to add the words "assign" and "responsibly direct" as independent indicia of supervisory status.

In an early effort, the NLRB attempted to distinguish those registered nurses (RNs) who truly are part of management—"nurse supervisors"—from other professional RNs who primarily perform nursing functions but who, incidental to their exercise of professional or technical judgment, occasionally make patient care decisions that require them to make assignments, or otherwise direct, less skilled workers, such as licensed practical nurses (LPNs) or nurse assistants. The NLRB held that these incidental patient care assignments given by RNs to less-skilled employees do not result in RNs being properly classified as "supervisors" because these actions are in the interest of patient care, not "in the interest of the employer" as required by § 2(11) for one to be classified as a supervisor. The Supreme Court disagreed, holding that all on-the-job, work-related, professional decisions are made "in the interest of the employer" and that, in effect, the Board had made a special exception for nurses, contrary to congressional intent.[74]

Subsequently, again in an attempt to prevent the supervisor exclusion from consuming the protection of the NLRA that Congress intended for professional employees such as nurses, the NLRB narrowly defined the third element of the § 2(11) definition of supervisor. The NLRB held that the RNs' incidental assigning of tasks, or otherwise directing LPNs and nurse assistants, as part of routine patient care is not the exercise of "independent judgment" as defined in § 2(11), but rather is conduct that is "informed by professional or technical training and experience."[75] Accordingly, such assigning and directing by RNs does not deny them the protections of the NLRA by placing them in the category of a "supervisor." Again, the Supreme Court disagreed. In *NLRB v. Kentucky River Community Care, Inc.*, in a 5–4 decision written by Justice Antonin Scalia, the Supreme Court was unwilling to defer to the NLRB in its effort to harmonize the language of § 2(11) with the stated goal of the NLRA to include professional employees such as RNs within the act's protection and by recognizing that professional employees periodically need to make assignments and direct lower-skilled workers incidental to their exercise of ordinary professional judgment. The effect of the decision in *Kentucky River* was to create a "barrier to unionization [of RN nurses] in almost all cases" and to provide health-care industry employers "essentially uncontrolled discretion to fire nurses who oppose the[] laudable goals [of] fight[ing] to improve nursing ratios and patient care."[76]

Following the Court's *Kentucky River* decision, the NLRB under President George W. Bush, in *Oakwood Health Care, Inc.*, added "charge nurses" to the growing list of "supervisors" who are denied the NLRA's protections. Charge nurses primarily engage in the normal patient-care professional functions of an RN—caring for sick, disabled, or elderly patients—but occasionally, for only a fraction of their shift, "assign other RNs, . . . LPNs, nurs[e] assistants, technicians, and paramedics to their shifts."[77] The Bush NLRB held that this slight degree of "assigning" and "directing" was sufficient for charge nurses to be designated as supervisors. As the NLRB general counsel summarized the Board's decision in *Oakwood Health Care*, the Board's view is that one is a supervisor when a person, using independent judgment, designates a lower-skilled worker to a place to work (e.g., a particular work location) or a time to work (e.g., a particular shift), or otherwise assigns "significant overall duties, *i.e.*, tasks, to an employee." Such assigning constitutes a supervisory function, so long as the assigning is more than an "*ad hoc* instruction that the employee perform some discrete task (such as a one-time instruction to empty a bedpan or give a particular patient a pill."[78] Even a slight portion of a person's workday devoted to such assigning or directing of others qualifies the person possessing such oversight as a "supervisor." The NLRB general counsel explained that "individuals have been found to be supervisors where they have [engaged in assigning or directing others] for as little as 10–15 percent of [a person's] total work time"[79] (i.e., as little as one hour or less per eight-hour work shift).

The criteria for determining supervisory status, as articulated in *Oakwood Health Care*, has had the effect of removing much of the nursing profession from the protection of the NLRA.[80] It is hard to disagree with the dissenters in *Oakwood Health Care*, who concluded that the Board's decision had far-reaching negative implications for many professional employees whose responsibilities include directing the work of lesser-skilled employees. The dissenters concluded that the decision had "created a new class of workers under Federal labor law: workers who have neither the genuine prerogatives of management nor the statutory rights of ordinary employees. Into that category may fall most professionals (among many other workers)." The dissenters in *Oakwood Health Care* estimated that as early as 2012, the NLRB's expansive definition of "supervisor" could result in excluding nearly thirty-four million professionals and others, accounting for 23.3 percent of the workforce.[81] RNs, for example, comprise one of the largest segments of the US workforce. Currently, there are more than 3.8 million RNs nationwide, 84.5 percent of whom are employed in various aspects of the healh-care profession. Through 2026, the number of RNs is projected to grow by more than 200,000 new positions annually, a growth rate of 15 percent.[82] Nurses in nursing homes, in particular, are undercompensated and require the benefits of collective bargaining. Nationwide, according to the Bureau of Labor Statistics, RNs in the US who are union members "can earn an average of $200–$400 more per week than non-unionized nurses."[83]

But it is not just the millions of nurses who are harmed by the expansive definition of "supervisor." It has been estimated that "thirty percent of workers in at least twenty-four professions could be severely affected by [*Oakwood Healthcare*]. . . . Essentially, the Board's rulings permit employers to make a supervisor out of any employee who uses independent judgment or has authority to assign or direct other employees."[84] One exhaustive study concluded that "especially [for] low-level supervisors who themselves often suffer low pay and poor working conditions, [misclassification of employees as supervisors] is part of a 'divide-and-conquer' strategy to weaken workers' bargaining power."[85]

A legislative solution is needed because the NLRB and the courts are not likely over time to consistently limit the scope of the terms "assign" and "responsibly to direct" in NLRA § 2(11). The proposed changes to the NLRA's definition of "supervisor," as set forth in this discussion, return the definition to its pre-1947 meaning by eliminating "assign" and "responsibly to direct" from the indicia found in § 2(11) for independently and sufficiently determining who is a supervisor.

Moreover, as stated here, the historical purpose of the supervisor exclusion was that those excluded as supervisors should *not* include straw bosses, leadmen, set-up men, and other minor supervisory employees. Rather, it should be limited to those persons, like foremen, whose primary function is directing the work of others on an ongoing basis rather than doing the work themselves. For a short period, the NLRB had respected this congressional distinction by *not* excluding as supervisors those "whose primary function is physical participation in the production or operating processes of their employers' plants and who [only] incidentally direct the movements and operations of less skilled subordinate employees [in the performance of that person's own nonsupervisory functions]"[86] Since its decision in *Oakwood Health Care,* the NLRB has lost sight of the historical purpose of the supervisor exclusion since now millions of workers, such as charge nurses, are viewed as supervisors by the NLRB, notwithstanding the fact that their "primary function is physical participation in the . . . operating processes of their employers' [business] and . . . [only] incidentally direct the movements and operations of less skilled subordinate employees." Accordingly, the definition of "supervisor" in § 2(11) needs to be amended to require that to be classified as a "supervisor," the individual's supervisory activities must be executed for a majority of the individual's work time. This change will go a long way to limit the exclusion to those whom Congress intended to define as "supervisors" in 1947—those who have authority to exercise a broad, managerial type of direction requiring most of the person's work time.

In combination, the independent contractor and the supervisor exclusions, as the NLRB and the courts have interpreted them, have "withered the number of workers eligible for [inclusion in] bargaining units that function as sources of countervailing power."[87] Adoption of these changes addresses these deficiencies.

Preventing the Misclassification of Workers

The NLRA also needs to be clarified to provide that an employer violates the NLRA by misclassifying an employee. Reforming the NLRA in this way will overturn the NLRB's 2019 decision in *Velox Express*,[88] which held that misclassification is not a violation of the NLRA.

Two arguments dominate the view that an employer's misclassification of its employees as independent contractors, standing alone, violates § 8(a)(1) of the NLRA. The first is the reality that by misclassifying employees as independent contractors, an employer, regardless of its motive or intent, inherently interferes with, restrains, and coerces those employees in the exercise of their § 7 rights because the employer effectively conveys that the misclassified employees do not have any rights or protections under the act when in fact they do.[89] Relatedly, misclassification can be understood as interfering with employees' rights of self-organization protected by the NLRA because misclassification effectively conveys to employees that engaging in union or other protected activities is futile[90] and preemptively prevents the misclassified employees from engaging in § 7 activity.[91]

The NLRB majority in *Velox Express* rejected all these arguments, concluding that they are grounded in the proposition that the misclassification of employees as independent contractors is inherently coercive. As the Board majority stated:[92]

> An employer's mere communication to its workers that they are classified as independent contractors does not expressly invoke the Act. It does not prohibit the workers from engaging in Section 7 activity. It does not threaten them with adverse consequences for doing so, or promise them benefits if they refrain from doing so. . . . If the employer responds with threats, promises, interrogations, and so forth, then it will have violated Section 8(a)(1), but not before.

In short, the majority viewed misclassification as no more than the employer's communication of its "legal opinion" that its workers are independent contractors, an "opinion" whose expression the majority views as a protected free speech right.

The dissent in *Velox Express* focused on the facts of the case. It explained that the employer in that case imposed a contract on its drivers that contains a clause that "acknowledges that [the driver] is an independent contractor and is not an employee of Company." By requiring employees to sign this contract, the employer conveyed to Velox drivers that they had no rights under the NLRA when, in fact, the drivers were employees who possessed NLRA rights. By forcing employees with rights to sign a document stating that they had no such rights, the employer was not simply expressing a legal opinion, but rather was unlawfully coercing its employees. These actions by the employer, the dissent argued, had a predictable "chilling effect" on employees by incorrectly communicating to them that because they had no NLRA rights, any attempts to exercise such rights would be futile. Section 1 of the NLRA declares that the policy of the US is to protect "the exercise by workers of full freedom of association, self-organization, and designation of representatives of their own choosing, for the purpose of negotiating the terms and conditions of their employment or other mutual aid or protection." The dissent argued that "taking the proper statutory perspective—by focusing on the rights Congress gave employees—reveals the defects in the majority's position."[93] There is support for the dissent's view in the academic literature,[94] and in the PRO Act.[95]

Protecting Employees Who Have Multiple Employers

An important change to the NLRA, which is particularly needed because of changes to the modern workplace, is to provide that two or more persons shall be employers under the act if each codetermines or shares control over the employees' essential terms and conditions of employment. In applying this standard, the NLRB or a court would be required to consider as relevant direct control, indirect control, reserved authority to control, and control exercised in fact. This approach to defining joint employers codifies the joint employer standard that the Board adopted in its 2015 *Browning-Ferris* decision,[96] which was overturned by the Trump NLRB in 2020 through rulemaking.[97]

For the nonlabor law specialist, it is all too easy to overlook the significance of a reform that expands the criteria for establishing the joint employer status of two companies that share control over employees' essential terms and conditions of employment. Yet, in the modern digital economy, with an increasing number of workers being contingent employees, expanding the criteria for establishing the joint employer status of two companies removes one of the most important barriers that denies employees their aspiration to obtain the benefits of collective bargaining.

Earlier, this chapter discussed companies that engage in fissuring—outsourcing by a lead company by contracting with a staffing agency to provide workers to perform the outsourced functions or by hiring a management company to provide and oversee leased employees. Such outsourcing excuses the lead company from many legal and financial obligations, such as making contributions to Social Security and Medicare, purchasing workers' compensation insurance, paying minimum wage and premium pay for overtime, and incurring liability arising from claims of employment discrimination. Employers typically also deny contracted workers health insurance, pensions, and other benefits that are available to its regular full-time employees. In addition, such outsourcing has provided lead companies the argument that they may refuse to recognize a union that seeks to represent the workers performing outsourced work, even when this work is done at the premises of the lead company, because these workers are not the lead company's employees but rather are the employees of a staffing agency. If, however, the lead company and the staffing agency are "joint employers," then both companies are considered the employer of those performing the outsourced work. This precludes the lead company from validly claiming no responsibilities under the labor and employment laws for these employees.

It is a mistake to view the "temporary employees" (temps) whom a staffing agency provides to a company as simply workers whose tenure with a host company is for a short term. Indeed, many temps who are referred by staffing agencies have worked for the same company for many years.[98] In February 2021, the Labor Department reported that employers in the US employed 3.7 million such "temporary" employees, an increase of 1 million just since 2010. Temporary employees are becoming a dominant force in the US economy. The number doubled between 2000 and 2008, fell during the 2008–2010 Great Recession, and then doubled again between 2010 and 2020. The increase in the number of temps since 2010 represents a 4 percent annualized increase, twice the 2 percent annual rate of increase for all employment during that period.[99]

It also is a mistake to think of temps as day laborers looking for an odd job from a passing contractor or the occasional office help associated with the Kelly Girl image from the past. As one commentator has explained:[100]

> The overwhelming majority of th[e] growth [in temps] has come in blue-collar work in factories and warehouses. . . . [M]ore than one in every 20 blue-collar workers [is] a temp. . . . They are regular employees . . . working in the supply chain of many

> of America's largest companies—Walmart, Macy's, Nike, Frito-Lay. They make our frozen pizzas, sort the recycling from our trash, cut our vegetables and clean our imported fish. They unload clothing and toys made overseas and pack them to fill our store shelves. They are as important to the global economy as shipping containers and Asian garment workers.

The highest utilization rates of temps are in the manufacturing and transportation and utilities industries and, of these, the largest industry share of temps is concentrated in manufacturing.[101]

For the millions of temps to obtain union representation and effective access to the benefits of collective bargaining, it is necessary for temps to be classified as employees of the host employer (i.e., the lead company that contracts for their services with a staffing agency). Theoretically, the temps could organize the staffing agency, but that would not be effective because the host employer could simply contract with a different, nonunionized staffing agency to secure its needed temps. Moreover, organizing the staffing agency's employees is unrealistic in most cases because those employees typically work for a variety of different employers at different places, have different types of work assignments, and most likely possess a variety of skill and work experiences. Consequently, all the temps employed by a staffing agency are unlikely to share a community of interest needed for effective union organization.

There is no theoretical barrier to two employers being viewed as joint employers of a single group of employees. The Supreme Court recognized this possibility more than half a century ago.[102] In the first decade after the enactment of the NLRA, the NLRB expansively construed its "joint employer" doctrine, finding that two companies were joint employers even when only one in practice controlled the employees' conditions of employment, so long as the other company possessed the authority to do so, even if that authority in fact had been unexercised.[103]

By 1984, however, the Board had developed a much more constricted view of the test for the creation of joint-employer relationships—one that limited joint employer status to business relationships where each employer in practice exercised actual significant control over the same employees. As the Board would later explain in *Airborne Express*, "[t]he essential element in [the] analysis is whether a putative joint employer's control over employment matters is direct and immediate."[104]

In short, beginning in 1984, a joint employer relationship depended on evidence of direct and immediate control over key employment terms, control that was actually exercised. Indirect control alone, an unexercised potential right to control, or the "limited and routine" control inherent in a service arrangement was insufficient. This approach to joint employer status made it easy for a company to contract with a staffing agency, prescribe the wages to be paid, and set other basic conditions of employment, but turn over all day-to-day supervision of the temps to the staffing agency and then claim that it, the host company, did not employ any of the temps as a joint employer because it did not exercise direct, day-to-day control over them.

Browning-Ferris Industries of California, Inc.[105] is a good example of a triangular structure, in which a host company contracts with a staffing agency to hire temps, with the host company substantially controlling the economic realities but doing so indirectly to avoid being viewed as a joint employer with the staffing agency and thus being subject to union organizing of its temp workers.

"The facts of BFI [*Browning-Ferris Industries*] are fairly representative of joint-employer cases brought before the Board from across the American economy [where] the companies tr[y] to construct an invisible wall between each other ensuring that [the host company] retain[s] no direct control over [the staffing agency's] employees even while employees of each company worked side by side."[106] In *Browning-Ferris Industries*, a recycling facility contracted with a staffing agency, Leadpoint, to provide screen cleaners, housekeepers, and most recycled material sorters who worked at the same facility as BFI's own full-time employees. The details of the arrangement were set forth in a "temporary labor services agreement." Leadpoint's own managers supervised the workers that it provided to BFI, exercising "the sole responsibility to counsel, discipline, review, evaluate, determine pay rates, and terminate" these employees. But the temporary labor services agreement reserved considerable indirect control over the economic realities of the arrangement. The agreement provided that Leadpoint was required to screen those it hired to ensure that the employees that Leadpoint provided were free from the effects of alcohol and illegal drug use on the job. In addition, BFI reserved the right to reject or request the termination of the temp workers "for any or no reason," and indeed did on occasion influence the terminations of some. Moreover, the agreement between BFI and Leadpoint included a rate schedule that provides that Leadpoint "solely determines the pay rates paid to its Personnel," but without BFI's approval, Leadpoint was prohibited from "pay[ing] a pay rate in excess of the pay rate for full-time employees of [BFI] who perform similar tasks." BFI set the hours of operations and shifts, decided when the production line would continue running for overtime purposes, and determined when breaks occurred. As stated by Van Wagtendonk (2018), "Taken together, Browning-Ferris exerted substantial control over the employees, albeit always with a Leadpoint supervisor as an intermediary."[107]

A local of the Teamsters Union filed a representation petition to represent a bargaining unit consisting of 240 "full-time and regular part-time employees" who were "employed by [Leadpoint] and [BFI], joint employers." Both BFI and Leadpoint sought dismissal of the petition on the ground that they were not joint employers of those whom Leadpoint referred to work at the BFI facility, because BFI had no direct control over the substantial terms and conditions of the employees that Leadpoint referred to it. Under the standards in place since 1984, BFI, as well as dozens of other employers and staffing agencies with functionally similar arrangements, had a strong argument.

However, the NLRB changed direction in its 2015 *Browning-Ferris Industries of California, Inc.* decision.[108] The NLRB concluded that BFI and Leadpoint were joint employers and that the union's representation petition sought an election in an appropriate bargaining unit. In so finding, the Board relied, among other things, on BFI's possession of control over those whom Leadpoint may hire to work at its facility; BFI's direct *and* indirect control over work processes and task assignments; and BFI's significant role in determining employees' wages. In concluding that BFI and Leadpoint were joint employers, the NLRB held that the issue is whether a putative joint employer possesses sufficient control over employees' essential terms and conditions of employment to permit meaningful collective bargaining. The Board held that it no longer will require that a joint employer must not only *possess* the authority to control employees' terms and conditions of employment, but also must *exercise* that authority. Reserved authority to control terms and conditions of employment, even if not exercised, is now relevant to the joint-employment inquiry. The Board also held that control that is exercised indirectly—such as through an intermediary—may now establish joint-employer status.

The D.C. Circuit Court of Appeals enforced the board's decision in *Browning-Ferris Industries of California, Inc.* with respect to its determination that both reserved authority to control and indirect control are relevant factors in the joint-employer analysis.[109] The D.C. Circuit reasoned that the "common-law element of control is the principal guidepost" for determining whether an entity is an employer of another and at common law the relevant inquiry is whether the servant "is controlled or is subject to the right to control by the master." In addition, "[t]raditional common-law principles of agency do not require that 'control . . . be exercised directly and immediately' to be relevant to the joint-employer inquiry. . . . In fact, the National Labor Relations Act itself expressly recognizes that agents acting 'indirectly' on behalf of an employer could also count as employers."[110] Thus, the act indicates that the NLRB is to examine all indicia of employer status, whether that status is exercised directly or indirectly.

According to Warner (2019), the Board's *Browning-Ferris* decision does not specify a test to determine whether an employer exercised *sufficient* indirect control for a joint employer relationship to be established, leaving room "for arguments to be made in the future disputing whether joint-employer status exists in particular situations."[111] What is clear is that the changes made in *Browning-Ferris* enable hundreds of thousands of temporary employees who are provided to a company by a temporary staffing agency to have an enhanced opportunity to secure union representation and the benefits of collective bargaining.

However, four years after the *Browning-Ferris* decision, in a 3–2 decision in *Hy-Brand Industrial Contractor's, LTD.*, the Trump NLRB overruled *Browning-Ferris* and returned to the pre–*Browning Ferris* standard for making joint employer determinations—namely, requiring proof that a company actually exercise some "direct and immediate control" over the essential employment terms of another company's employees.[112] In a vigorous dissent, two Board members argued that

> [t]ellingly absent from the majority's endless recitation of potential hardships for employers [especially the alleged absence of predictable results] is any mention of the concern that should undoubtedly be foremost: ensuring that the statutory promise of collective bargaining extends to as many workplaces and working arrangements as the Act contemplates. . . . The predictability that the majority achieves here is a one-sided assurance to employers that, by retaining a nominal distance from the supervision of workers, they can exert control and still avoid statutory bargaining obligations.

The NLRB subsequently vacated its decision in *Hy-Brand* because a Board member voting with the 3–2 majority was disqualified from participating in the case.[113] However, *Hy-Brand* and its dissenting opinions are discussed here because *Browning-Ferris* was overturned in 2020 by the Trump NLRB through rulemaking that adopted the majority's position in *Hy-Brand*.[114] The reasoning of the *Hy-Brand* dissent, quoted here, remains relevant both with respect to deficiencies in the Trump NLRB's administrative rule and because in September 2022, the NLRB issued a Notice of Proposed Rulemaking, which would rescind the joint-employer rule issued in 2020 by the Trump NLRB and replace it with a rule that provides that an employer is a joint employer of particular employees if the employer has an employment relationship with those employees under established common-law agency principles and the employer shares or codetermines those matters governing at least one of the employees' essential terms and conditions of employment.[115]

The NLRA should be amended to adopt the *Browning-Ferris* standards for determining joint employer status. It is unseemly for the US to proclaim in the NLRA that the national labor policy is to encourage the practice and procedure of collective bargaining, and at the same time adopt joint employer standards that permit—indeed invite—employers to avoid statutory bargaining obligations over workers whom they control by adopting the subterfuge of retaining a nominal distance from the supervision of workers. There already are an estimated 3.7 million "temporary" employees, an increase of 1 million just since 2010. With the prediction that this number will continue to increase faster than the overall growth of the workforce, it is time to incorporate the *Browning-Ferris* standards into the NLRA.[116] Otherwise, labor relations law will continue to vacillate with presidential politics, and millions of "temporary" workers will be denied the opportunity to choose collective bargaining.[117]

In summary, studies repeatedly show that a majority of nonunion workers desire unionization and the benefits of collective bargaining, but their desire remains unsatisfied. There are many reasons for this unsatisfied demand, and subsequent chapters will detail more of them. But one important explanation is inherent in the structure of the NLRA itself as interpreted by the NLRB and the courts: the exclusion of millions of workers who are classified as independent contractors and low-level supervisors, combined with the effective exclusion of millions of temporary employees who work for two employers (e.g., a staffing agency and its host employer client). By one estimate, for example, "more than half of women workers are excluded from coverage under the . . . NLRA [and thus are] stripped of the right granted under the [A]ct to choose independent workplace representation."[118] Just widening the range of workers permitted the legal protection of efforts to achieve collective representation would go a long way toward bringing the promise of industrial democracy to millions of American workers.

5 Opportunities in the NLRA during the Representation Process for Employer-Created Delay and Interference with Employee Free Choice

Labor Law Reforms Needed[1]

Remove employer standing in representation cases.

Prevent employers from gerrymandering union representation elections.

Permit offsite union representation elections.

Provide for electronic voting in union elections.

Streamline election procedures.

Change notice-posting requirements and the requirement that the employer provide the union a list of bargaining unit employee names and contact information.

Provide for civil penalties for violations of the posting requirements and voter list requirements.

* * *

Chapter 4 demonstrated that, as currently written and interpreted, the National Labor Relations Act (NLRA) excludes millions of US workers from its protections. The reforms proposed in that chapter redress some of the most important of those coverage deficiencies by widening the range of protected employees.

But increasing the range of choice is only part of what is needed to redress the problem of US workers in the private sector being denied their aspiration for collective representation. National labor policy also must reduce the direct costs associated with such choices. Over 600,000 private-sector workers lined up to vote in National Labor Relations Board (NLRB) elections during the past decade (see table 1.3 in chapter 1). And there are millions more outside the ranks of organized labor who would line up to vote in union representation elections if they did not feel that the potential costs in terms of employer retaliation outweighed the benefits of collective representation. But "[various] levels and kinds of employer resistance to [unionization] clearly impose direct costs on employees and corrupt the process of deliberation [over whether to choose union representation]."[2] In a variety of ways, the NLRA has been complicit in facilitating, or even encouraging, this employer resistance. One deficiency is the myriad of opportunities that the act provides for employers to create delays during the representation process. According to Hurd and Uehlein (1994), "Legal delays are a major barrier to organizing [because] delay buy[s] time for a union-resistance campaign."[3] What follows is a discussion of how the NLRA permits the employer to use delaying as an anti-union tactic.

Three reforms in the NLRA are needed to combat delays by the employer during the representation process: (1) removing employer standing in representation cases, (2) preventing employers from gerrymandering a bargaining unit as a way both to cause delays and to include individuals in the unit who have no interest in joining the union, and (3) streamlining election procedures by codifying portions of the NLRB's 2014 regulations that modernized its representation election procedures. To more fully appreciate how and why these proposed changes are needed and are well designed to encourage and facilitate employees' free choice, it is necessary to understand how employer delay—even if it is legal—interferes with employees' right to choose collective bargaining.

Employer Motivations to Delay the Representation Process

Beginning in the late 1970s, as global competition intensified and employers escalated what is benignly referred to as "union avoidance" efforts, companies increasingly retained law firms and management consultants to advise them on how to stop unions.[4] At the same time, employer lawbreaking increased. This is evidenced by the increased number of meritorious unfair labor practices filed against employers compared to the number of representation election petitions filed.[5] Lane Windham (2017), who has examined this data carefully, concludes that "the increased use of antiunion management consultants and lawyers . . . helped shift the paradigm of acceptable employer behavior . . . [t]hrough an avalanche of seminars, training, books, and speeches [making] mainstream the level of antiunionism that had once been extreme in the midcentury labor-management arrangement."[6]

One anti-union technique recommended by management consultants is that companies should limit the employment of women, Blacks, and Hispanics because research showed that statistically, these groups tend be more prone to unionization.[7] Business schools and professors added their voices by inserting union avoidance into the course of instruction for their students, many of whom would become corporate managers. These future business executives were taught that unions are an unnecessary expense to be avoided at all costs. Business schools taught that "it is almost negligent to allow unionization to happen, that it is a 'rookie mistake' to confront a union-organizing drive without the assistance of a management consultant, [and that] it is quite possible for management to effectively destroy an organizing effort [given the reality that] the NLRB response to employer unfair labor practices [is] so lengthy and the penalties quite mild."[8]

It was in this context that management consultants and management lawyers taught corporate clients to "make good use of the predictable patterns in an NLRB election process," especially the ready availability of legal delay.[9] Management consultants widely deployed what has been described as a "textbook union-resistance campaign."[10] First, employers are urged to discourage employees from signing union authorization cards or petitions, which typically state an employee's desire that the soliciting union serve as the employee's bargaining representation. The authorization cards are used to meet the union's obligation to present to the NLRB a 30 percent showing of interest, which is required for the NLRB to process the union's representation election petition.[11] Employer statements to employees discouraging them from signing union authorization cards can be very intimidating, but they are legal nevertheless. For example, the NLRB has permitted employers to tell employees, "Don't sign any cards; they can be fatal to a business." The Board found that this and similar statements associating "fatal" consequences with signing a union authorization card did not reasonably intimidate or threaten employees: these statements, it concluded, merely expressed the company's position that the employees would be better served in terms of benefits by rejecting the union, and the use of the word "fatal" was a neutral reference to the possibility that unionization could lead to difficulties if the union struck to obtain unreasonable demands.[12]

If, notwithstanding employers' efforts, employees sign a sufficient number of cards to provide the required showing of interest, the next phase in the textbook anti-union campaign is to do everything possible to delay as long as possible the subsequent steps in the NLRB representation process. The NLRB's current procedures provide many possibilities for such delay. For example, the employer presently is a party in the representation election process and has a right to demand a preelection hearing, in which the employer typically will contest the scope of the bargaining unit, which defines the employees who will be provided the right to vote in the upcoming union representation election. Often, employers also will seek to litigate voter eligibility issues at this hearing. The standard advice that management consultants and lawyers give to clients is to always request a preelection hearing. As one consultant stated, "'I have yet to see a situation where time worked against the employer in an election. . . . Suffice it to say that you have at least 500 issues. So, you litigate those issues. . . . You could come up with them for almost a year. As we did in one case.'"[13]

Another delaying tactic is to refuse to agree to a consent election, or even if consenting, agree only to a "stipulation for consent election," for then preelection and postelection disputes that arise are not resolved expeditiously by the NLRB's regional director; rather, they are referred to the NLRB in Washington, D.C., adding considerable time to the process. Once employers more routinely began to engage management consultants, "stipulations for consent elections" more than tripled. One study showed that "[s]uch delay costs organizing workers dearly. [E]ach month of delay between the filing of the petition and the election decreased the workers' chance of winning their union election by 2.5 percent."[14]

One useful indicator of the utility of delay for employers, in addition to the fact that their highly experienced management consultants always recommend it, is that on average, there is a 17 percent overall drop between the percentage of bargaining unit members who sign union authorization cards at the time that the union filed the representation petition and those who end up voting for the union in the NLRB representation election.[15] Employers argue that this drop shows solid proof of the value of delay—that it provides the employer an opportunity to show employees why unionization is not in their best interest. From that perspective, delay is not only benign, but also helpful in educating employees and promoting free choice. It is this "don't muzzle employers" argument that is the cornerstone of the case *against* reducing delay.

Proponents of amending the NLRA to reduce delay in the representation process need to answer this core employer claim that reducing delay denies employees access to both sides of the argument regarding the decision whether to unionize. Even with an expedited representation election, employers have ample opportunity to present their side. First, employers typically know quite early, through information gathered by their front-line supervisors or anti-union employees, that an organizing drive is underway and that the union is in the process of soliciting signatures on union authorization cards among its employees.[16] This advanced knowledge gives the employer a head start in perfecting and communicating its anti-union message to employees. Indeed, before the representation petition is even filed, it is not unusual for an employer to initiate a pattern of retaliation against those of its employees who are the organizing leaders. This is done in an effort to undermine the unionization effort before it takes root.

Obtaining signatures on authorization cards can take considerable time because, while the union needs only to obtain cards from 30 percent of the bargaining unit employees to satisfy the "showing of interest" requirement, it will insist as a rule on signed cards from a majority or more of the employees before filing an election petition with the NLRB, since there is an inevitable attrition of support as the organizing drive continues.[17] Thus, this time-consuming process of securing signatures on authorization cards provides the employer additional time to communicate its anti-union views to the employees to "educate" them.

Moreover, the authorization cards that give evidence of the union's showing of interest must accompany the petition that the union files with the NLRB or be provided soon thereafter. The regional office then must investigate. An NLRB agent must acquire a current payroll list of employees furnished by the employer and then check the cards against that payroll list to ascertain whether the cards are current and sufficient in number. This investigation of the showing of interest normally occurs before a preelection hearing is held. And the investigation may be time-consuming, depending on how many employees are in the bargaining unit. This delay provides even more opportunity for the employer to communicate its views on unionization to the employees.

The point is that quite early during the union-organizing campaign, the company normally has considerable time to assemble an anti-union campaign and disseminate its arguments against unionization, all prior to the NLRB regional director even scheduling the preelection hearing. Moreover, even with an expedited timetable for conducting representation elections, there is much additional time between the filing of the representation election petition and the scheduling of the election, which provides the employer ample opportunity to communicate its point of view on unionization to employees. Take, for example, the procedures for streamlining representation elections in the NLRB's 2014 regulations to modernize representation election procedures.[18] Under these expedited procedures, once a union files a petition for an election, the NLRB must schedule a preelection hearing within eight days from the date that the notice of the hearing is served on the labor organization. This prelection hearing can be time-consuming, as the regional office needs to assemble the evidence needed to make an informed decision whether the petition filed by the union raises a "question concerning representation (QCR)." That inquiry entails requiring a determination of whether the employer satisfies the NLRB's statutory and discretionary jurisdiction, whether the bargaining unit proposed by the union constitutes "an appropriate bargaining unit," and whether, as a matter of law, there is any bar to the conduct of the election. Under the reform discussed here, the employer would not be a party at this hearing, but the time required to compete a preelection hearing still would provide the employer additional opportunities to advance its point of view to the bargaining unit employees.

When (if) the NLRB regional director concludes that the union's petition raises a real QCR and directs an election, the NLRB's 2014 expedited procedures provide that its regional office is required to transmit the notice of election at the same time as the direction of election, and the employer must post that notice within two days after it is served in a place where employees will see the notice. The NLRB's regional director must then schedule the election for the earliest date practicable, but not later than twenty *business* days (about one calendar month) after the direction of election. The delay in scheduling the election following the preelection hearing and subsequent issuance of the direction of election, of course, will vary depending on the circumstances of each case. However, it is likely that altogether there will normally be at least thirty to forty-five calendar days between the scheduling of the preelection hearing and the date set for the conduct of the election.

Combined with the time that is available to the employer during the period when the union is gathering authorization card signatures and the NLRB is ascertaining the adequacy of the showing of interest, there is ample opportunity for the employer to convey its point of view to the employees. Charges that these expedited procedures muzzle the employer are hyperbolic. The charge that they provide for "ambush elections" equally lacks merit.[19]

The desire for additional time to coerce employees is the real reason that many employers and their management consultants so strongly insist on additional delay. Delay provides employers enhanced opportunities to engage in "strong-arm tactics such as firing, demoting, and suspending workers involved in organizing drives," conduct that occurs frequently.[20] Retaliation against the leaders of a unionization effort often occurs early in the organizing drive, but it takes time for the intimidating impact of this action to take hold among rank-and-file employees, create high levels of anxiety, and effectively erode employees' support for the union. Preelection delay provides that time.

Moreover, delay provides increased opportunities for employers to engage in "payroll stacking."[21] Regular part-time employees are permitted to vote in the representation election if they are actively working during the payroll period immediately preceding the date of the direction of election and are still employed by the company at the time of the election.[22] Consultants urge employers to take advantage of this loophole in the present NLRB election procedures, which allows employers to "seed the voting group with as many 'no' votes as possible [by hiring, before the date of the direction of the election,] relatives on a regularly scheduled part-time basis. [Consultants advise companies to hire] even a hell of a lot of people if you need to. . . . 'Stacking' a payroll is permitted."[23] This payroll-stacking strategy works only if there is sufficient delay between the date that the union files the representation petition and the date that the NLRB regional office issues an order directing an election, since time is needed for the employer to organize a new hiring effort that is designed to seed the bargaining unit with sufficient "no" votes to affect the outcome of the election. Under current rules, any reasonably well qualified management labor lawyer can gain the necessary delay by raising a myriad of issues at the preelection hearing, usually challenging the appropriateness of the bargaining unit proposed by the union, raising issues regarding the voting eligibility of certain employees, and then appealing any adverse ruling by the regional director to the NLRB in Washington.

A variation of this payroll-stacking tactic is evidenced in an organizing drive that occurred at HarperCollins, San Francisco, by the Communications Workers of America. Company lawyers challenged the eligibility of sixteen employees to be included in the bargaining unit, thereby prolonging a preelection period for months. The tactic worked; the challenges litigated at the preelection hearing delayed the election by five-and-a-half months. The NLRB found all sixteen challenges to be groundless, but HarperCollins, San Francisco, used the time gained by this delay to its advantage because during the period of delay, the employer eliminated six of eighty-three members of the bargaining unit, each a leading union supporter (two promoted out of the unit and four laid off). Then the employer hired eleven new employees, all of whom voted in the election. The union lost the election by a margin of five votes.[24] If the NLRA were reformed to eliminate the employer as a party in preelection representation proceedings, employers would be unable to raise frivolous claims at the preelection hearing that are calculated to buy time for payroll stacking and other nefarious actions that distort the election process or intimidate employees.

In sum, delay that is used to provide time to fire and otherwise discriminate against union activists and to seed the voting group with anti-union votes is highly useful to the employer. But these uses of delay represent only part of its utility in defeating unionization. Robert A. Penney (2004) has explained how consultants have elevated anti-union campaigning to a science by adopting a set blueprint for an anti-union campaign that is "'battle-tested.'" These well-honed anti-union campaigns have proved to be effective and may include, but do not require, illegal employer conduct such as discriminatory discharge and overt intimidation. This blueprint entails "tactics and strategies [that] revolve around a constant barrage of propaganda that can basically be divided into positive and negative incentives to vote against the union . . . The themes and messages contained within this propaganda can be described as a 'carrot and stick' approach to union avoidance."[25] But to be effective, this "barrage of propaganda" requires time—time that is gained by delaying the NLRB's preelection process.

The "carrot" side of the standard anti-union campaign involves persuading employees that the employer has learned its lesson, has received a "wake-up call," and will do better in the future in terms of treatment of employees, but it just needs a second chance to demonstrate this epiphany to the employees. Employees are called together in repeated meetings during work time, called "captive audience" meetings (more on this in chapter 7), in order to be propagandized with management promises to improve conditions. Or employees receive repeated letters sent to their homes, or text messages or emails, all containing this same message of a rational, fair, and benevolent employer who may have made past mistakes but is now being victimized by the union.[26] Although it is illegal for an employer to grant or promise benefits during an election campaign in an effort to influence employee voting in the upcoming election,[27] employers often do just that by announcing pay raises and new benefits—perhaps, for example, enhanced vacation time or a grievance system where employees can resolve workplace disputes with management. Although illegal, these grants and promises of benefits during the election campaign "are strategically difficult for a union to challenge," according to Penney.[28] The union is understandably reluctant to challenge a wage increase or an extra vacation day and thus be tarred as the source of denying employees some desired benefit granted by the employer. Management consultants can show their clients that such "carrot" propaganda tactics are effective. Many employees are persuaded to withhold support for the union by the promise of management's newfound commitment to employee welfare and the need to give the company another chance.

Supplementing the carrot is the stick—implied threats centered on the pitfalls of choosing a union. Through communications that emphasize disempowerment and the threatening implications of choosing union representation, the employer attempts to create anxiety among employees. The goal is for this anxiety to take root to a sufficient extent that many employees who initially desired collective bargaining representation will fear its consequences and end up voting against the union. Time is key. Time is needed for the anxiety and fear created by the employer's messaging to permeate the workplace and gain control over large numbers of bargaining unit employees. Delaying the representation election process buys that time. Employer labor consultants typically recommend that employers impliedly threaten employees through communications that emphasize three themes: strikes, dues, and management prerogatives.[29]

The employer's message of choice is conveying the real likelihood that the union will "call you out on strike" to achieve its collective bargaining goals. Management consultants teach the company to create anxiety among the bargaining unit employees by stressing, through leaflets, text messages, emails, and captive audience speeches, the length of strikes that the union seeking recognition had engaged in at other companies, the adverse economic impact of the strike on the strikers and their families, and the disloyalty and harm to the employer's business caused by striking. The linguistic choices are critical, such as phrasing the communication as the union will "take you out on strike," suggesting a degree of coercion by the union and the concomitant loss of personal choice, even when the union's constitution and bylaws provide that no strike can be called unless authorized by a strike vote among the affected employees.

The objective of this employer propaganda is for employees to be intimidated. The employer's explicit assertion of the inevitability of job loss if employees unionize constitutes unlawful intimidation.[30] But the employers are advised to choose messaging designed for employees to conclude that strikes and their economic hazards, including job losses, are inevitable and unionization is futile, without the employer ever *explicitly* making either statement.

Predictions by the employer are permissible but hazardous, for to be lawful, a prediction as to the precise effects of unionization "must be carefully phrased on the basis of objective fact to convey an employer's belief as to *demonstrably probable consequences beyond his control*."[31] The trap that employers are taught to avoid is making a prediction in the absence of "objective fact" upon which to base it. The solution that management consultants have honed for companies is to avoid stating what "would" or "will" result from unionization, for that is a prediction that the employer often lacks an objective basis to make.[32] The phrasing that has withstood the test of time is to state a hypothetical—statements that proclaim what "could" occur "if" some event occurs, such as stating that "if" the employees engaged in an economic strike, the employees "could" be subject to permanent replacement. The NLRB has concluded that such "if/could" hypothetical statements are lawful.[33] It is critical that the employer never state that a union *would* call a strike if employees unionized or that permanent replacement of the employees *would* occur. But the clear implication that the employer hopes that employees will draw from the employer's lawful hypothetical statements that a strike and permanent replacement *could* occur is that unionization is futile—namely, employees will need to strike to get what they want from the employer, and if they strike, they will lose their jobs because the employer will exercise its legal right to hire permanent replacements. Perhaps the best evidence of the implied threat contained in these hypothetical messages is how often employers use them during unionization campaigns.

Linking employees' decision to unionize to job losses resulting from lost customer patronage is a good example of how the NLRA currently creates opportunities to design lawful implied threats. It is well established that predicting lost customers and lost jobs because of unionization is unlawful if there is no objective basis for the prediction, which seldom is available.[34] But it can be lawful to state that loss of customer patronage as a result of unionization *could* occur, with job losses resulting from cutbacks in production, *if* certain eventualities arose. For example, in *Freeman Manufacturing Co.*, the NLRB concluded that it was lawful for the employer to send letters to employees that stated:[35]

> [M]ost of you work for one customer [Sears]. *If* Sears were dissatisfied with our quantity, our deliveries or our prices, they *could* dump us as a supplier in a moment. We have no long term contract with them. We depend upon this business almost on a day to day basis. *If* they switched to another supplier, imagine how many jobs would be discontinued. . . . This same thing *could* happen with our other products, our other customers. *If* the customers do not buy, there are no jobs and hence no job security. There is no way in the world a union can make our customers continue to buy from us. But a union can make jobs insecure *if* it insists that an employer engage in practices which adversely affect quality, delay deliveries or result in higher prices for the product. The customer is the boss. He will place his business where he wishes.

There is a high likelihood that this communication was crafted by an experienced management consultant or lawyer who instructed the company to phrase its warning to employees in terms of "if" and "could"; and that this instruction was followed and paid dividends: the NLRB concluded that the communication did not constitute a threat. However, there can be little doubt that many workers read past the equivocation contained in the sentences using the words "if" and "could" and understood the employer to be warning that the union *will* likely make demands and engage in actions that *would* lead to lost customers and job losses. Otherwise, why send the letter? Crafting predictions as "if" and "could" hypotheticals has become an art form for management consultants to permit the company to legally communicate implied threats.[36] But, again, delay is needed to provide time for these implied threats to take hold.

Many employees are conflict adverse, and employers take advantage of this. A standard anti-union strategy used by employers during union representation campaigns is to "create anxiety about workplace life in a unionized future [and] [i]n particular portray union adherents as committed to a confrontational approach that will translate into a state of perpetual conflict if the organizing campaign succeeds." Research shows that creating the specter of perpetual conflict accompanying unionization, causing dissention, tension, and loss of friendships, is often a successful anti-union tactic. Many employees, especially those who initially are uncommitted and are the swing voters that the employer needs to recruit, tend to be disproportionately conflict adverse, and they will withdraw support for unionization if they can be convinced that supporting unionization will create conflict at the workplace between employees and management and among the employees themselves.[37] Aware of this, management consultants advise employers that the specter of disruption and increased tension accompanying unionization needs to be deployed as a valuable "tool for management." Thus, employer propaganda dwells on the disloyalty of unionizing and the inevitability of conflict if employees unionize, notwithstanding the infrequency of strikes and the peaceful and mutually productive labor relations climate that the union may have created with many other companies. According to Cohen and Hurd (1998), "The uncommitted middle in organizing campaigns is more likely to be affected by the conflict generated during the [organizing] campaign than they are to be intimidated by perceived threats of retaliation."[38] Once again, time is critical. Delay in the representation election process provides the time needed for the anxiety created by the employer-fabricated specter of ongoing conflict resulting from unionization to seep in, particularly among those who are most conflict adverse.

Company propaganda also often focuses on union dues, again pushing the theme of loss of personal control by inferring that the union will "take" the employee's money, even though dues paying is voluntary in a majority of states that have enacted "right-to-work" laws. And even in non-right-to-work states, dues payments cannot be made mandatory unless the employer agrees to include a union security clause in the collective bargaining agreement. But even in right-to-work states where dues paying is completely voluntary, employers harp on the theme of a union "taking" the employees' money through union dues. Often, employers will circulate charts among the employees showing the amount of money that employees will lose as a result of dues payments per month, per year, and even over the course of an employee's career. From annual reports that unions must file with the US Department of Labor, management consultants obtain access to the amount of money that a local union has sent to the headquarters of the international union with which it is affiliated. These fund transfers are communicated to employees, along with the inference that the employees' dues will be used to finance lavish salaries for "fat cat" union officials in Washington rather than benefiting the employees who pay the dues. The subliminal message is that the union is an outsider group that is in business to make a profit, is solely motivated by a desire to capture the employees' dues, and has little, if any, interest in advancing the employees' welfare.

Employees are barraged with such propaganda through repeated letters sent to their homes and speeches at repeated captive audience meetings that employees are required to attend during work hours and on work time. In one case, the NLRB held that it was lawful for the employer to state during a campaign that "the union *might* send someone out to break the employees' legs in order to collect dues." The NLRB reasoned that this was not a coercive statement or an unlawful threat of violence because the employer was not in a position to carry out the threatened conduct and the statement was an expression of opinion protected by the employer's free speech rights.[39]

Companies also point out the risks to personal safety that can arise in labor relations disputes, inferring that the employees should avoid unionization out of concern for their own personal safety. For example, the NLRB has permitted employers to postulate on the violent proclivities of unions, such as management falsely implying that union supporters had been bullying and threatening other employees.[40] A recurring assertion during unionization campaigns is the employer warning that "[i]f the union were to get in here, it would not work to your benefit but to your serious harm." The view of the NLRB is that these words alone "*can be given* a noncoercive and nonthreatening meaning" and thus do not constitute illegal threats "in the absence of conduct or other circumstances supplying a particular connotation [of threat]."[41]

Since 1982, the NLRB has adhered to the rule that there will be no negative consequences when parties engage in misleading campaign statements or misrepresentations of fact, even those made with knowing falsity. The employer may assert any falsehood or misrepresentation about the union that it desires. The NLRB will generally not probe into the truth or falsity of statements during a unionization campaign.[42] This opens creative opportunities for propagating unlimited falsehoods about unionization in general and a specific union in particular. Repeated often enough, the "big lie" can gain currency and overwhelm the truth.

One of the most powerful claims that a company advances to dissuade workers from unionizing is communicating the implied futility of unionization. It is unlawful for the employer to state explicitly, or by clear implication, that choosing unionization would be an exercise in futility.[43] The illegality in the futility cases arises from the employer conveying the message that it will not bargain in good faith with a union, even if the employees choose unionization. However, management consultants have crafted ways for the company to lawfully communicate the futility of unionization to its employees. The trick is to frame communications to employees that convey accurate statements of the law relating to management prerogatives as a way to demonstrate the union's impotence to effect meaningful change. For example, one lawful message to employees is that management has, and will continue to exercise, the full prerogative to manage—to hire, fire, discipline for cause, promote, lay off, set the hours of operation, and make other decisions affecting employees. And because the employer is not required to agree to the union's demands, the union cannot gain anything for the employees through collective bargaining without the concurrence of management. To this message, the employer is permitted to add that employees could lose some of what they now have because the employer has as much right during bargaining to ask for wage and benefits reductions as the union has to ask for increases.[44] And in a case where the employer stated the potential for "long and bitter negotiations," the NLRB found the statement lawful, reasoning that the employer may tell employees how the NLRA operates: "If parties are sharply divided . . . negotiation can indeed become protracted and bitter."[45] Moreover, as discussed here, the employer may state that *if* the union's demands are excessive, that *could* result in lost customer patronage and the need for downsizing, with concomitant reductions in staff.

Fear of job loss is widespread among workers, especially during the current era of deindustrialization, memories of the Great Depression of 2008, knowledge that many employers have replaced employees with contingent workers, and memory of the impact of the COVID-19 economic downturn. Economic changes loom large in the minds of many and create anxiety. Many employees desire better conditions of employment through collective bargaining, but not at the cost of the permanent loss of their current livelihood if they attempt to improve those working conditions.

These examples demonstrate some of the ways that the NLRA, as interpreted by the NLRB and the courts, provides employers with opportunities to design carefully crafted anti-union communications that deceive, misrepresent, and implicitly intimidate. Much of the employers' success in generating chilling but legal implicit threats can be traced to expert advice that employers receive from management consultants who have perfected ways to exploit job loss anxiety among the bargaining unit employees. For example, in one study, researchers conducted after-voting polls in 360 certification elections involving more than fifty unions and featuring 150,000 in-depth telephone interviews. Employees were asked what they thought was the "most important reason" that coworkers would vote against union representation. Comstock and Fox (1994) report, "Without prompting, a total of 31 percent of respondents made direct reference to pressure from management, including, specifically, fear of job loss. [And in polls among employees,] 68 percent of the workers identified employer coercion as the key to the union's loss."[46] The authors of this study conclude that their data "strongly indicate that workers feel employer coercion is increasing and that this tactic [of coercion] frustrated demand for union representation. [Moreover,] as desire for representation has increased, so has the frequency and extent of employer coercion."[47] One research study has described a "climate of fear" among nonunionized workers. Polls demonstrate that "approximately 70 percent of Americans think that workers in general will be subject to economic coercion by their employers for attempting to unionize. And approximately 45 percent of workers fear that they themselves would be so treated for exercising collective bargaining rights."[48] And Adams (1994) says, "[A]n enormous amount of research carried out over the past few decades . . . indicates that intimidation and fear of reprisal [by employers] are rampant in the United States and that the true choice is between accepting the status quo or being victimized."[49]

Attempts to protect employees from harm during an organizing campaign by changing the rules regarding the permissible and impermissible content of preelection speech is not a realistic option. The courts might well conclude that the effort violates employers' free speech rights. And, in any event, the next NLRB majority appointed by an anti-union president and composed of former management labor lawyers could find workarounds, and the implicit threats and intimidation of employees would continue. The preferred reform strategy is to leave in place the substantive law regarding what is permissible for an employer to communicate during a union-organizing campaign, but to reshape the legal environment of the representation process to reduce the opportunities and incentives to inflict harm.[50]

Removing Employer Standing in Representation Cases

Denying party status to employers in union representation proceedings foils the most commonly deployed strategies now used by employers to create preelection delays in an effort to buy the time needed to thwart employees' free choice. Without party status, employers lack the standing to drag out preelection hearings by raising frivolous arguments that certain groups of employees should be barred from voting in an upcoming election because they are either supervisors or independent contractors. In addition, employers would no longer be able to prolong a preelection hearing by advancing groundless claims disputing the appropriateness of the bargaining unit in which the union seeks an election.

An organizing drive by the Communications Workers of America at Harper-Collins, San Francisco, discussed earlier in this chapter, is a good example of the delaying tactics that labor law reform should eliminate. The union obtained authorization cards from sixty-two of the bargaining unit's eighty-three employees and filed a representation petition on December 18, 1992. The employer claimed that twenty of the eighty-three employees whom the union sought to represent should be excluded from the bargaining unit, and after some negotiation, sixteen employees remained in dispute. Then the employer's delaying tactics at the preelection hearing began in earnest:

> The NLRB held eight days of hearings in January and February 1993. The hearings were prolonged by management lawyers, who, for example, questioned a receptionist for three hours about her duties. The NLRB ultimately ruled with the union and included all sixteen contested employees in the unit. The [NLRB's] decision was not issued until May 28, however, and the election was scheduled for June 18 [six months after the union had filed its representation petition].[51]

The union lost the election by five votes, and the nearly six-month delay achieved in this case greatly assisted the employer in recruiting anti-union votes.

In a study of a random sample of 261 NLRB certification elections that occurred between July 1986 and June 1987, Kate Bronfenbrenner (1994) found that the union win rate is much higher when "the election was held less than two months after the petition was filed (53 percent) than when the election was held two to six months after the petition was filed (41 percent)."[52]

In other words, delay provides employers a clear competitive advantage. According to Gould (1996), in addition to providing opportunities for deceit, misrepresentation, and intimidation, delay "has a direct relationship to the ability of unions to keep employees' interest in unionization . . . If . . . there arises substantial delay in . . . the handling of representation petitions . . . employees will simply lose interest and draw the conclusion—sometimes with the subtle assistance of employer communications—that they can more effectively address employment concerns in a nonunion environment."[53] An effective way to neutralize the advantages that employers gain from the ability to delay the representation election process is to deny employers standing in the preelection hearing. Employers will then be unable to mount baseless preelection arguments that create months of delay, as occurred in the HarperCollins, San Francisco case and thousands of other cases.

Employer groups protest that removal of employer standing in representation cases denies employers due process and a fair opportunity to campaign for employee allegiance.[54] However, as noted previously, the expedited election procedures that have been proposed leave extensive opportunities for an employer to communicate its anti-union views; typically, employers would have between thirty and forty-five days to do so. And removing employer standing in representation cases is not a denial of due process because the employer is not on the ballot. The decision about whether to choose a union to represent employees is a matter of free choice for workers, not managers. According to Comstock and Fox (1994), "[E]very other industrialized democracy excludes employers from workers' deliberations about union representation."[55] As James Gross (1994) has argued, "A national labor policy favoring collective bargaining should minimize employer involvement in the process of employee choice [and by] shorten[ing] the period of pre-election campaigning[, we] enable the Board to avoid the bottomless pit of litigation over the meaning and intent of speech and its effect on employee choice."[56]

One of the more convincing rejoinders to the claim that it is somehow un-American or a denial of due process to deny employers standing in union representation proceedings is that such a denial of standing is exactly how labor relations under the Railway Labor Act (RLA) have been conducted since 1934. Section 2, Ninth of the RLA, which was added in 1934, provides that "the Mediation Board shall be authorized to take a secret ballot of the employees involved, or to utilize any other appropriate method of ascertaining the names of their duly designated and authorized representatives in such manner as shall insure the choice of representatives by the employees *without interference, influence, or coercion exercised by the carrier*."[57] In *Railway Labor Executives' Association v. National Mediation Board*, the D.C. Circuit held that the language of § 2, Ninth "makes perfectly clear that, the term 'parties' [in the RLA] includes neither carriers nor the [National Mediation Board (NMB) and the legislative history of the RLA substantiates that Congress did not want an employer] to thrust itself into the center of a representation fray and thus attempt to influence the outcome of any subsequent election."[58] Removing employer standing in representation election procedures simply harmonizes the NLRA and the RLA with respect to the employer's role in "influencing" certification election outcomes by participating as a party in preelection proceedings. Paul Weiler (2001) correctly states that "[i]t is time for American labor law to recognize that employees alone are the constituency that should be involved in the judgment about whether they need union representation to persuade corporate management to enhance their pay and working conditions."[59]

Employers are guaranteed due process: employers will continue to have an opportunity to advance arguments challenging the validity of the certification election process following the election. Obviously, if the union loses the election and that loss is not due to any election interference by the employer, then the employer will have no duty to bargain with the union, and therefore removal of employer standing to participate as a party in the election process will have caused employers no adverse consequences. Under the most enlightened labor law reform proposals, such as the Protecting the Right to Organize Act (PRO Act), when a majority of valid ballots have been cast in favor of the union, the NLRB is to issue an order requiring the parties to bargain. That order is self-enforcing and may be challenged by the employer by initiating a petition for review in the courts of appeal within thirty days. In that forum, the employer is able to raise challenges to the validity of the election, such as the appropriateness of the bargaining unit and the voting eligibility of those whom the employer believes should have been excluded from the eligibility to vote.[60]

Streamlining Election Procedures and Permitting Offsite Union Representation Elections

Prior to the 2014 reforms in election procedures, delay was a chronic problem. After the filing of the representation petition, the range of delay prior to the holding of the election was fifty-nine to seventy days. Most of that time was consumed by the need for the NLRB regional office to resolve preelection disputes. In most years during that period, contested elections took between sixty-four to sixty-seven days.[61] The 2014 reforms reduce this delay by two to three weeks.[62] As discussed in this chapter, decreasing preelection delay promotes uninhibited employee free choice.

The reason that there is a need to codify the procedures of the 2014 election reforms by amending the NLRA is that on December 13, 2019, the Trump NLRB announced a final administrative rule that overrode most of the Board's 2014 election regulations. These 2019 regulations reinstated most of the delays that the 2014 regulations had sought to eliminate. When the 2019 final rule was announced, the NLRB's only Democrat at that time said in dissent to the rule that "the GOP majority inserted unnecessary delays at every step of the election process—adding nearly two months even in straightforward cases that don't have disputes requiring litigation."[63] The Trump NLRB's 2019 final rule was to take effect on May 31, 2020.[64] On May 30, 2020, a federal district court judge in Washington, D.C., issued an order enjoining implementation of five aspects of the 2019 final rule, holding that the changes violated the "notice-and-comment" provisions of the Administrative Procedure Act.[65] These five changes that were enjoined included some of the most delay-causing changes that the Trump NLRB had proposed in 2019.[66]

By the fall of 2021, Democratic appointees constituted a majority of the NLRB. The battle over the Board's certification election procedures that has been waged since 2014 will likely continue. It is time for Congress to weigh in and decide that expedited representation elections are in the nation's best interest. The procedures contained in the NLRB's 2014 election reforms are well balanced. They excised most of the delay that has interfered with employees' free choice. They also retained ample opportunities for employers to communicate their views about unionization to employees and to raise postelection judicial challenges to any NLRB representation election decisions alleged to have violated the NLRA.

Moreover, the NLRA should provide that the employees petitioning for a representation election can choose whether the election will be conducted electronically, through certified mail, or at a location other than one owned or controlled by the employer. This range of choices is a way to ensure that employees can cast their ballots in neutral, noncoercive environments.

The NLRB's longstanding past policy strongly favored paper-ballot elections. During the COVID-19 pandemic, however, the Board increasingly permitted mail-ballot elections. Beginning in March 2020 and continuing throughout 2020, approximately 90 percent of NLRB representation elections were conducted by mail.[67] In *Aspirus Keweenaw*,[68] the Board approved mail-ballot elections broadly during the COVID-19 pandemic. In a separate opinion in this case, the Board's sole Democrat concurred in the result but advocated that the Board should "modernize its election methods," arguing that holding manual elections at the employer's place of business, "a space controlled by the employer," creates the potential for compromising employees' free choice. This concurring opinion urged that the NLRB institute permanent changes to implement "mail, telephone, and electronic voting."[69] The concurring opinion in *Aspirus Keweenaw* pointed out that electronic voting is the practice adopted for elections conducted by the Federal Labor Relations Authority, which conducts representation elections for federal public employees and also is used by the NMB, which conducts representation elections in the airline and rail industries. The concurring opinion in *Aspirus Keweenaw* argued that e-voting would not decrease voter participation, as some management opponents to e-voting have claimed,[70] citing NMB data showing an 85 percent participation rate using e-voting between 2010 and 2013.

Then e-voting in NLRA elections received a vote of confidence by the House of Representatives in 2021, as evidenced by the House's FY 2022 appropriations bill that expressly included "not less than $1 [million]" of the NLRB's annual budget to be "used to develop a system and procedures to conduct union representations electronically."[71] Mail and electronic voting in representation elections has become mainstream in much of US labor relations law and deserves congressional endorsement through amending the NLRA to provide for such voting.[72] From a fairness point of view and to encourage full participation, moving beyond voting by paper ballot at the employer's place of business is needed to permit voting by employees who are ill, are laid off, or are on leave of absence.[73]

Preventing Employers from Gerrymandering Bargaining Units

Inclusion disputes during NLRB representation proceedings involve disagreements over which categories of employees should be included in the bargaining unit. These are the employees who will vote in the representation election and will be represented by the union should a majority of valid votes be cast for the union in the election. These inclusion disputes are most often referred to as "bargaining unit disputes." The NLRA states that the NLRB may hold an election only in "an appropriate bargaining unit." Historically, the preelection hearing has been the forum for protracted and delaying litigation over bargaining unit disputes. Often, but not always, employers claim that the unit proposed by the union is smaller than it needs to be for it to be an appropriate bargaining unit.

The 2017 *PCC Structurals* case is a classic example.[74] There, the union sought an election among 102 welders employed at the employer's three facilities, all located within a five-mile radius in Portland, Oregon. The employer contended that the smallest appropriate unit was a wall-to-wall unit of 2,565 workers, essentially all the company's production and maintenance employees at its three Portland facilities. As is nearly always the case, the dispute had significant strategic implications. First, the 30 percent showing of interest required of the union for the 103-person unit that the union proposed was satisfied by the union producing 31 signed authorization cards, whereas the union would need authorization cards from 770 workers to satisfy the 30 percent showing of interest if the smallest appropriate unit was 2,565 employees. Moreover, securing majority support in an election among 103 workers, all of whom were involved in the organizing drive and had the cohesion gained from working in the same profession—welding—would be far easier than securing majority support among 2,565 employees who had not been involved in the organizing drive as of the date that the petition was filed and who were spread out in three locations performing a wide variety of production and maintenance tasks.

Studies have identified what is referred to as a "size gap." Union win rates are lower in larger bargaining units,[75] so it is understandable that employers fight for such units. The standard for determining if a bargaining unit is appropriate is whether a particular group of workers share a "community of interest," which is determined by a similarity or dissimilarity of many aspects of their conditions of employment, including wage structure, common supervision, skills, interaction, and even such things as where on the employer's property employees are permitted to park their vehicles and the colors of the badges and the hard hats that they must wear.[76] Sorting out the differences or similarities in the conditions of employment among 2,565 workers scattered among three facilities is calculated to consume a considerable amount of time at a preelection hearing. What often happens is that the employer's demand for a much larger bargaining unit forces the union to make a choice: whether to litigate the unit question for weeks or perhaps months, creating a delay that the employer can take advantage of to intensify its anti-union campaign, or to agree to the larger unit demanded by the employer to keep the election process moving. But agreeing to a much larger unit places the union at a great disadvantage since now it is required to begin organizing perhaps thousands of employees who had not previously been approached about the organizing campaign and likely have never indicated any interest in union representation.[77]

What complicates bargaining unit disputes is that at a single facility, several bargaining units often constitute "an appropriate unit" because several combinations of workers share a community of interest. The law is well settled that the election can be held in any unit if it is "an appropriate" bargaining unit, but the unit need not be the most appropriate bargaining unit. The legal question is whether the unit selected in the union's representation petition is *an* appropriate unit under the NLRA, not whether the unit is the one that either the NLRB or the employer would prefer. The fundamental question then is whether employees should be permitted to seek union representation in the bargaining unit that they prefer, so long as the unit that they prefer is "an appropriate unit" under the NLRA's statutory standards—even if another, larger unit also is appropriate and is preferred by the employer.

Unit disputes will continue to cause delays even if the NLRA is amended to provide expedited election procedures. Unit disputes will not delay the conduct of the election because when the employer is not a party in the representation election proceedings, it cannot delay the holding of the election through protracted preelection litigation over unit appropriateness. But the employer will retain the right to insist that it be obligated to bargain only with a union representing employees in an appropriate unit. So if a union prevails in an election and the NLRB orders an employer to bargain, under the reforms discussed in this chapter, that order is self-enforcing and the employer then has a window of thirty days to challenge the order to bargain in a circuit court of appeals. A valid basis for such a challenge is that the NLRB had ordered bargaining to occur in a bargaining unit that is not appropriate. In short, adopting expedited election procedures does not eliminate unit disputes; instead, they just defer them to after the election.

In 2011, in *Specialty Healthcare & Rehabilitation Center of Mobile*,[78] the NLRB adopted an approach that is designed to limit litigation over bargaining units. There, the Board held that if a union petitions for an election among a particular group of employees who share a community of interest under traditional standards, but the employer takes the position that the appropriate bargaining unit must include additional employees who are not included in the unit proposed by the union, the Board will find the petitioned-for unit appropriate unless the employer is able to prove that the excluded employees share an "overwhelming" community of interest with the petitioned-for group.[79] Employers challenged the validity of *Specialty Healthcare* in eight circuits, all of which upheld the ruling.[80]

Nevertheless, in 2017, in *PCC Structurals, Inc.*, the Trump NLRB reversed *Specialty Healthcare* in a 3–2 decision.[81] Among other things, the majority in *PCC Structurals* held that *Specialty Healthcare* focused on the unionization interests of employees who sought to organize in the petitioned-for unit, but it failed adequately to consider the statutory interests of employees excluded from the proposed unit. As the dissent in *PCC Structurals* pointed out, "the majority's view, in other words, [is that] the statutory right of employees to seek union representation, as a self-defined group, is contingent on the imputed desires of employees outside the unit who have expressed no view on representation at all—with the employer serving as their self-appointed proxy."[82] The Supreme Court has held that § 9(a) "implies that the initiative in selecting an appropriate unit resides with the employees [and] suggests that employees may seek to organize 'a unit' that is 'appropriate'—not necessarily the single most appropriate unit."[83] To be clear: historically, the policy of the NLRB has been "to consider only whether the unit requested is an appropriate one, even though it may not be the optimum or most appropriate unit for collective bargaining."[84]

The NLRA should be amended to codify the NLRB's 2011 decision in *Specialty Healthcare*.[85] Such a codification would reduce significantly the protracted litigation spawned by unit disputes and would prevent employers from gerrymandering a bargaining unit as a way to defeat unionization by including individuals in the voting unit who have no interest in being represented by the union. Codifying the NLRB's 2011 decision in *Specialty Healthcare* into the statutory language of the NLRA would be in accord with the views of eight circuit courts of appeals and would give primacy to the wishes of employees who desire union representation and collective bargaining, rather than the preferences of employers whose primary motive is to operate their businesses unencumbered by any collective bargaining responsibilities.

Notice Posting, Transparency, and Penalties for Noncompliance

In addition to requiring the NLRB to promulgate regulations requiring employers to post and maintain notices to employees of their rights under the NLRA, and to notify each new employee of the information in the notice, amendments to NLRA should adopt the portion of the NLRB's 2014 Election Rule that requires employers to provide unions with a list of all employees in the bargaining unit no later than two business days after the NLRB directs an election. This list should contain the employees' names, home addresses, work locations, shifts, job classifications, and, if available to the employer, personal landline and mobile telephone numbers and email addresses. The Trump NLRB's 2019 Election Rule, which rescinded much of the 2014 Election Rule, provides employers five business days to provide the voter list rather than two business days as provided in the 2014 Final Rule, but it does not change the scope of the information that needs to be included with the voter list.[86]

Later chapters of this book will discuss in detail the need for amendments to the NLRA that provide for civil penalties designed to strengthen enforcement for the NLRA. One such change in the NLRA's remedial scheme should be a civil penalty for violations of the posting requirements and voter list requirements. This reform has been proposed, for example, in § 109 of the PRO Act. Under that proposal, upon failure to post a notice or to inform new employees of their rights under the NLRA, or failure to produce the voter eligibility list on time, the NLRB "shall" order the employer to provide the information to employees and "shall" impose a civil penalty not to exceed $500 for each violation.

6 Opportunities in the NLRA for an Employer to Retaliate without Fear of Significant Consequences

Labor Law Reforms Needed[1]

Enhance remedies to prevent serious unfair labor practices.

Enforce compliance with orders of the National Labor Relations Board (NLRB) by making orders self-enforcing, with expedited court of appeals review.

Provide for mandatory request for injunctive relief against unfair labor practices involving discharge.

Provide for civil penalties to remedy violations of employees' rights.

Provide for a private right of civil action if the NLRB does not expeditiously seek an injunction to protect an employee's right to engage in protected activity.

Clarify the Labor Management Reporting and Disclosure Act (LMRDA) to require the disclosure of arrangements with consultants to directly or indirectly persuade employees on how to exercise their rights under the National Labor Relations Act (NLRA).

Reinstate the NLRB's Congressional Reporting Requirement.

* * *

Suppressing Union Organizing through Employer Illegal Conduct: The Evidence

There is perhaps no more widely criticized feature of the current structure of the NLRA than the absence of effective remedies to deter employer intimidation, retaliation, and other illegal activities directed at employees for engaging in protected § 7 activities—illegal activity by employers that occurs most often during union organizing. Chapter 5 includes a discussion of opportunities that the NLRA provides employers to stay within the letter of the law but nevertheless engage in conduct that intimidates employees. Those deficiencies in the NLRA are remedied by reducing delay during the representation process. But employers also openly employ blatantly illegal tactics to suppress union organizing, as Hurd and Uehlein (1994) describe, "most often by discriminating against leaders of the organizing drive."[2] For example, a study published in 2019, reviewing union elections in 2016 and 2017, found that employers were charged with NLRA unfair labor practice violations in 41.5 percent of all union election campaigns. And, in one out of five organizing campaigns (19.9 percent), employers were charged with firing pro-union workers. Often, such firings occur early in the organizing campaign, soon after the initial union contact or the first union meeting, with the intent to intimidate the workforce and effectively quash the incipient organizing drive before it has a chance to take root.[3] Moreover, in nearly a third of all union election campaigns, employers also are charged with making threats, engaging in surveillance activities, harassing workers, or a combination.[4]

These 2019 findings are consistent with other findings of employer illegal conduct during election campaigns. In 2009, Kate Bronfenbrenner analyzed unfair labor practice charges during union elections in relatively large bargaining units (i.e., having more than fifty workers) that were conducted between 1999–2003 (a sample of 1,004 election campaigns). She found that there were charges of illegal firing in 19.0 percent of these election campaigns.[5] Other studies have found even higher rates of termination for union activities (26 percent).[6]

Findings vary, but there is evidence that the NLRB has found merit in a large percentage of these charges of unlawful employer retaliation. In 1994, the Dunlop Commission found that as of 1990, 25 percent of the elections that the NLRB conducted produced reinstatement orders, evidencing the Board's conclusion that there was merit in many hundreds of claims of unlawful discriminatory discharge for union activity during these elections.[7] In one study of 261 certification election campaigns, there were charges of discriminatory discharge in 87 percent of the campaigns (227), and sufficient merit was found in 43 percent of these (97) that the NLRB general counsel issued a complaint. In other words, in 97 of the 261 campaigns analyzed (37 percent), the NLRB general counsel's investigation found merit in claims of discriminatory discharge and other retaliation because of union activity.

One way to gauge the merit of the thousands of charges of illegal discharge and similar discrimination by employers is the number of NLRB reinstatement orders and back-pay awards that the Board issues annually. In 1983, Paul Weiler consulted NLRB data and found that in 1980, the Board had ordered reinstatement of about 10,000 employees, most discharges arising during organizing campaigns, and this was in a year that unions had obtained approximately 200,000 votes in representation elections. He thus concluded that "[a]stoundingly, then, the current odds are about one in twenty that a union supporter will be fired for exercising rights supposedly guaranteed by federal law a half-century ago."[8]

As table 6.1 shows, over the ten-year period from 2011 to 2020, the NLRB ordered the reinstatement of 18,001 workers and $621.3 million in back pay. These numbers include reinstatement and back pay for both workers who were illegally fired and victims of discriminatory layoffs. The level of union organizing and the number of NLRB representation elections have decreased significantly since the late 1970s and early 1980s, when Weiler conducted his research. However, the 18,001 orders of reinstatement and $621.3 million in back pay over a decade represented in table 6.1 demonstrates the

Table 6.1
NLRB reinstatement offers and back-pay awards, 2011–2020

Fiscal Year	Number of Reinstatement Offers	Back Pay (in millions)
2011	1,644	$58.7
2012	1,254	$44.2
2013	2,729	$109.7
2014	3,240	$43.8
2015	2,109	$94.3
2016	1,648	$52.3
2017	1,716	$70.8
2018	1,270	$54.0
2019	1,431	$55.6
2020	960	$37.9
Total	**18,001**	**$621.3**

Source: Lynn Rhinehart and Celine McNicholas, "Shortchanged—Weak Anti-retaliation Provisions in the National Labor Relations Act Cost Workers Billions." Economic Policy Institute (April 22, 2021).[9]

enormity of the continuing problem of employer discrimination—most of it arising out of union-organizing campaigns.

In June 1993, the Industrial Union Department of the AFL-CIO initiated a project that collected data on 167 organizing campaigns involving twenty-one national unions in thirty-six states and the District of Columbia. These case studies document a pattern of openly unlawful discriminatory actions against leaders of union-organizing drives. The following examples are just a sample of what was uncovered in this study, but they provide useful insight for understanding how workers place themselves in harm's way if they decide to act on their desire for collective bargaining by exercising their federally protected right to engage in union organizing:[10]

- International Association of Machinists, Wichita, Kansas (April 1991): "The two most vocal union supporters fired."
- United Food and Commercial Workers Union, Hamtramck, Michigan (May 1992): "discipline and dismissal of vocal union advocates."
- Communications Workers of America, San Francisco (December 1992): "Two workers were promoted out of the unit, and four were laid off. Five of these were on the organizing committee."
- Amalgamated Clothing and Textile Workers Union, Cincinnati, Ohio (February 1993): "Eight workers passed out organizing leaflets at the plant gate [and] an hour later all eight were either laid off or had their hours reduced. This scenario was repeated over the next few days until twenty-six union supporters were laid off. The organizing campaign had been stopped cold [and] [s]ix months later [the employer paid] $70,000 in back pay [but the employer] avoided unionization by breaking the law quickly, scaring the workers into retreat."
- Communication Workers of America, Buffalo, New York (January 1993): In late 1992 the union began an organizing campaign among licensed practical nurses (LPNs) and in early January the company "fired sixteen of its twenty-one LPNs; . . . with no explanation."
- United Mine Workers, Osceola Mills, Pennsylvania (December 1988): Sixty days after the petition was filed and thirteen days before the election, the company "laid off thirteen workers, all of them union activists, including the leaders of the organizing campaign [who voted by challenged ballot], the company [committed additional unfair labor practices,] including

laying off twelve additional union supporters." Three-and-a-half years after the petition was filed, the NLRB found most of this conduct unlawful, the challenged ballots were counted and were found to be for the union, and the NLRB certified that the union had won the election. The company continued to refuse to bargain and challenged the NLRB's findings in court.

- International Ladies Garment Workers Union, Brooklyn (December 1989): "A key union supporter with twenty-seven years' seniority informed the owner's son that the union was there to see him. Fifteen minutes later, the union supporter was fired. That afternoon the employer's attorney told the union's attorney that he was not worried because even if the employer had to reinstate the discharged worker, the back-pay liability would not amount to much." Within two months, the company "fired two more pro-union workers" and after much litigation during the ensuing three years, "the NLRB took a consistent stance in opposition to [the employer's] blatant disregard for the law." When the election was held in 1992 "only a third of the original union supporters still worked [for the employer]," and the union lost the election. The NLRB overturned that election but, still refusing to bargain, the employer appealed.
- United Paperworkers International Union, Columbus, Indiana (July 1989): Evidence that the NLRA's modest remedies do not deter, and that many employers combine discriminatory discharge with other NLRA violations, is documented in a case of an employer that, soon after initiation of the union campaign, discharged eight pro-union employees and placed union supporters under surveillance at work.

The Cost-Benefit Advantages for Employers to Illegally Retaliate against Workers

Employers engage in illegal retaliation because it makes sense economically. The benefits exceed the costs, which are relatively minimal. The philosophy of the original NLRA was remedial, not punitive. The act currently does not provide for civil or criminal sanctions or penalties in unfair labor practice cases. An employer that commits an unfair labor practice, such as terminating an employee for union activities, must "cease and desist" and post a notice in the workplace promising not to repeat the offense. Steps must also be taken to repair the harm done, such as reinstating the discharged workers and providing back pay, calculated as lost wages and benefits, less the amount of any interim earnings obtained by the worker.[11] The data in table 6.1 show that the total of $621.3 million for 18,001 reinstatement orders represents an average of $34,515 in back pay per reinstatement order. This is not an insubstantial amount of back pay liability, but the high continuing incidence of unlawful discharges during union campaigns shows that employers calculate that the business benefit derived from an unlawful retaliation is well worth the price. Morris Kleiner (1994) has demonstrated that under the current NLRA regime, there "exist[] huge economic incentives for management to commit [discriminatory discharge] violations."[12]

If a society were serious regarding its commitment to support and encourage the practice and procedure of collective bargaining, it would adopt remedies to ensure that violators cannot profit from their violations.[13] Yet, Kleiner argues that under the NLRA as currently written, mid- and upper-level plant management "see the use of unfair labor practices as a tool that can stop organizing with little economic costs but with potentially huge opportunities for career advancement [especially because studies have shown that] managers who were in charge during organizing drives leading to elections suffered dire consequences, such as a greatly increased likelihood of being fired or demoted."[14] One chilling threat that will motivate supervisors to redouble their anti-union efforts is to threaten to fire all supervisors if nonsupervisory workers unionize.[15] Employers choose to provide back pay rather than obey the law because in most cases, terminating the union leadership reduces union win rates. Why? In only a small percentage of the illegal discharge cases does the NLRB order reinstatement before the election takes place.[16] Ordering reinstatement *after* the election has taken place, which is what occurs in two-thirds of the cases, "is too late for those workers to vote and too late to affect the election outcome positively."[17] The reality is that "the employer does not [normally] face a legally-enforceable reinstatement order until 1,000 days or more after the original firing. And even if the employer is prepared to settle earlier (if only to avoid its expanding legal bills), this almost invariably takes place after the pro-union employees have lost their organizing campaign." By contrast, preelection reinstatement is correlated with increasing union win rates. Returning a key union supporter to the workplace where the illegal discharge occurred shows the bargaining unit employees both the need for and the potential value of the collective power of unionization to challenge management's absolute authority, and thereby mitigates the intimidation effect of the discriminatory discharges on other employees.[18]

In a study of 261 elections, Kate Bronfenbrenner (1994) found that the union won 44 percent of the elections when unlawfully discharged bargaining unit employees (normally the strike leaders) were reinstated prior to the election, but only 37 percent when unlawfully discharged workers were not reinstated until after the election.[19] Research demonstrates that the NLRA's remedies are so mild that a company "is indifferent in its choice between providing an increase in wages [resulting from its employees unionizing] and paying additional penalties, legal fees, and other costs related to a potential unfair labor practice charge or violation."[20] In other words, noncompliance with the law produces substantial economic benefits. Management calculates the cost of lawbreaking and readily concludes that the NLRA creates an economic incentive to violate the law. Employers and their labor consultants often compute the cost of unionization by comparing the wage differential between becoming unionized and remaining a nonunion employer, and they frequently conclude that the price of NLRA noncompliance is less than the price would be of complying with the NLRA and risking becoming unionized. In short, public policies should price lawlessness at a sufficiently high level that, from a cost-benefit perspective, employers are incentivized to comply with the NLRA.[21]

Beefing up NLRA Remedies

Four changes to the NLRA will go a long way toward deterring employer discrimination of employees for engaging in union activities by increasing the costs of noncompliance to a level that reduces substantially employers' incentive to engage in such unlawful conduct.[22]

First, when an employee has been discharged or suffers serious economic harm in violation of the NLRA, it should provide that the NLRB shall award the employee back pay (without any reduction based on the employee's interim earnings, as is now the case), front pay, consequential damages, and an *additional amount* as liquidated damages equal to two times the amount of damages awarded.[23] Lynn Rhinehart and Celine McNicholas (2021) have explained that if the 18,001 workers who received reinstatement offers over the ten-fiscal-year period from 2011 to 2020, as summarized in table 6.1, had also received double back pay as liquidated damages, "this would have translated into an *additional* \$1.24 billion in damages to affected workers, or \$69,030 in additional damages per affected worker [in addition to the \$621.3 million in back pay that was awarded]."[24] In other words, had this reform been in effect, the total back-pay liability of the employers who had directed their unlawful retaliatory conduct to the 18,001 workers who received reinstatement orders would have been over \$1.86 billion (\$.62 billion in back pay plus \$1.24 billion in liquidated damages). This does not include any "consequential damages" owed.[25] This modification substantially changes the cost-benefit calculation for employers that are contemplating engaging in retaliatory discharges of employees who are active in union-organizing campaigns.[26]

Increasing the financial costs of retaliating against employees during a union-organizing campaign will not resolve the current problem of discharged strike leaders typically not being reinstated until after the election has been conducted. Without preelection reinstatement, the unremedied discriminatory discharges intimidate other workers and send the message that the union is weak. As has already been discussed, union win rates decrease substantially when discharged workers are not reinstated until after the election. Accordingly, the second change needed to minimize the harm from discriminatory discharges and reduce employer incentives to act unlawfully is requiring the NLRB to seek temporary injunctive relief whenever it determines that there is a reasonable basis to find that an employer unlawfully terminated an employee or significantly interfered with an employee's rights under the NLRA (e.g., by threats, surveillance, or interrogation). The presumption should be that temporary injunctive relief is appropriate in these circumstances and should be granted by the district court for the duration of the Board proceedings unless the court concludes that there is no reasonable likelihood that the NLRB will succeed on the merits of its claim. Currently, § 10(j) of the NLRA authorizes the Board, *in its discretion*, to request preliminary injunctive relief in a federal district court where it concludes that an expeditious remedy is needed. But, historically, seeking § 10(j) preliminary relief has been spotty: some NLRB general counsels have shown little interest in seeking § 10(j) authorization from the Board.[27] Aggressively seeking § 10(j) relief is highly correlated with NLRB general counsels who have been appointed by presidents from the Democratic Party. The proposed modification of § 10(j) would change that by making it mandatory for the Board to seek preliminary § 10(j) relief in federal district court in all cases when the NLRB general counsel determines that there is a reasonable basis to find that an employer unlawfully terminated an employee or otherwise significantly interfered with an employee's rights under the NLRA. This change will dramatically increase the number of preelection reinstatement orders and, concomitantly, will increase union win rates in representation elections and reduce the incentives for employers to engage in lawbreaking. Later in this chapter is a discussion of a reform that provides for a remedy if the NLRB general counsel fails to seek injunctive relief.

Third, the NLRA should be modified to permit the NLRB to seek civil penalties for invasion of employee rights. The Protecting the Right to Organize Act (PRO Act) proposes a civil penalty not to exceed $50,000 for each incident of invasion of employee rights, though the NLRB would have authority to double that penalty in any case where the employer has committed another such violation in the previous five years and where the penalty arises from discharge or serious economic harm to the employee.[28] In addition, the PRO Act proposes that the NLRB should be permitted to hold an officer or director of an employer personally liable and assess a civil penalty against that person. This reform changes the underlying philosophy of the NLRA from being solely a remedial statute to a law that punishes unlawful conduct.[29] Such a change is necessary because, as the previous statistics plainly show, the NLRA's current remedial approach has not deterred employers' unlawful conduct, especially during union-organizing campaigns. And moving to a philosophy of punishment as a strategy to disincentivize unlawful employer behavior is consistent with the approach taken in modern employment law.[30]

Fourth, a fully functioning NLRA remedial scheme needs to provide a private right of civil action in federal district court when the NLRB fails to seek an injunction expeditiously (i.e., within sixty days) following the filing of a charge alleging retaliation against the employee's right to join a union or engage in protected activity. In such a civil action, the district court would award the relief that would be available to employees who file a charge before the NLRB, which includes preliminary and then permanent injunctive reinstatement relief, back pay, double back pay liquidated damages, front pay, and consequential damages. This provision for a private right of action to remedy violations of the right to engage in protected § 7 activities, when the NLRB itself does not act to enforce § 7 rights, should go a long way toward neutralizing the adverse effects of appointing NLRB general counsels who adopt a policy to underenforce rights guaranteed by the NLRA.

In addition, § 203(c) of the LMRDA needs to be amended to require employers and their outside labor consultants, including attorneys, to disclose arrangements they undertake to, directly or indirectly, persuade employees how to exercise their rights to union representation and collective bargaining. This reporting obligation should require disclosure of all fees paid and services provided. LMRDA § 203(c), referred to as the "advice" exemption, currently provides in pertinent part that "nothing in this section shall be construed to require any employer or other person to file a report covering the services of such person by reason of his giving or agreeing to give advice to such employer." In addition, LMRDA § 204 exempts from reporting any attorney-client communications, which are defined as "information which was lawfully communicated to [an] . . . attorney by any of his clients in the course of a legitimate attorney-client relationship."

Initially, the Department of Labor interpreted the § 203(c) "advice" exemption to require employers to report any "[a]rrangement with a 'labor relations consultant' or other third party to draft speeches or written material to be delivered or disseminated to employees for the purpose of persuading such employees as to their right to organize and bargain collectively." By contrast, there was no obligation to report arrangements with a labor relations consultant, including attorneys, "related exclusively to advice, representation before a court, administrative agency, or arbitration tribunal, or engaging in collective bargaining on [the employer's] behalf."[31] In 1962, the Department of Labor interpreted § 203(c) to create a loophole that excluded most reporting by labor consultants or other third parties by categorically exempting from reporting any activities in which a consultant has no direct contact with employees.[32]

In 2016, the Department of Labor promulgated a final rule, titled "Interpretation of the 'Advice' Exemption in Section 203(c) of the Labor-Management Reporting and Disclosure Act," ("2016 Persuader Rule").[33] The 2016 Persuader Rule revised the department's interpretation of the advice exemption in an effort to require employers and their consultants to file a report not only when they make agreements or arrangements pursuant to which a consultant directly contacts employees, but also when a consultant engages in activities behind the scenes if an object of those activities is to persuade employees concerning their rights to organize and bargain collectively. The 2016 Persuader Rule defined reportable activities to include recommending drafts of or revisions to an employer's speeches and communications if those drafts or revisions were designed to influence employees' exercise of their organizational rights.[34] Employer groups challenged the 2016 Persuader Rule in three district courts.[35] In June 2016, a federal district court in Texas issued a nationwide permanent injunction.[36] The Department of Labor appealed to the Fifth Circuit, which held the matter in abeyance pending the department's rulemakings in 2018 under President Donald Trump, which ended up rescinding the 2016 Persuader Rule.[37]

The 2016 Persuader Rule should be reinstated legislatively, thus eliminating the categorical exemption of activities in which a consultant has no direct contact with employees. The Department of Labor also should be directed to make this information available through a searchable electronic format.[38] Reporting arrangements should include planning or conducting employee meetings, drafting speeches or presentations to employees, training employer representatives, identifying employees for disciplinary action or targeting, or drafting employer personnel policies. If enacted, this reform undoubtedly would be opposed vigorously, as was the 2016 Persuader Rule, on a variety of theories, including free speech and association grounds, and in particular that the Persuader Rule impinges on the attorney-client relationship.[39]

7 Opportunities in the NLRA for Employers to Indoctrinate Employees through Work-Time Captive Audience Meetings while Denying Unions Workplace Access to Employees

Labor Law Reforms Needed[1]

Prohibit captive audience meetings.

Protect employee concerted activity conducted electronically using workplace email or other employer-provided electronic communication systems.

* * *

The Ban on Captive Audience Meetings

The former Yale law professor Charles Black once observed that "unreplying attention to the words of another is known immemorially as an individual badge of servility."[2] Workplace captive audience meetings fix such badges of servility onto workers. Captive audience meetings are assemblies of employees during paid work time, at which employers compel employees to listen to anti-union and other types of proselytizing on pain of discharge. During the weeks preceding a union representation election, when communicating with bargaining unit employees is most critical, the workplace captive audience meeting is the employer's anti-union tactic of choice.[3] A total of 90 percent of employers involved in union-organizing campaigns require employees to attend captive audience meetings, and two-thirds require employees to meet one-on-one with supervisors at least weekly during the election campaign.[4] At training sessions, supervisors are taught that they are "expected to convey to workers [the four supposed losses from unionization]: plant closings, strikes, the end of open relationships with supervisors, and discord."[5] The reason that employers so widely incorporate captive audience meetings into their anti-union strategies is that the captive audience meeting furnishes employers with a "decided advantage over the union."[6] With the captive audience meeting, the employer gains "virtually complete access to the minds of [the employees] during paid work hours,"[7] while the union normally is not entitled to a similar opportunity.[8] The reason that employers so determinedly defend their legal prerogative to conduct these compulsory employee meetings is that they are so highly correlated with election-day outcomes that are favorable to employers.[9] Consultants advise employer clients to schedule captive audience meetings early and often.[10] In one study of 261 union representation elections, employers held an average of 5.5 captive audience meetings per election campaign, and there was a high correlation between the number of captive audience meetings conducted and employers' likelihood of defeating employees' efforts to unionize. When employers held no captive audience meetings, unions won 42 percent of the elections studied, and when the number of captive audience meetings rose to twenty or more, the union win rate declined dramatically, to 18 percent. Bronfenbrenner (1994) reports, "[F]or every additional captive audience meeting, the proportion of union votes declined by 2 percent and the probability of the union winning the election declined by 1 percent."[11]

The captive audience meeting should not be confused with an assembly designed to promote a bilateral exchange of ideas or otherwise be misunderstood as a forum for free and open debate. As interpreted by the National Labor Relations Board (NLRB) and the courts, the National Labor Relations Act (NLRA) permits employers to compel employees to listen to anti-union proselytizing—under threat of discharge—in mandatory assemblies during paid work time. The employer is entitled to discipline employees who leave the captive audience meeting[12] or who insist on participating by asking questions or manifesting disagreement with the views being force-fed to them.[13] Further, the employer may prevent pro-union employees from attending such meetings, deliberately isolating employees from coworkers who might be able to rebut the employer's claims.[14] It is not unprecedented for an employer to lock all the exits at the workplace during a captive audience meeting and physically restrain those attempting to leave.[15] In short, the NLRB and the courts have found nothing incongruous between such forced anti-union indoctrination at the workplace and our national labor policy's commitment to employee free choice regarding union representation.

It was not always this way. The legal test for whether employer behavior interferes with employees' protected § 7 rights is objective: the Board asks whether "it may reasonably be said [that an employer's action] tends to interfere with the free exercise of employee rights under the Act."[16] In 1946, prior to the Taft-Hartley amendments to the NLRA, the NLRB in *Clark Brothers* concluded that captive audience meetings constitute unlawful employer interference with freedom of association and employees' free choice.[17] That conclusion rested on two alternative grounds. The first is that the captive audience meeting interferes with employees' protected right to choose not to listen to employer views regarding unionization. Employees enjoy the statutory right to receive aid, advice, and information from others concerning the right to self-organization, and the necessary corollary to this is that the NLRA protects employees' free choice regarding which aid, advice, and information to seek in deciding how to exercise their freedom of association.[18] The second reason was the intimidating effect on employees resulting from the employer's deployment of its superior economic power to force ideological listening.[19] One commentator has summarized the intimidating effect of such employer use of superior economic power to influence the election outcome as follows:[20]

> The CAM [captive audience meeting] is a display of employer power, demonstrating at once the employer's position of dominance at work and the employees' vulnerability. It is difficult to think of other examples workers would experience in their lives in which they could be forced to sit and listen to opinions with which they may strongly disagree. Due to the very uniqueness of the experience, the CAM transmits an extremely potent signal to employees that is quite distinct from the content of the speech. It is a message about where power in the employment relationship rests, about the limits of a union's power . . . , and about the state's opinion of this imbalance of power and communicative access in the workplace.

Because, on its face, the captive audience tactic of forcing employees into ideological listening is so inherently coercive, the *Clark Brothers* precedent might have survived, but in the end it did not. The 1947 Taft-Hartley amendments added the § 8(c) free speech proviso to the NLRA, which states: "The expressing of any views, arguments or opinions, or the dissemination thereof, whether in written, graphic, or visual form, shall not constitute or be evidence of an unfair labor practice under any of the provisions of this Act, if such expression contains no threat of reprisal or force or promise of benefit.[21] By its terms, § 8(c) speaks to limitations on the NLRB's ability to regulate the *content* of the speech that an employer disseminates, not the *manner* of such dissemination, such as forced anti-union indoctrination at the workplace through captive audience speeches. Yet one line in the report by the Senate Labor Committee on the then-pending Taft-Hartley amendments states an intention to overrule *Clark Brothers*.[22] There is no other legislative history manifesting that the House of Representatives or the Congress as a whole intended that enactment of § 8(c) was intended to overrule *Clark Brothers*. Nevertheless, within one year following the addition of § 8(c) to the act, the NLRB reversed *Clark Brothers* in *Babcock & Wilcox Co.*, concluding that "the language of 8(c) of the amended Act, and its legislative history, make it clear that the doctrine of the *Clark Bros.* case no longer exists as a basis for finding unfair labor practices."[23]

Babcock left unresolved the issue of whether the employer violates § 8(a)(1) when it conducts a captive audience meeting but then refuses the union a similar opportunity to address employees. Initially, the NLRB oscillated on this issue,[24] but in *Livingston Shirt Corporation*,[25] it finally established that in the absence of either an unlawful no-solicitation/no-distribution rule or a "broad but privileged" no-solicitation rule,[26] holding a captive audience meeting creates no concomitant obligation to provide the union an opportunity to address employees on the employer's premises. *Livingston Shirt*, decided in 1953, still stands as the controlling rule.[27]

The asymmetrical right of employers to schedule an unlimited number of "regular, often incessant, often intensive meetings with employees" during work time, while denying unions a similar opportunity creates enormous advantages for employers during election campaigns.[28] This advantage gained from employers' disproportional access to employees at the workplace, a time when employees are focused on the work aspects of their lives, is exacerbated by the company's right in most cases to ban unions entirely from its property, even from unutilized spaces such as parking lots. It is well established that although the NLRA confers rights only on employees, not on unions or union organizers, the "right of self-organization depends in some measure on [employees'] ability . . . to learn the advantages of self-organization from others."[29] While this labor relations reality provides the foundation for the Supreme Court to conclude that the NLRA may restrict a company's right to exclude union organizers from its property, in practice union organizers virtually always are denied access to the employer's property. This is because, in *Lechmere, Inc. v. NLRB*,[30] the Supreme Court in effect limited union access to company property to remote mining camps, lumber camps, and mountain resort hotels, work locations that "are isolated from the ordinary flow of information that characterizes our society. The union's burden of establishing such isolation is, . . . 'a heavy one,' . . . and one not satisfied by mere conjecture or the expression of doubts concerning the effectiveness of nontrespassory means of communication." To gain access, the union must show that options to communicate with employees that are an alternative to access are "infeasible."[31]

It would be a serious miscalculation to amend the NLRA to remedy abuses resulting from captive audience meetings by providing unions greater access to company property to answer employer claims advanced in captive audience meetings, as that remedy subjects the reform to claims of "taking" property in violation of the Fifth Amendment.[32] Reform rather should attempt to reduce the current asymmetry of access to employees by prohibiting employers from using express or implicit threats to compel employees to attend captive audience meetings. Such a reform would clarify § 8(c) of the NLRA to establish that § 8(c) does not provide a statutory basis for employer claims of a right to hold mandatory captive audience meetings. What remains, however, is whether an employer's constitutional right to free speech precludes government from punishing an employer for requiring employees, on pain of discharge, to attend captive audience meetings designed to indoctrinate them with the employer's view on unionization.

The constitutional right of free speech does not immunize captive audience meetings from statutory proscription. Bans on captive audience meetings are not content regulations that qualify for "the most exacting [judicial] scrutiny." Strict judicial scrutiny is reserved for regulations motivated by the suppression of the content of what one wishes to express—the views sought to be expressed.[33] Captive audience meetings are not banned to suppress an employer's viewpoint regarding unionization. That is, captive audience meetings are not banned because the government disagrees with the viewpoint presented by employers at those meetings. The employer remains free to choose the substantive content, the viewpoint, of its expression related to the merits of proposed unionization and disseminate it through emails, texts, letters sent to employees' homes, newspaper advertisements, or a myriad of other means. The government's interest in banning captive audience meetings is to promote an employee's freedom to choose which advice to seek in deciding how to exercise freedom of association, unencumbered by coerced listening to propaganda from any source regarding how to exercise that choice. A complete ban on captive audience meetings is content neutral;

the ban is applicable regardless of whether the content of the expression at the meeting is favorable or unfavorable to unionization. The reform simply bans one manner of dissemination—forced indoctrination.

The ban on captive audience meetings is a classic example of a time, place, and manner regulation evaluated by using a less stringent "intermediate scrutiny" standard that permits restriction if the regulation (1) is content neutral—the restriction is justified without reference to the content of the regulated speech, (2) is narrowly tailored to serve a significant government interest, and (3) leaves available ample alternative channels for communication of the information.[34]

As previously noted, the proposed ban on captive audience meetings is content neutral. Captive audience meetings are not banned because of government disagreement with the message conveyed, but rather to protect the unwilling listeners' freedom to choose which advice to receive in making a decision regarding unionization.[35]

Moreover, the ban on captive audience meetings is narrowly tailored to serve significant government interests. The government has a strong interest in the plight of the unwilling listener. As the Supreme Court has stated, "our cases have repeatedly recognized the interests of unwilling listeners in situations where 'the degree of captivity makes it impractical for the unwilling viewer or auditor to avoid exposure.'"[36] The constitutionally guaranteed free speech right does not privilege one to compel unwilling employees to listen, for as the Court has made plain, "no one has a right to press even 'good ideas' on an unwilling recipient."[37]

And, as has been detailed, a ban on captive audience meetings leaves employers ample alternative means to convey their views on unionization. Banning captive audience meetings maintains the NLRA § 8(c) protections that bar the NLRB from finding that noncoercive speech constitutes, or is evidence of, unfair labor practices. The captive audience ban does nothing to modify the substantive content of employer speech that the NLRB and the courts have previously found to be lawful.

In April 2022, the NLRB general counsel Jennifer Abruzzo announced her intent to urge the NLRB to hold that captive audience meetings violate the NLRA.[38] Subsequently, an NLRB regional office issued a complaint alleging that a captive audience meeting held by Amazon violated the act.[39] Her view of the illegality of captive audience meetings has been challenged on free speech grounds.[40] But even if the NLRB under President Joe Biden's administration agrees to reverse precedent with respect to captive audience meetings, and the courts sustain the reversal of captive audience precedent, the next probusiness NLRB will no doubt reverse course. Thus, national labor policy again would be determined by presidential politics. To gain stability, Congress needs to amend the NLRA to ban captive audience meetings and then obtain a definitive ruling on the First Amendment implications by putting the issue before the courts in that context.

Protecting Employees' Access to Workplace Email and Other Employer-Provided Electronic Communication Systems

The advent of the widespread use of email and other information technology (IT) systems has raised the question of whether an employer may lawfully deny employees the use an employer's email system and other electronic communication systems to communicate with coworkers about unionization or other § 7 activity. This issue is the most recent variation of one that is as old as the NLRA: how to accommodate the employer's property interest in things it owns and controls with the national commitment to "encourage and protect" workers' aspirations for industrial democracy through the declared national policy of protecting the exercise by workers of "full freedom of association [and] self-organization."

In 2007, the NLRB resolved that accommodation in *Register Guard*[41] by giving primacy to employers' property rights and holding that employers generally have the right to impose nondiscriminatory restrictions (including outright bans) on the use of employer-owned IT systems for nonwork purposes. In 2014, the NLRB overruled *Register Guard* in *Purple Communications, Inc.*,[42] recognizing that with the emergence of the digital workplace, employees' work locations now are often widely dispersed. In addition, there has been a momentous change in the nature of workplace communications. In *Purple Communications, Inc.*, the NLRB held that if an employer grants employees access to its email system for any personal use, then it must let them use the system (on nonworking time) to communicate with each other for statutorily protected purposes unless the employer can prove that the need to maintain production or discipline, or to preserve the efficiency of the system itself, justifies restricting or prohibiting the use of the system. In 2019, in *Caesar's Entertainment*,[43] the NLRB under President Donald Trump overruled *Purple Communications, Inc.* and returned to the standard in *Register Guard*. In

Caesar's Entertainment, the Board held that employers have no legal duty "to permit access to their IT systems for Sec. 7 purposes [except] in those atypical and rare situations in which employees otherwise would be deprived of 'adequate avenues for communication' necessary for the exercise of their Sec. 7 rights."[44] Moreover, the majority in *Caesar's Entertainment* held that, because in a "typical workplace," oral solicitation and face-to-face-literature distribution are sufficient to allow employees to exercise their § 7 rights, an employer's restriction on the use of its electronic communications system does not generally "unreasonably imped[e]" the exercise of the right to self-organization.[45]

Caesar's Entertainment and its return to the framework of *Register Guard* seem inconsistent with the balancing test articulated in *Republic Aviation Corp. v. NLRB*,[46] an early Supreme Court case adjusting the competing legitimate interests of employer property rights and employees' right to self-organization under the NLRA. Early on, the Board had held that the NLRA represents a judgment by Congress that there need to be limits on an employer's property right to control the use of its premises. Accordingly, employers may not ban employees' oral solicitation during nonworking time or the distribution of literature during nonworking time in nonworking areas.[47] In *Republic Aviation*, the Supreme Court agreed that the enactment of the NLRA required the need for an adjustment that balanced employer property rights and employee § 7 rights. The Court has stated the standard for that adjustment in unequivocal terms: "No restriction may be placed on the employees' right to discuss self-organization among themselves unless the employer can demonstrate that a restriction is necessary to maintain production or discipline."[48] The Board's holding in *Register Guard*, that employers generally have the right to impose nondiscriminatory outright bans on the use of employer-owned IT systems for nonwork purposes, is not grounded in any special circumstances that make the rule necessary to maintain production or discipline. Instead, the NLRB adopted its *Caesar's Entertainment/Register Guard* framework based on the bare property interest of corporate ownership of IT equipment. That ownership alone, without the need for an employer to show any other interest, was found to be sufficient in most cases to justify banning employee use of IT equipment for purposes related to protected § 7 activities.

The majority in *Caesar's Entertainment* acknowledged that its rule was uncoupled from *Republic Aviation*'s requirement that restrictions on employee communications at the workplace during nonwork time need to be justified by the employer's interest in promoting production or discipline. However, the *Caesar's Entertainment* majority ruled that the *Republic Aviation* framework was limited to employer-imposed restrictions on face-to-face communications, "not, as here, the right to use employer-owned equipment."[49] In support of this constricted view of *Republic Aviation*, the majority in *Caesar's Entertainment* cited a long line of cases holding that employees do not have an NLRA-based right to use other employer equipment, such as televisions, bulletin boards, copy machines, telephones, or public-address systems.[50]

The effects of *Caesar's Entertainment* are likely to be significant, given the reality that in many modern workplaces, the only feasible way for employees to communicate with each other—especially with coworkers they don't know and never see—is via the company's intranet email system.[51] When the NLRA was enacted, employees did not work via computer in disparate locations many miles from the company's main production facility. And, of course, in 1935 the word "email" did not even exist in the English language. The NLRA needs to be updated to reflect the changing realities of the American workplace. *Purple Communications* was a reasonable effort to balance employers' property rights and employees' § 7 rights in the context of contemporary work life. But if, as it appears, the *Purple Communications* effort to provide meaningful communication opportunities among large groups of geographically separated employees via a company's email system is doomed to become yet another example of the NLRA's meaning depending on the results of the most recent presidential election, then Congress needs to step in. It should amend the NLRA by incorporating the NLRB's 2014 *Purple Communications, Inc.* decision. This revision will help keep the pledge that employees are to be provided meaningful opportunities to engage in concerted activity, which includes discussions of wages and working conditions.

III The Role of Contemporary Labor Relations Law in Creating Obstacles to Employees' Ability to Secure Favorable Collective Bargaining Terms

8 Opportunities in the NLRA for Employers to Deny Workers an Initial Collective Bargaining Agreement

Labor Law Reforms Needed[1]

Provide for a bargaining order to remedy employer interference with employee free choice in representation elections.

Facilitate initial collective bargaining agreements by providing for interest arbitration.

Permit the National Labor Relations Board (NLRB) to engage in economic analysis.

* * *

If the union manages to win an election, the current National Labor Relations Act (NLRA) framework provides employers many options to resist their employees' choice to unionize by delaying the commencement of collective bargaining negotiations. The first option is to administratively challenge the validity of the election and, should that fail, to then judicially appeal the NLRB's certification of the union as the exclusive bargaining representative. In almost all cases, the motive for initiating these postelection challenges is to delay bargaining, perhaps for years in some cases. The second opportunity to continue delaying is to engage in "hard bargaining" once collective bargaining begins—that is, meet but refuse to reach any agreement. Here, the goal is to deny employees even a first contract in order to weaken employee support for the union as part of a larger strategy to eventually decertify the union.[2] Labor law reform needs to counter both of these anti-union tactics.

Reducing Opportunities to Delay Initiating Collective Bargaining

Under current NLRB representation election procedures, employers raise two types of postelection issues. Each is deployed to delay the Board from certifying the results of an election and thereby postpone the onset of a legally enforceable duty to bargain. First, employers challenge individuals' eligibility to vote in the election; and second, employers advance objections to conduct that affects the results of the election.

Challenges concerning individuals' eligibility to vote must be lodged before the questioned ballots are dropped into the ballot box. Each challenged ballot is placed in an envelope bearing the name of the challenged voter and is investigated following the voting if the challenges are sufficient in number to affect the results of the election. Challenges may be resolved either administratively by the NLRB regional director without a hearing, or in a nonadversarial hearing if the director determines that the challenges raise substantial and material factual issues. Following the postelection hearing, the hearing officer prepares a report recommending the disposition of the challenges, and exceptions may be filed with the regional director, who then decides the matter.[3] Once the regional director decides the challenges, the envelopes of challenged voters who are ruled eligible to vote are opened and counted, and the regional director issues a tally of ballots. In most cases, NLRB review of decisions concerning challenged ballots can be obtained by filing a request for review, thereby further delaying the process. Only after the Board rules on the challenges and issues a revised tally of ballots does the NLRB certify the results of the election. It is not difficult to appreciate the abundant opportunities that this procedure presents for an employer to use the challenged ballot tactic to postpone for many months the NLRB's certification of the union as the exclusive bargaining representative, thereby postponing the legal obligation to commence bargaining.

A related delaying tactic available to employers following a union victory in the representation election is to file postelection objections to conduct that affects the results of the election within seven days of the tallying of ballots.[4] If, by a written offer of proof, the objections provide a prima facie case that there was conduct interfering with employees' free and uninhibited choice in the selection of a bargaining representative, thus warranting setting aside the election, the NLRB regional office is required to investigate the objections, including conducting a postelection hearing to resolve any substantial and material factual issues.[5]

Except in elections held by consent election, the regional director's resolution of postelection objections, challenges, or both may be appealed to the Board. The NLRB's final disposition of election objections and challenges is not subject to direct judicial review,[6] but the NLRA provides the employer with a simple expedient to continue to delay bargaining. The employer can judicially challenge the Board's decisions with respect to all the issues raised during the representation election process through an indirect procedure commonly referred to as a "technical 8(a)(5)." Once the union is certified as having won the election, the employer can simply refuse to bargain, forcing the union to protest by filing unfair labor practice charges against the employer. The ensuing NLRB order finding that the employer has unlawfully refused to bargain is a final order that may be reviewed in the circuit courts of appeal. At the courts of appeal, as a defense to the NLRB's finding of an unfair labor practice for refusing to bargain, the employer can challenge the correctness of the certification of the union as the collective bargaining representative by placing in issue all the claims previously raised during the representation process. From the date that the election was conducted until a court of appeals upholds the NLRB's final order directing the employer to bargain, the delay can, and often does, take years. In one study of 261 certification elections, 23 percent of the employers refused to recognize and bargain with the union that won the election but instead initiated the abovementioned delaying tactics by filing election objections and challenges with the NLRB and then judicially litigating the issues raised through the expedient of the technical 8(a)(5). In this study, all these administrative and judicial challenges to the correctness of the election were found to be without merit, but the effort was effective from the employer's viewpoint. Unions were able to obtain a first contract in only 70 percent of the cases in which the employer deployed the election objection/technical 8(a)(5) tactic, compared with an 83 percent first-contract success rate when election objections were not filed.[7] In addition, the worst penalty that the employer can suffer for refusing to come to the table to bargain as soon as the NLRB certifies the union as the employees' bargaining representative is an NLRB order to meet with the union and begin bargaining and to post a notice promising that going forward, the employer will not continue its unlawful conduct of refusing to bargain. However, even when the employer's litigation effort is unsuccessful, the delay that the unfair labor practice litigation caused erodes support for the union among the employees because, perhaps for years, the union is unable to show that it has participated in even a single bargaining meeting with the employer or produced a single benefit for the bargaining unit employees.[8]

Labor law reform should reduce this delay in commencing initial bargaining. A balanced approach for incorporating this reform goal into the NLRA can be found, for example, in several sections of the Protecting the Right to Organize Act (PRO Act). First, § 105(e) provides that after the election, if the results are in dispute, the NLRB must schedule a postelection hearing to resolve factual issues in dispute no later than fourteen days after the filing of objections. Second, when the tally of ballots shows that a majority of valid ballots has been cast in favor of the union, § 105(d) provides that the NLRB shall issue a bargaining order requiring the parties to begin bargaining immediately. That bargaining order is a *self-enforcing* final order. Section 107 provides that within thirty days of the issuance of the bargaining order, the employer may file a petition for review with a federal court of appeals as a means of challenging the bargaining order, but during such an appeal, the order must be complied with.[9] If the employer refuses to commence bargaining in compliance with the bargaining order, the NLRB may initiate contempt proceedings in federal district court. In addition, § 109 requires the NLRB to seek temporary injunctive relief whenever it determines that there is a reasonable basis to find that an employer has significantly interfered with employees' rights under the NLRA. The district court is required to grant this temporary relief unless the court concludes that there is no reasonable likelihood that the NLRB will succeed on the merits of its claim. Implicit in these provisions is that refusal to comply with the NLRB's bargaining order triggers this obligation by the Board to seek § 10(j) injunctive relief. Finally, § 109(b) provides that if an employer commits a violation of employees' rights under the NLRA, the employer shall be subject to a civil penalty not to exceed $50,000 for each violation. The NLRB may double that penalty where the employer has committed another such violation in the previous five years, and where such additional violation involves serious economic harm. The NLRB also may, under certain circumstances, hold an officer or director of an employer personally liable and assess a civil penalty against that person. Since noncompliance with an NLRB bargaining order is a paradigmatic example of a violation of employees' rights under the NLRA, an employer who refuses to comply with an NLRB bargaining order would be subject to a $50,000 civil fine, and the provision for doubling that fine might also apply.[10]

Under current NLRA law, when the union fails to obtain a majority of votes due to employer interference with a fair election, the NLRA remedies the employer misconduct simply by ordering a new election.[11] The act should be amended to change that anemic remedial approach by providing for a bargaining order in these circumstances. PRO Act § 105 represents a good model for this purpose, as it provides that if, due to election interference by the employer, a majority of valid ballots has not been cast in favor of union representation, and if a majority of employees in the voting unit have signed authorization cards designating the union as their representative, then the NLRB is required to issue a bargaining order compelling the employer to bargain with the union. The appeal rights and the duty to comply immediately with this bargaining order are the same as when the Board issues a bargaining order following the union's victory in the election.

Ordering bargaining based on authorization cards is not a novel NLRB remedy. Prior to the Taft-Hartley amendments, the NLRB certified unions based on authorization cards.[12] And for twenty years, beginning with the 1949 *Joy Silk* decision, the Board applied its "good faith doubt" test. The so-called *Joy Silk* doctrine provided that the NLRB would order an employer to recognize and bargain with a union when the union presented evidence of an authorization card majority and the employer refused recognition but lacked a good faith doubt as to the union's majority status.[13] The Supreme Court never endorsed the *Joy Silk* "good-faith-doubt" test for ordering bargaining based on authorization cards, largely because NLRB counsel during oral argument in *NLRB v. Gissel Packing Co.* misstated that the NLRB had abandoned its *Joy Silk* test.[14] Believing in error that the *Joy Silk* doctrine was being jettisoned, the Court in *Gissel* established a new test for determining when the NLRB could rely on authorization cards to issue a bargaining order. Rather that focus on the employer's motivation at the time of its refusal to bargain—as was the approach under the *Joy Silk* doctrine—the Court in *Gissel* focused on the remedial question of whether the NLRB should order bargaining based on authorization cards because the extensiveness of employers' unfair labor practices made it highly unlikely or even impossible that a future election could be fairly conducted.[15] However, the critical point is that, while never endorsing the *Joy Silk* good faith doubt test, the Supreme Court's 1969 *Gissel* decision did affirm the Board's decades-recognized authority to issue a bargaining order—under some circumstances—based on the union having secured evidence of majority support through authorization cards.

The rule in *Gissel* should be modified legislatively to remedy effectively all employer interference with employees' free choice during a representation election when the union has obtained evidence of majority support through authorization cards. Currently, the NLRB and the courts will remedy employers' unfair labor practices by issuing a bargaining order only if the employer has engaged in one or more of the "hallmark" unfair labor practices: discriminatory discharge, layoffs of union activists, and threats to close unionized facilities.[16] The NLRA should provide that issuance of a bargaining order is mandatory whenever the union's loss in the election is due to election interference by the employer and the union is able to demonstrate majority support through authorization cards. Otherwise, anti-union NLRBs and judicial panels will find ways to avoid providing the bargaining order remedy.[17]

Limiting bargaining orders to unions that have demonstrated majority support at some point through authorization cards might incentivize some employers to aggressively coerce the workforce early in the organizing campaign with the objective of preventing the union from ever obtaining signatures on a majority of authorization cards, thereby precluding it from qualifying for a bargaining order should it lose the election due to employer interference. However, the choice to provide bargaining orders only for unions that at one time were able to obtain evidence of majority support through authorization cards represents an intelligent political compromise. The principle of majority rule is foundational in our political culture. Thus, labor law reform should preserve the majority-support principle by limiting bargaining orders to circumstances where the union has at some point gained majority support from the bargaining unit employees.[18]

Facilitating Negotiation of the Initial Collective Bargaining Agreement

One of the least-understood deficiencies of the current NLRA collective bargaining regulatory system is its failure to fulfill the promise of industrial democracy for the thousands of workers who successfully choose collective representation but never can obtain even a first collective bargaining agreement. Even when an employer's purposeful delay to forestall negotiations ends and the employer finally is forced to meet with the union to begin collective bargaining, it is not unusual that employers engage in sham bargaining, with the result that no first contract is ever executed.

Estimates of unions' inability to obtain a first contract vary. The late 1970s is generally recognized as the onset of employers' intensification of hostility to unionization. Even after enactment of the Taft-Hartley amendments in

1947, and until the late 1970s, roughly 70 percent of employers and newly certified unions were able to reach a first contract (i.e., the no-first-contract rate was about 30 percent).[19] Beginning in the 1980s, however, that no-first-contract rate steadily increased.

In 1994, the Federal Mediation and Conciliation Service (FMCS) calculated first-contract estimates for the Commission on the Future of Worker-Management Relations (known as the "Dunlop Commission"). The FMCS reviewed 10,783 union elections certified by the NLRB between 1986 and 1993 in which the FMCS assisted. In this report to the commission, the FMCS concluded that 44 percent of certifications in which the FMCS was contacted to assist never resulted in a first contract.[20] In 2008, John-Paul Ferguson published a study of 8,155 elections won by unions in the period of 1999–2004. This study also found that 44 percent of these certifications resulted in the union failing to achieve a first contract within two years of the election.[21] In 1994, Joel Rogers concluded that "[a]t present, in the United States, only about half the units won by unions in representation elections before the National Labor Relations Board ever make it to first contract."[22]

Compounding the indictment of the current NLRA representation system because it results in low rates of first contracts is the even greater inability of unions that win representation elections to ever obtain a second contract, and thereby establish normal, long-term stable labor relations with employers. Studies by the Industrial Union Department (IUD) of the AFL-CIO in 1975, 1988, and 1993 defined "stable labor relations" as "maintaining a continual bargaining relationship for at least five years following the NLRB election." A union fails to establish such stable labor relations either because it never obtained a first contract or, even if a first contract had been executed, it was unable to negotiate a successive collective bargaining agreement within five years of winning the representation election.[23] These studies showed that "65.4 percent of the workplaces that voted for unions in 1982 *did not have a union contract after five years*, compared with 35.9 percent in 1970." Moreover, although the results were somewhat improved five years later, even among unions that won elections in 1987, the majority (52.9 percent) had no collective bargaining contract after five years.[24]

It is clear that the NLRA, as interpreted by the NLRB and the courts, has greatly contributed to this spike in the inability of recently elected unions to establish stable labor relations with employers. Since the early 1980s, employers have intensified their desire to operate free of the employee rights contained in collective bargaining agreements. The NLRA's pallid remedial structure facilitated employers' ability to achieve this goal of operating free of such obligations by permitting employers to engage in virtually risk-free sham bargaining—meeting with unions but lacking a sincere desire to accommodate differences and find common ground with the other side. Indeed, a convincing case can be made that the current NLRA framework actually creates incentives for employers to engage in bad-faith collective bargaining as part of a strategy to eventually decertify the union.

The incentives that the current NLRA creates for employers to engage in sham bargaining are grounded in the policy that so long as the employer does not engage in behavior that the NLRB concludes consists of "bad faith bargaining," the act permits employers to lawfully engage in hard bargaining—going through the motions of good faith bargaining but never in fact agreeing to mutually acceptable contract terms. The NLRA's governing principle is freedom of contract: the employer is never *required* to consent to a proposal or make concessions,[25] and the NLRB lacks the statutory authority to direct the contract terms that employers must offer.[26] According to Pavy (1994), employers increasingly hire labor relations consultants and lawyers who "offer their services on the premise that no place of work is unionized until a contract is signed and that . . . employers can and should avoid signing a union contract."[27] These labor consultants become expert at devising bargaining tactics that frustrate the bargaining process by deploying negotiation strategies that walk a thin line between lawful hard bargaining and unlawful bad faith bargaining. For example, a labor consultant, acting on behalf of the employer, might agree to meet with the union perhaps dozens of times over a course of many months, or even years. But the employer never agrees to any contract terms proposed by the union and may respond to the union's proposals by an offer such as a management rights provision that confers virtually all power and discretion to the employer and provides little, if anything, of value to the workers.[28]

It is unlawful to engage in the formalities of negotiation, the externals of collective bargaining, while lacking a bona fide and serious intent to "adjust differences and reach an acceptable common ground [through] a shared process in which each party . . . plays an active role."[29] This is referred to as unlawful "surface bargaining." But surface bargaining is hard to prove. In one set of 1993 negotiations in Uniontown, Pennsylvania, for example, the labor relations consultant hired by the employer met with the union monthly over a period of two-and-a-half years—meetings that

> resulted in no agreement on even basic issues. During bargaining the consultant display[ed] a lackluster attitude by reading the newspaper while the union present[ed] its proposals or engag[ed] in idle banter about cattle ranching, skiing, or amusement parks to kill time and prolong the process. The union . . . repeatedly filed ULPs only to be told that "hard bargaining" is not a violation.[30]

The employer's long-term strategy when engaging in such surface bargaining is to stall negotiations for a year or more in order to frustrate the workers, who come to regard the union as feeble, incompetent, or both. The failure of the union to produce results at the bargaining table dissipates rank-and-file support for the union and opens opportunities for the employer to provide encouragement to decertification efforts by employees who have become disgruntled.[31] Or, in the alternative, the employer's strategy may be to force the union to strike to obtain reasonable concessions. Then, as one manager told the employees, if they do not like the company's bargaining position, the employees could strike, "and [then] I will replace every goddamn one of you."[32]

If labor consultants are skilled, it is very difficult (and some say often nearly impossible) for the NLRB to prove that this stalling approach to collective bargaining negotiations constitutes unlawful bad-faith bargaining.[33] A sham bargaining strategy rewards the employer by allowing it to work to rid itself of a union. As one United Steelworkers organizer explained, after a year or more of unsuccessful bargaining, "a lot of the folks that wanted the union are gonna get dissatisfied because they haven't got a contract yet and quit the union, and then you can't do anything."[34] Sham bargaining that has the effect of dissipating employee support for the union represents an overwhelming victory for the employer.

But even if the NLRB concludes that the employer has crossed the line from lawful hard bargaining to unlawful bad faith bargaining and that the employer therefore has committed an unfair labor practice, there are no meaningful adverse consequences for the employer. As previously stated, upon finding that the employer bargained in bad faith, the Board normally is able to remedy this violation of federal law only by ordering the employer to cease and desist from engaging in bad faith bargaining and to post a notice stating that the employer will not continue its unlawful behavior.[35]

Litigating a bad faith bargaining unfair labor practice before the NLRB, and then appealing the Board's decisions through the courts, may take three or four years to complete, providing the employer additional time to dissipate union support among the understandably frustrated employees, who are then more inclined to support an effort to decertify the union.[36] In short, in most cases, the NLRA currently fails to provide remedies that are adequate to thwart a motivated employer who is determined *never* to agree to an initial collective bargaining contract with a union that has recently won a representation election.[37]

Labor law reform needs to focus on modifying the NLRA's postelection procedures in ways that are designed to create disincentives for an employer to engage in unlawful surface bargaining during first-contract negotiations. One effective approach is to provide what is referred to as "interest arbitration" for first contracts. This is the approach taken by § 104(h) of the PRO Act, for example, which provides that once a union has been recognized or certified as the employees' bargaining representative, the employer and the union must commence bargaining within 10 days of the union submitting a written request. If the parties fail to reach an agreement after 90 days of bargaining, or for additional periods as the parties may agree, then either party may request mediation facilitated by the Federal Mediation and Conciliation Service (FMCS). If the parties cannot reach an agreement within 30 days after mediation is requested, or for additional periods as the parties may agree, then the FMCS is required to refer the dispute to a tripartite arbitration panel. This panel consists of one member selected by the employer, one selected by the union, and one mutually agreed to by both the employer and union. The employer and union must agree to this panel within 14 days of the referral. A majority of the panel is required to render a decision settling the dispute within 120 days, absent extraordinary circumstances or an agreement between the parties. The findings of this panel are binding upon the parties for a period of two years unless the parties mutually agree in writing to amend during that period. In addition, the enhanced NLRA remedies discussed here also would apply to employer violations of these postelection procedures that provide first-contract interest arbitration, including the possibility of a $50,000 civil penalty (or perhaps double that), injunctive relief, and an order of contempt.

First-contract arbitration has been a staple under Canadian labor law for many years in jurisdictions that cover 80 percent of the Canadian workforce.

Employers' unwillingness to bargain in good faith during first-contract negotiations "led to first-contract arbitration . . . in British Columbia in 1973," and then in the Canadian federal sector, and then in most Canadian provinces. The goal of the Canadian legislation, as well as all proposals for first-contract arbitration, is to "lay the foundation for establishing a mature bargaining relationship, and [create] a deterrent effect, that is to pressure employers to bargain with newly certified unions by raising the possibility that [a third party] will impose a costly first agreement if a [voluntary] settlement is not reached."[38]

In addition to providing a deterrent to sham bargaining by the employer during first-contract negotiations, first-contract arbitration addresses a key concern of some workers—namely, that the union that they recently voted to represent them may end up being a do-nothing entity. Do-nothing unionism is a big fear of workers contemplating whether to vote for the union—taking a worker's dues but providing no compensable benefit to the worker in return. Some unions, to combat this anxiety, have a rule that the "union will not collect any dues until workers approve the first contract. In other words, workers would not pay a dime until they approved a contract they were happy with."[39] By assuring workers and unions that there will be a first contract relatively soon after the union is certified, first-contract arbitration is calculated to reduce worker anxiety at the preelection stage that voting for a union will not bring about positive changes at work. First-contract arbitration also assures unions that soon after being certified, a first contract will be in place, and the union will be able to begin charging monthly dues, thus placing the bargaining unit on a more sound financial footing.

The arbitration of first contracts is not a panacea and is no substitute for a mutual desire by unions and employers to create a long-term and productive institutional relationship. For example, first-contract arbitration does not eliminate the risk of ongoing employer obduracy in refusing to accept the union as the bargaining representative, a problem that could manifest itself during subsequent contract negotiations. But first-contract arbitration provides the parties a "trial marriage" of sorts, and that represents progress.

Some argue that "the principal problem" with first-contract arbitration is that no real bargaining will take place prior to the first-contract arbitration because both parties, "anticipating the entry of an impartial third party, [will] rigidly preserve their position so that a compromise of it will not be harmful to them [once arbitration commences]."[40] This risk will need to be managed as arbitration policies and procedures develop. One answer could be an evidentiary rule that offers of compromise during prearbitration collective bargaining negotiations will be inadmissible as evidence during arbitration hearings. Alternatively, the arbitration could take the form of final-offer arbitration, as used for decades in baseball salary disputes, or some variation of that arbitration format, as former NLRB chair William Gould has suggested.[41] Final-offer arbitration has been used to resolve emergency disputes in the rail industry under the Railway Labor Act (RLA) and is a preferred dispute resolution mechanism in some public-sector labor relations legislation. The idea is that the parties will be incentivized to compromise when presenting their final offers in arbitration because the arbitrator's role is only to choose, in total, one side's best, final offer.[42]

Other specifics will need to be worked out to implement first-contract arbitration. If the NLRA is amended to provide first-contract arbitration, it will be necessary to address the union's right to strike prior to referral of the first-contract dispute to arbitration or during the arbitration process itself. In addition, the first-contract tripartite arbitration panel and the parties will need to work out the standards to be applied by the arbitration panel in resolving the first-contract dispute. And what, if any, judicial review of the arbitration panel's work should be permitted, using what standards of judicial review? Posing these questions is not intended to undermine the merits of proposals for first-contract arbitration, but rather to acknowledge that after labor law reform creates a framework for first-contract arbitration, many details still need to be filled in.[43]

9 Opportunities in the NLRA Permitting Employers to Destabilize Existing Bargaining Relationships

Labor Law Reforms Needed[1]

Protect the collective bargaining process after the first contract.

Prohibit employers from permanently replacing employees who strike (the full discussion of this point is deferred to chapter 10).

Prohibit offensive lockouts (the full discussion of this point is deferred to chapter 10).

Eliminate employers' ability to unilaterally withdraw union recognition without an election to decertify the labor organization.

Restore longstanding bars to the raising of a question concerning representation (QCR) as a means to protect collective bargaining.

* * *

The establishment of stable and productive collective bargaining relationships is a fundamental objective of the National Labor Relations Act (NLRA), which states that "it is . . . the policy of the United States [to] encourage[] the practice and procedure of collective bargaining."[2] Even after an initial contract (and even after a second contract), some bargaining relationships remain unstable. Responding to this labor relations reality, five labor law reform provisions are needed to promote stability in existing bargaining relationships. These provisions are discussed next.

Banning the Unilateral Implementation of New Terms or Conditions of Employment

National labor policy currently recognizes the destabilizing effect on the collective bargaining process when employers initiate unilateral changes in terms and conditions of employment. For many years, the NLRA has placed some limitations on unilateral changes. For example, § 8(d)(4) of the NLRA bars unilateral implementation of modifications of terms and conditions in existing contracts during the term of the contract.

But § 8(d)(4) is a very limited unilateral implementation ban; its proscription applies only to conditions of employment that are addressed in the provisions of an existing agreement. However, no collective bargaining agreement addresses all terms and conditions of employment. For example, a contract may contain provisions providing for a basic wage structure but remain silent with respect to merit pay increases or bonuses, matters that were not discussed during the negotiations that led to the current agreement. In this example, absent waiver, there would be an ongoing duty to bargain over merit increases, even during the term of the existing agreement.[3] But under current law, an employer's unilateral implementation of changes regarding a provision such as merit increases would not be barred by NLRA § 8(d)(4) because merit increases in this example are not "terms or conditions of an existing contract."

More common is the situation where the parties are in the process of negotiating a first contract. During these negotiations, there are existing conditions of employment (i.e., those that existed before the union was elected as the bargaining representative), but these employment conditions are not yet contained in any "existing contract." Thus, prior to a first contract, § 8(d)(4) is inapplicable as a bar to an employer's unilateral implementation of changes in existing conditions of employment.

Finally, it is not unusual that while the parties are renegotiating an existing contract, the current contract expires. Once that happens, there no longer is an "existing contract" on which the § 8(d)(4) bar can operate. In short, in a variety of contexts, the employer is able to engage in the destabilizing conduct of unilaterally implementing working conditions without violating any language currently contained in the NLRA.

In circumstances when the § 8(d)(4) implementation bar is inapplicable, unilateral changes are regulated by the rule that the Supreme Court approved in *NLRB v. Katz*.[4] *Katz* provides that an employer may lawfully make unilateral changes during the course of the bargaining relationship with respect to mandatory subjects of bargaining not contained in an existing contract once an impasse in bargaining occurs. The *Katz* rule might appear benign, but in fact it is the keystone of a strategy adopted by employers to rid themselves of a union. It is no exaggeration that in the hands of an employer committed to frustrating the bargaining process and undermining an incumbent union, the *Katz* unilateral implementation rule "gives employers the power to destroy collective bargaining."[5] Their strategy for doing so is described next.

During the negotiation of a first contract or the renegotiation of an existing agreement, the employer decides to willfully refuse to engage in good faith bargaining but couches its negotiation posture as legal "hard bargaining." Without crossing the line barring bad faith bargaining—or at least not getting caught by the National Labor Relations Board (NLRB) when crossing that line—the employer meets and confers with the union but relies on its NLRA § 8(d) right not to be compelled "to agree to a proposal [from the union] or . . . mak[e] a concession." After bargaining negotiations have taken place for a suitable period of time needed to make a case that the employer has been bargaining in good faith, the employer makes a final offer—one that no self-respecting union would likely accept because it contains a broad, but lawful, management rights clause reserving to the employer unilateral control over the most significant aspects of the employment relationship and provides little, if anything, of value to the employees. Once the union predictably rejects the employer's final offer and a bona fide bargaining impasse exists, and assuming that any existing collective bargaining agreement has expired by then, the employer is privileged to unilaterally implement its final offer.

The union then is left with three options, each of which is untenable. It could do nothing, at which point the employer could lawfully lock out the employees as an offensive weapon to pressure the union to accept a collective bargaining agreement containing the employer's final offer.[6] When an employer deploys a lawful offensive lockout, the employer may continue business operations by hiring temporary replacements for the locked-out workers.[7] The employer may condition the locked-out employees' right to return to work upon their making an unconditional offer to return and on the union accepting the employer's final bargaining offer.[8]

Or, following the employer's implementation upon impasse, the union could avoid a lockout, concede defeat, and end negotiations by accepting the final offer that the employer made during bargaining. The result, then, is a collective bargaining agreement whose provisions, for the duration of the contract (normally two or three years), track the employer's unilaterally imposed terms, which the union in effect is forced to accept. At that point, the union's "power and the allegiance of its members would be severely reduced," and conditions become ripe for the union to be decertified.[9]

Or the union could try to resist and attempt to persuade the employees to strike for better contract terms than those contained in the employer's final offer. But striking is not a viable option in these circumstances, or in most circumstances today, even if the employees were sufficiently unified to vote to do so. This is because in an economic strike, which this would be, the employer is permitted to hire permanent replacements for the strikers under the *Mackay Radio* rule,[10] which is discussed in more detail in chapter 10. When an employer has decided not to reach agreement with the union, but rather to reach impasse in order to be able to deploy the *Katz* implementation upon impasse rule to frustrate collective bargaining and thereby undermine the union, the employer surely would move quickly to permanently replace the strikers soon after the strike was called. Once permanent replacements are hired, the employer may refuse to reinstate the economic strikers who have been replaced. Even following an economic striker's unconditional offer to return to work, permanently replaced economic strikers are entitled only to be placed on a preferential hiring list. Full reinstatement, then, is available only upon the departure of the replacement or another circumstance that creates an opening in the bargaining unit, which could be years after the strike occurred, and then only if the striker has not acquired regular and substantially equivalent employment and the employer is unable to show a legitimate and substantial business reason for failing to reinstate that person.[11]

In short, the *Katz* implementation upon impasse rule, working in conjunction with the offensive lockout and the *Mackay* permanent striker replacement rule, permits many employers to negotiate with the certainty that they will be able to dictate contract terms largely without concern for the workers' desires because in many cases, there is little that the union can do to resist. In this way, as currently interpreted, the NLRA permits—indeed may invite—the undermining of the collective bargaining process.

The combination of the *Katz* rule, the offensive lockout, and the right to permanently replace economic strikers not only permits a motivated employer to sabotage the bargaining process, it also is an effective way for an employer to rid itself of the union entirely when combined with the right of the employer to withdraw recognition upon evidence that the union has lost majority support among the bargaining unit employees. Here is how this union-elimination strategy operates.

The employer's implementation upon impasse and the union's inability to prevent it provide a clear object lesson to employees about the union's impotency, especially if the terms that the employer unilaterally implements contain a wage cut as part of an anti-union low-wage strategy. Implementation upon impasse dissipates union support among the bargaining unit employees and fortifies the arguments advanced by those in the bargaining unit who support decertifying the union by arguing that unionization is futile because even though the employees have chosen unionization, the employer effectively retains control over the employees' terms and conditions of employment.[12] Although permanently replaced economic strikers may vote in a union decertification election for twelve months after commencement of the strike, the employer can simply wait a year after the start of any economic strike where the employer has permanently replaced strikers. Then, a combination of workers (i.e., permanent replacements and those who were never replaced because they did not strike or they returned to work before being replaced) can file a petition with the NLRB requesting an election to decertify the union.[13] Once presented with a decertification election petition that shows by a preponderance of the evidence that the union has lost its support among a majority of the bargaining unit employees, the employer may lawfully withdraw recognition of the union under current law or announce its intention to do so if there is an existing contract that is about to expire.[14]

To encourage stability in bargaining relationships, labor law reform should include amending the NLRA to prevent employers from declaring an impasse in bargaining and then unilaterally implementing new terms or conditions of employment while the parties are in the midst of collective bargaining negotiations.[15] This reform would force each side to work together to find a compromise agreeable to both rather than permitting the employer to dictate the outcome of a bargaining dispute through unilateral implementation. In addition, bargaining relationship stability would be greatly enhanced by prohibiting employers from permanently replacing employees who strike and by prohibiting the offensive lockout, These provisions are taken up in detail in chapter 10.

Banning Unilateral Withdrawal of Union Recognition

Labor law reform should reverse the effects of *Johnson Controls, Inc.*,[16] a particularly pernicious 2019 decision of the NLRB during President Donald Trump's administration. In *Johnson Controls*, the Board held it permissible for an employer to announce that it will withdraw recognition of a union within a ninety-day time frame before the expiration of an existing collective bargaining agreement based on evidence that the union has lost majority support. Once the employer has announced its intent to withdraw recognition, the holding in *Johnson Controls* provides that the union thereupon is provided no way to regain recognition except by filing for and prevailing in another NLRB-conducted representation election.

Prior to *Johnson Controls*, the rule had been that if the employer were presented with evidence of a union's loss of majority support during the final months of a collective bargaining agreement—for example, by a decertification petition supported by a majority of bargaining unit employees—the employer could lawfully announce its intention to withdraw recognition once the current collective bargaining contract expired and then refuse to meet to renegotiate the current contract. This is referred to as "anticipatory withdrawal of union recognition." The union then often would attempt to reacquire majority status by an action such as obtaining signatures on union authorization cards from a majority of the bargaining unit employees. If that effort by the union failed, the employer could withdraw recognition of the union after the current contract expired and could unilaterally implement new employment conditions. Often very favorable for the employees, these new conditions of employment are calculated to demonstrate that the employees do not need a union after all to obtain benefits such as a wage increase. If, however, the union succeeded in reacquiring majority support prior to the time that the current contract expired, the employer would not be permitted to unilaterally withdraw recognition upon the expiration of the contract, would not be permitted to refuse to meet to negotiate a new contract, and (most important) would not be permitted to unilaterally implement new conditions of employment prior to an impasse in bargaining. If the union reacquired majority support and the employer nevertheless refused to bargain, unilaterally implemented new employment terms prior to a bargaining impasse, or both, that would constitute a refusal-to-bargain unfair labor practice that the NLRB would remedy by issuing a bargaining order and a ban on withdrawal of recognition for one year.[17]

Johnson Controls is particularly pernicious because a sophisticated employer (especially one that hires a competent and aggressive labor consultant) possesses the ability to manipulate dissention and dissipate union support among the workers by refusing to agree to any contract other than one that provides little of value to the employees. This tactic encourages disgruntled employees to organize anti-union groups and to work to persuade coworkers to support a union decertification effort. If there is no option for the union to regain recognition following a lawful anticipatory withdrawal of recognition by the employer, other than to win a subsequent representation election, and if in the meantime, the employer is free to implement unilateral changes in employment terms without the need to first bargain to impasse with the union, the union is at an almost insurmountable disadvantage in being able to win a subsequent representation election.

Reform is needed to reverse the process.[18] The NLRA should be amended to ban unilateral withdrawal of recognition, to require the employer to bargain in good faith to renegotiate contracts, to bar unilateral implementation of working conditions, and to respond to the interests of any disgruntled employees who want to be rid of the union by making available to them the ability to file a petition requesting the NLRB to conduct a union decertification election.

Protecting Existing Collective Bargaining Relationships by Codifying Bars to the Raising of a QCR

This book endeavors to avoid as much as possible any discussion of "inside baseball"—that is, getting bogged down by needlessly discussing the intricacies of NLRA labor relations law. Some discussion of labor law minutiae is unavoidable, however, to properly address the reforms that are needed to preserve the law creating certain "bars to the raising of a QCR" and the so-called blocking charge rule.[19] The bars to the raising of a QCR are particularly important to maintain stable bargaining relationships because when one of these bars is in place, it bars the NLRB from processing a petition for a representation election and, by extension, precludes the employer from withdrawing recognition from the union.

The NLRA already contains one important bar to the raising of a QCR, found in § 9(c)(3) of the act—the election bar, referred to as the "one-election-per-year rule," which was added in the 1947 Taft-Hartley amendments. The election bar precludes the NLRB from conducting any election more often than once a year in any given bargaining unit. Prior to the addition of § 9(c)(3), the NLRB had long protected the majority status of a certified union—a union that had won a representation election—by adopting what is referred to as the "certification bar," which bars the filing of a representation petition during the one-year period following the certification of a union.[20] The addition of the election bar in 1947 in effect codified the certification bar and also applied it to cases where the union lost the election.[21] The certification bar is designed to stabilize labor relations during the union's certification year to give the parties a reasonable opportunity to negotiate a first contract without the distraction of an election petition challenging the union's representational status. As a corollary, the certification bar also creates an irrebuttable presumption of a certified union's majority status during the initial one-year period following certification. Accordingly, an employer is barred from withdrawing recognition during the certification-bar year, even if presented with evidence that the union has lost majority support.[22]

However, the certification bar applies only to unions that are certified by the NLRB as the exclusive bargaining representative, a status conferred on a union after it prevails in a union representation election. Unions also obtain recognition as the employees' bargaining representative in additional ways, such as through voluntary recognition and when a majority of the employees hired by a successor employer are the employees of the predecessor who are represented by a union. Longstanding NLRB precedent requires that, by operation of the "recognition bar," the Board must dismiss a petition for a decertification or other election for a reasonable time after the employer voluntarily recognizes the union so the employer and the union can focus on collective bargaining.[23] In addition, the "successor bar" prevents elections for a reasonable time after a successor employer begins bargaining with the union.[24] Moreover, the "remedial bargaining order bar" prevents elections for a reasonable time after the Board issues a remedial bargaining order so the employer and union can develop a stable bargaining relationship.[25] Finally, the "contract bar" prevents elections for up to the first three years of a bargaining agreement to allow the union to focus on implementing the agreement.[26] In addition to the bars to the raising of a QCR, the Board's "blocking charge" policy suspends the processing of any election until after it resolves any pending unfair labor practice charges to prevent any alleged coercion from undermining the integrity of the election.[27]

These bars to the raising of a QCR, the associated bars on the employer withdrawing recognition, and the Board's blocking charge policy operated well for many decades without the need to codify them in the NLRA. But now the need for codification has arisen because the Trump NLRB undermined the continued viability of these bars. First, on April 1, 2020, the Trump NLRB filed a Final Rule that adds several amendments to the Board's current rules and regulations governing the filing and processing of representation petitions.[28]

The first amendment in the Trump NLRB's April 2020 Final Rule modifies the election blocking charge policy by ending the policy of suspending elections during the pendency of unfair labor practice charges that, if valid, would interfere with the ability of the NLRB to hold a fair election. Instead, the Trump NLRB's Final Rule provides that the Board will proceed with processing the petition, conducting the election, and counting the ballots except in a certain limited type of case in which the unfair labor practice charges are far more likely to be filed against the union than against the employer. In those cases, if a complaint on the pending unfair labor practice charges has not been issued prior to the conclusion of the election, the NLRB will impound the votes and delay the vote count or certification of results for a maximum of sixty days.[29] The blocking charge policy that this rule abandons dates from 1937, shortly after the act went into effect.[30]

The second amendment modifies the current recognition bar policy by establishing a notice requirement and forty-five-day open period for filing an election petition following an employer's voluntary recognition of a labor organization as employees' majority-supported exclusive collective-bargaining representative.[31] This forty-five-day open period for filing an election petition is created to provide disgruntled employees time to organize an anti-union campaign and file a decertification election petition. In November 2022, the NLRB issued a proposed rule to reinstate the blocking charge rule and reverse other changes contained in the Trump Board's April 2020 Final Rule, as discussed here.[32]

In addition to the changes made by the rulemaking described here, the Trump NLRB, in July 2020, announced that it was considering eliminating or weakening the eighty-one-year-old contract bar. Following the election of President Joe Biden in 2020, the NLRB, with the addition of Democratic member Lauren McFerran as chair of the NLRB, decided to make no changes to the contract bar "at this time."[33] Codifying the longstanding contract bar precedent will preserve bargaining relationship stability during the term of an existing collective bargaining agreement.

In sum, there are many opportunities in the current NLRA, as interpreted by the NLRB and the courts, for an employer to destabilize an existing collective bargaining relationship, undermine the collective bargaining process, and rid itself of a union that has been freely chosen by employees as their collective representative. Amending the NLRA to ban unilateral implementation upon impasse, banning offensive lockout, banning permanent replacement of economic strikers, and banning the withdrawal of union recognition without a decertification election will go far in promoting bargaining relationship stability. Moreover, to protect future NLRB majorities from eroding or eliminating the bars to the raising of a QCR and the protections of the blocking charge rule, labor law reform should include codification into the NLRA of these bars and the blocking charge rule. This chapter demonstrates why these reform proposals deserve the support of those who are committed to the pledge to American workers that national labor policy is to encourage the practice and procedure of collective bargaining.

10 Opportunities in the NLRA Permitting Employers to Limit Workers' Economic Actions

Labor Law Reforms Needed[1]

Prohibit employers from permanently replacing employees who strike.

Clarify the scope of the right to strike.

Prohibit offensive lockouts.

Remove limitations on secondary picketing and strikes and repeal NLRA § 303 (private right of action for an employer to sue unions that conduct secondary strikes and other activities).

End prohibitions on collective and class action litigation.

Repeal § 14(b), which permits states to pass laws that prevent unions from requiring union membership as a condition for employment.

* * *

Prohibiting the Permanent Replacement of Employees Who Strike

The right of employers to permanently replace economic strikers is a judicially created policy. Nothing in the National Labor Relations Act (NLRA) privileges the employer to unleash this economic weapon. Of the many judicially created labor policies that have aided employers to defeat workers' desire for meaningful protection through the collective bargaining process, none has harmed workers more than the striker replacement rule created by the Supreme Court in its 1938 *Mackay Radio* decision.[2]

It is hard to disagree with Ahmed White (2018), who argues that "the rule established in *Mackay Radio* came out of the blue. It was set forth in a case which required no such question to be resolved, in a manner that drew no support from the text of the Wagner Act, and on the basis of legislative history that was ambiguous at best."[3] In addition, the *Mackay* rule is in direct conflict with NLRA policies that bar employers from retaliating against employees who exercise the right to strike.[4] The *Mackay* rule is particularly problematic because the text of the act, in § 13, states that "[n]othing in the Act, except as *specifically provided for herein*, shall be construed so as either to interfere with or impede or diminish *in any way* the right to strike."[5] Forcing strikers to gamble with job loss due to permanent replacement interferes with, impedes, and diminishes the right to strike. It is hardly surprising, therefore, that the eminent labor law scholar Paul Weiler (2001) has concluded that the *Mackay Radio* rule is "the worst contribution that the Supreme Court has made to the current shape of labor law in this country."[6] Other authorities in the field of private-sector labor relations law "have made the restoration of the right to strike a cornerstone of [their] scholarship. [They] strongly criticize the arguments that judges, legislators, and others have used to justify their degradation of the right to strike."[7]

"Permanent replacement" may be the technical term for the economic weapon that the Court handed to employers in its *Mackay* decision, but as Weiler (2001) says, "[f]rom the employee's perspective, there would seem to be little tangible difference between being discharged for striking or being permanently replaced in one's job."[8] To be clear, according to Gould (1996), "[p]ermanent strike replacement means the loss of jobs for the strikers for the foreseeable future [and] [i]t is difficult to imagine a prospect more likely to dissuade employees from exercising their statutory protected rights than the loss of jobs and the benefits bound up with them."[9]

Because of this risk of permanent replacement, the strike has become a rarity in many industries regulated by the NLRA. As White (2018) has explained, "For most people, strikes are hardly more than historical relics or quaint curiosities" due to "the near extinction of this form of protest."[10] This observation is certainly accurate with respect to major work stoppages in NLRA-regulated industries. For example, in 2021, the US Labor Department reported that there were only eight major work stoppages that began in 2020. This was the third-lowest number of major work stoppages since the Labor Department first began keeping track of such strikes in 1947.[11] For most employees, the strike is seldom a realistic option as a means to secure favorable contract terms because the employers' use of permanent replacements creates such a devastating effect on the workers who strike, as well as on their unions.[12]

Initially, employers seldom used the right of permanent replacement as an economic weapon, although it has been in the employers' arsenal since 1938 when the Court decided *Mackay Radio*. By the mid-1970s, according to White (2018), "the labor movement found itself . . . locked in bitter conflicts [with employers] increasingly over . . . fundamental issues, including the movement's very right to exist in a meaningful way."[13] This emerging, no-holds-barred assault on unions, combined with the Ronald Reagan administration's public willingness in 1981 to fire more than 11,000 striking air traffic controllers, made resistance to unions more fashionable and permanent replacement of strikers less stigmatizing.[14] There is no question that the permanent replacement of strikers occurred in proportionately more strikes beginning in the 1980s.[15]

One should not conclude that the labor relations quiescence brought on by the relative absence of strikes is cause for celebration. Productive, good faith collective bargaining can, and often does, proceed without the strike, but that depends on the credible threat of the strike. As the Supreme Court has recognized, the right to strike is integral to the collective bargaining process.[16] The country is now reaping the economic whirlwind from employers' increased use of permanent striker replacement to crush any realistic option by workers to choose whether to strike in support of bargaining objectives. The resulting relative demise of collective bargaining in the US has resulted in wage stagnation, economic inequality, the collapse of the middle class, and social unrest.[17]

One irony regarding this occurrence is that there is almost never a business justification for permanently replacing economic strikers, and the law does not require that employers demonstrate such a justification. Indeed, hiring temporary striker replacements has proved adequate in other circumstances, such as during an offensive lockout and during an unfair labor practice strike, when only temporary replacements may be hired. But even when permanent replacement is lawful, temporary replacement normally is sufficient to pressure workers to settle a bargaining dispute: the employer maintains operations with temporary replacements and the strikers suffer increasingly from lost wages as the strike continues.[18] This is particularly true, as White (2018) states, "in a context where workers far outnumber decent jobs, where mechanization and automation have steadily eaten away at the centrality of skill, [and] where employers wield overwhelming advantages in wealth and power over workers."[19]

In two cases decided after *Mackay Radio*, the Supreme Court interpreted the NLRA to make the need for permanent replacement even more unnecessary. First, the holding in *Pattern Makers League of North America v. NLRB*[20] permits striking union members to resign from the union at any time during a strike, become "crossovers" who quit the strike and return to work, and remain insulated from union discipline resulting from their decision to abandon the strike. By barring unions from enforcing members' agreements not to break ranks during a strike, the Court in *Pattern Makers* encouraged striking union members to quit the strike and return to work.

In the second case, the Court's ruling actually creates incentives for strikers to break ranks and return to work during a strike. In *TWA, Inc. v Flight Attendants*,[21] the Court held that strikers who made an unconditional offer to return to work at the end of a strike not only may not displace permanent replacements, but also may not insist on exercising their seniority to displace less-senior strikers who crossed the picket line to return to work during the strike. Quitting the strike and returning to work had the effect of providing less-senior workers the ability to retain their jobs following termination of the strike and thereby surmount the seniority rights of more senior workers who did not cross over. The *TWA* decision creates strong incentives for strikers to break ranks during a strike as a way to overcome the seniority system to protect their own jobs.

In sum, the permanent replacement of strikers has set up a one-sided contest in which many employers almost look forward to work stoppages as a weapon that they can use to crush unions. A strike provides employers with the option of permanently replacing strikers, and hiring anti-union permanent striker replacements conveys an object lesson to all the firm's workers that it is senseless to challenge the superior power of the employer. Maintaining solidarity is challenging when, by striking, workers place their jobs and financial fortunes in jeopardy, with only a vague anticipation of getting much in return.

Banning the permanent replacement of strikers reinstates the possibility of resurrecting a right to strike that "entails the ability to put real pressure on employers without the workers unduly sacrificing their jobs or needlessly compromising their material well-being." Workers deserve a right to strike that is "practical, functional, and legally legitimate, and not merely an artifact of rhetoric."[22]

Clarifying the Right to Strike

NLRA § 13 makes clear that nothing in the NLRA, "except as *specifically provided for herein*, shall be construed so as either to interfere with or impede or diminish *in any way* the right to strike.[23] Yet the right to strike needs to be clarified to redress erosions of the protected right to strike that have crept into the NLRA. The approach taken by the Protecting the Right to Organize Act (PRO Act) to address this need for reform is to make clear that the "duration, scope, frequency, or intermittence of any strike or strikes shall not render such strike or strikes unprotected or prohibited."[24]

Notwithstanding the broad language of § 13, the right to strike protected by the NLRA is not an absolute right. For example, the courts and the National Labor Relations Board (NLRB) have interpreted Congress's intent in protecting the right to strike in the NLRA as not protecting strikers' defiance of law, either state or federal. Examples are the unprotected status of strikes that violate the NLRA itself, such as unlawful jurisdictional strikes, secondary boycotts, and unlawful recognition picketing.[25] Other examples of unprotected strikes are mass picketing, which blocks ingress and egress; and disregard for state trespass laws when, for example, workers engage in so-called sit-down strikes, in which strikers take possession of an employer's property and refuse to remove themselves during a strike.[26] Proposals for labor law reform rarely propose disturbing these well-established limits on the right to strike.

However, over the years, the NLRB and the courts have only given lip service to the § 13 ban on interpreting the NLRA in ways that will "interfere with or impede or diminish . . . the right to strike." The NLRB and the courts have cast aside § 13 in many cases that have found peaceful and lawful work stoppages unprotected even when they fall short of a total strike; that is, if the strike "blurs the clear-cut boundary between working and [completely] stopping work."[27] Discussed next are examples of such peaceful and lawful concerted activities that have been found to be unprotected.

Disapproval of the Scope of the Strike: Refusals to Perform Specific Assigned Tasks and the Unprotected Status of the Partial Strike

One effective way to secure a favorable outcome during a labor dispute is to bring economic pressure on the employer by refusing to perform specific tasks[28] or refusing to work at specific times or on specific days (e.g., refusals to work overtime or on weekends).[29] These are described as "partial strikes," and the NLRB and the courts consider these strikes unprotected.[30] Under the current construction of the NLRA, therefore, the protected versus unprotected status of a work stoppage turns on its form. But the courts and the NLRB have "failed to articulate a comprehensive theory that justifies stripping . . . strikes of protection [because they constitute partial strikes]."[31] Accordingly. no coherent line separates protected from unprotected partial strikes.

For example, in *Harnischfeger Corporation*,[32] to determine whether a concerted refusal to work overtime was unprotected, the NLRB applied its "so-indefensible" standard to permit the employer to discharge of the strikers. In that case, the Board held that the refusal to work overtime there was *not* "so indefensible" that the strike was unprotected. The ruling offered no guidance for future cases to determine when such a strike is or is not "indefensible," other than stating that "calling a [total] strike would have occasioned much more serious difficulty" for the employer than the employees simply refusing to work overtime. However, following its decision in *Harnischfeger Corporation*, in its foundational decision in *Elk Lumber Company*,[33] the Board cited with approval *C. G. Conn, Ltd. v. NLRB*,[34] a Seventh Circuit case that categorically held that a refusal to work overtime constitutes unprotected concerted activity. Moreover, in *Elk Lumber*, the Board held that a slowdown constituted an unprotected partial strike, on the theory that the slowdown required the employer to pay workers for work not performed, a rationale that does not apply to concluding that refusals to work overtime are unprotected. The slowdown in *Elk Lumber* also was found to be unprotected because the workers intended to continue working at their own pace rather than at the pace set by the employer, contrary to the NLRA's underlying principle that employees must work at terms prescribed solely by their employer. But such an underlying principle is *ipse dixit* based on undiscussed and unexamined assumptions of employer hegemony over the production process, assumptions that "are not ratified in the NLRA, which, in fact, grants workers a role in setting these and other terms of employment."[35] Moreover, as Atleson (1983) has pointed out, "principles built upon such tenuous bases cannot help causing continued litigation and a series of [additional] unprincipled decisions."[36]

Disapproval of the Duration, Frequency, or Intermittence of the Strike: The Unprotected Status of the Intermittent Strike

An additional example of how the protected versus unprotected status of a work stoppage turns on its form is the current construction of the NLRA holding that the intermittent strike constitutes unprotected concerted activity, thus subjecting such strikers to discharge and other employer discipline. The NLRB uses the term "intermittent strike" to mean repeated short strikes. These strikes are not unlawful; indeed, the Supreme Court has stated that the intermittent strike is an accepted and integral aspect of the collective bargaining process, not an unfair labor practice when deployed as an economic weapon by a union.[37] Further, the intermittent strike is not subject to regulation under state law.[38] Neither can these strikes be criticized because they involve selectively choosing which assigned tasks to complete, nor can they entail objections to workers receiving pay for work not completed according to the terms and pace set by the employer. Yet, in *International Union, U.A.W.A., A.F.L., Local 232 v Wisconsin Employment Relations Board (Briggs-Stratton),*[39] the Supreme Court stated, in dicta, that a series of short, unannounced strikes constituted "intermittent strikes" that were not protected by the NLRA. Thus, an employer could lawfully discipline employees for engaging in an intermittent strike. This dictum has become a bedrock NLRA principle. However, as with the partial strike, nothing in the NLRA's language supports a finding that the intermittent strike is unprotected. Moreover, the courts and NLRB have provided no principled rationale explaining why a work stoppage that is intermittent rather than continuous is unprotected, other than the Supreme Court, in its *Briggs-Stratton* decision, referencing the NLRB's *Harnischfeger Corporation* case and stating the *ipse dixit* that engaging in short, repeated strikes was "so indefensible" as to permit the employer to discharge the strikers.[40]

This is no way to fashion a labor relations regime. Both employers and employees deserve a greater amount of structure and predictability. Moreover, the absence of principled and workable lines of demarcation between protected and unprotected concerted activity subjects the parties to the unarticulated policy preferences of Board members whose political leanings shift with the political winds. The remedy is to reject the view that it is appropriate to determine the protected status of strikes by applying the *ipse dixit* of whether the form of the strike is deemed "so indefensible" as to permit the employer to discharge the strikers. This reform objective can be achieved by clarifying § 13 by adding to the NLRA that the "duration, scope, frequency, or intermittence of any strike or strikes shall not render such strike or strikes unprotected or prohibited."[41]

Prohibiting Offensive Lockouts

It might initially seem anomalous to add a ban on offensive lockouts by an employer in a chapter devoted to reform proposals that are designed to address current opportunities in the NLRA for employers to limit workers' economic actions. But the offensive lockout is one way that employers are able to take control of employees' choice of whether and when to strike. Under current law, even in the absence of a strike, employers may offensively lock out employees by prohibiting them from returning to the work site, usually following an impasse in bargaining,[42] until their union agrees to a collective bargaining agreement that incorporates the employer's final bargaining offer.[43] This usurps workers' control over the timing and duration of any work stoppage, undercutting workers' bargaining power.

Current law also permits employers to continue operations during an offensive lockout by using supervisors and hiring temporary replacements, and there is no limitation on the duration of an offensive lockout.[44] In its decision in *Inland Trucking Co.*, the Seventh Circuit Court of Appeals explained the injustice of combining the offensive lockout with the employer's ability to hire replacements during the lockout. The court said that the offensive lockout, unlike the defensive lockout, "would not merely pit the employer's ability to withstand a shutdown of its business against the employees' ability to endure cessation of their jobs, but would permit the employer to impose on his employees the pressure of being out of work while obtaining for himself the returns of continued operation. Employees would be forced, at the initiative of the employer, not only to forego their job earnings, but, in addition, to watch other workers enjoy the earning opportunities over which the locked-out employees were endeavoring to bargain."[45] To these observations should be added the fact that the NLRB has held that an employer may initiate a partial lockout, pitting one group of employees against the other. For example, when a union strikes and the employer hires temporary replacements, and some strikers then quit the strike and become crossovers, the NLRB has ruled that if the union calls off the strike, the employer is permitted to decline the union's offer to return to work and initiate a partial offensive lockout of those still on strike, while not locking out those who quit the strike and crossed over prior to the lockout.[46] It is easy to understand how this creates a schism among the bargaining unit employees.

To counter the employer's deployment of the offensive lockout as an anti-union tactic, the NLRA should prohibit any lockouts from occurring prior to a strike, while maintaining the employers' right to respond to strikes with defensive lockouts.[47]

Removing Limitations on Secondary Picketing and Strikes

It is time to reverse one of the 1947 Taft-Hartley Act's most dramatic inroads on unions' ability to exercise the basic First Amendment right to publicize a labor dispute in an effort to secure public support and the support of other workers for union objectives during a labor dispute. The NLRA currently prohibits unions from engaging in secondary picketing, strikes, or boycotts, where workers of one company picket, strike, or support a boycott in solidarity with another company's workers to improve wages or conditions of employment. Private-sector labor relations law should permit this form of worker solidarity.[48]

It is worth repeating an observation made more than a quarter-century ago—namely, that "[t]he outcome of [the] economic contest [between workers and employers] is not simply a product of private resources [of each to resist the economic pressure exerted by the other]. It is also deeply influenced by the legal framework that determines what resources the parties start out with."[49] As construed, the NLRA starts the employer out with the right to continue to operate during a strike and to do so with permanent replacements. As discussed here, enlightened labor law reform should reverse that remarkable advantage currently provided to employers by proscribing the employer's use of permanent replacements to continue operations. But eliminating permanent replacements will not in itself level the playing field. Employers may continue operations during a strike with a combination of nonstrikers, crossovers, managerial personnel, and temporary replacements. But the current ban on secondary boycotts precludes strikers and their unions from attempting to interdict those continuing operations by the self-help tactic of appealing to workers at other firms to cease performing services required for the struck employer to continue normal, uninterrupted operations.[50]

Appealing to the public to boycott a struck employer's products and attempting to induce workers at other firms to cease performing services required for the struck employers to continue operations are effective and deeply rooted self-help options that unions deployed well before the advent of the modern, post–World War II, labor relations system. American labor law has not always banned secondary activity.[51] Nineteenth- and early-twentieth-century common law courts, in their zeal to promote market efficiency and "devotion to competition and freedom of contract," manifested hostility toward the activities of unions, in part by perfecting "government by injunction," which they deployed against labor[52] and by condemning secondary boycotts.[53] But secondary activity was never banned in all states. In New York, for example, state law permitted unions to exert pressure up to the point that "the union's . . . direct interests cease."[54] Further, in *United States v. Hutcheson*,[55] the Supreme Court finally held that union secondary activity does not violate federal antitrust laws, so long as labor acts in its own self-interest and does not combine with nonlabor groups. Even after the enactment of the 1947 Taft-Hartley Amendments, federal law did not bar all secondary boycotts and does not do so today.[56] As the Supreme Court has explained, the NLRA does not contain a "sweeping prohibition" of secondary activity; instead, it "describes and condemns specific union conduct directed to specific objectives."[57]

Indeed, it was not until the 1959 Landrum-Griffin amendments to the NLRA that it was unlawful under the NLRA to induce individual workers at other firms to cease performing services required for the struck employer to continue its normal, uninterrupted operations.[58] Even today, unions regulated by the Railway Labor Act (RLA)—unions representing employees of railroads and airlines—are free to advance lawful union objectives by means of secondary boycotts.[59] In practice, the RLA, enacted in 1926, has worked well without the need for a secondary boycott ban. As one observer has noted, "[i]n view of the interests of both parties in avoiding a strike . . . the availability of such self-help measures as secondary picketing may increase the effectiveness of [the RLA] in settling major disputes by creating an incentive for the parties to settle . . . The real oddity in federal labor law . . . is not the lawful status of secondary boycotts in the airline and railroad industries, but the illegality of secondary boycotts in nearly all other industries."[60]

In recent years, labor and constitutional scholars increasingly have made the case that "the secondary boycott prohibition contradicts the

Constitution's otherwise broad right of free speech."[61] For example, Catherine Fisk (2018) has made a convincing case that labor picketing should be accorded full First Amendment free speech recognition:[62]

> The Court and the NLRB have already recognized that most forms of labor advocacy other than picketing to encourage a full consumer and worker boycott are not coercive. Unions may picket to encourage consumers to boycott a product (though not a store that sells the product, and not even the product if a business is heavily dependent on the product). Unions have the right to distribute leaflets and display banners to publicize labor abuses, and to communicate via social media. Civil rights activists, immigrant rights activists, and all groups other than labor unions have the rights to picket and to urge secondary boycotts. While a labor picket line may convey a more forceful message than a labor banner or a civil rights picket line, now that labor unions lack the power to prevent those who cross from getting or keeping a job, [or from being disciplined by a union] a picket line has lost the power to coerce.

The risk of free speech violations in § 8(b)(4) adjudications has surfaced as a central consideration. In December 2021, in a statement of position to the Board on remand from the Ninth Circuit in the case of *Preferred Building Services, Inc.*, the NLRB general counsel advised the Board of the need for it to engage in a more fact-intensive, case-by-case approach to secondary picketing, cautioning it that any wide ban on secondary picketing may violate the First Amendment and arguing that union assembly should be presumed lawful "unless rebutted by clear and convincing evidence to the contrary."[63]

Reforming the NLRA to delete § 8(b)(4) removes from federal law limitations on secondary picketing, strikes, and boycotts, but this leaves unaddressed the effect on state regulation of secondary activity. The issue is whether by defederalizing the regulation of secondary boycotts, Congress would be understood as having intended to leave it to the states to regulate such activity. Or, if Congress defederalized the law of secondary boycotts, would courts find that Congress intended to legalize the secondary boycott nationwide? One possibility is that the federal courts would find that states are preempted from regulating labor secondary activity pursuant to the so-called *Machinists* branch of federal labor preemption doctrine.[64] *Machinists* preemption advances the congressional policy that when Congress chooses not to regulate some conduct, the intent is that such conduct should be left unregulated by *any* governmental body. *Machinist* preemption prohibits state and local regulation that the courts conclude "upset[s] the balance of power between labor and management expressed in our national labor policy"[65] by "introduc[ing] some standard of properly 'balanced' bargaining power . . . [or defining] what economic sanctions might be permitted negotiating parties in an 'ideal' or 'balanced' state of collective bargaining."[66] It has been argued that given many courts' decades-old propensity to view secondary activity as inherently coercive, *Machinists* preemption theory may be insufficient to block state regulation of secondary activity. Accordingly, congressional silence with respect to the preemptive effect on state law of defederalizing the regulation of secondary boycotts is ill advised. To protect all secondary activity from state regulation, an "effective repeal of the [NLRA's] secondary boycott prohibition [requires a provision] explicitly preempting any states' attempts to [regulate labor secondary activity]."[67] That precaution seems well advised in order to assure that labor secondary activity remains legal nationwide.[68]

Ending Prohibitions on Collective and Class Action Litigation

In 2018, in *Epic Systems Corp. v. Lewis*,[69] the Supreme Court held that, despite the NLRA's commitment to protect employee concerted activity for mutual aid and protection, it is lawful for employers to force workers into signing agreements that waive the right to pursue work-related litigation jointly, collectively, or in a class action. Labor law reform should overturn that decision by explicitly stating that, regardless of the unionized status of the employees involved, employers may not require employees to waive their right to collective and class action litigation.[70]

The NLRA protects employee concerted activity, rather than the activities of individual employees, because only through concerted group actions are employees able to make systemic changes at the workplace—changes that require restructuring employer practices. Collective bargaining is the NLRA's prime vehicle for effecting this restructuring, but only roughly 10 percent of the private-sector workforce in the US currently has access to that tactic. The other American workers depend on private rights of action contained in state and federal protective legislation to effect systemic changes at their places of work. The two best options under federal law for effecting systemic changes at the workplace are collective actions provided by the Fair Labor Standards Act (FLSA)[71] and pattern-or-practice class action suits brought pursuant to Title VII of the Civil Rights Act of 1964 (Title VII).[72] Class actions under state civil rights law and protective labor legislation may also provide opportunities for achieving systemic changes at the workplace.

For example, an FLSA collective action might challenge widespread employer misclassification of employees as independent contractors or an employer's failure to pay minimum wage or overtime pay.[73] Prospective injunctive relief is not available to private litigants under the FLSA, but groups of litigants can combine individual claims for monetary relief by bringing a collective action to redress past FLSA violations.[74]

Or employees who have been adversely affected by discriminatory business practices that harm all of an employer's minority employees might form a protest group that organizes mass actions to protest a pattern-or-practice of discrimination at the workplace, and then bring a pattern-or-practice Title VII class action seeking injunctive and monetary relief.[75]

Or women may organize to redress a pattern-or-practice of sexual harassment at the workplace and bring a Title VII sexual harassment class action seeking injunctive and monetary relief.[76] In these collective and class action suits, the employees bringing the actions might be unionized, but most often they are not. They look to the courts to provide the systemic changes that collective bargaining might have provided had unionization been available to them.

A decade of Supreme Court litigation has now provided employers a straightforward way to foil these litigation options to redress the denial of employees' state and federal rights. The simple solution now is for employers to require employees to sign mandatory arbitration agreements that include "class waivers." These arbitration agreements contain two powerful provisions. First, they waive an employee's right to initiate litigation that seeks judicial redress of employer unlawful conduct and require that all redress be sought exclusively through arbitration. Second, the arbitration agreement's "class waiver" provision precludes employees from joining claims in arbitration. This strategy to protect employers from judicial adjudication of systemic workplace violations of employee rights has correctly been summarized as follows: "[W]hen arbitration agreements include class waivers, employees cannot bring group actions via litigation or arbitration. And because Title VII pattern-or-practice claims must be brought as group actions rather than as individual claims, arbitration agreements prevent employees from bringing pattern-or-practice claims altogether."[77]

AT&T Mobility LLC v. Concepcion[78] was a pivotal decision in this area. In that case, the Supreme Court upheld the enforceability of class waivers in arbitration agreements, including contexts where state law rendered the waivers unenforceable. *Concepcion* incentivized employers to add arbitration agreements in employees' contracts of adhesion as a simple way to eliminate class action litigation. Mandatory arbitration agreements in employee contracts steadily accelerated following the Court's decision. One study concluded that "mandatory arbitration agreements rose from just over 2% [of all workers] in 1992 to around 25% in the early 2000s to over 55% in 2017. . . . Mandatory arbitration is more common in low-wage work and in industries with higher proportions of women and Black workers."[79]

There is evidence, contested by some, that arbitration is a less satisfactory option for employees than judicial relief: with mandatory arbitration, employees bring fewer claims, win less often, and receive lower awards.[80] What is uncontested is that "arbitration makes it impossible for plaintiffs to pursue structural reform via class litigation [depriving law of its ability to] be used to 'structure and reform institutionalized practices.'"[81]

In *Murphy Oil, USA, Inc.*,[82] the NLRB attempted to quell the rising forced waiver of employees' statutory right to seek judicial redress of violations of workplace rights. There, it held that an employer commits an unfair labor practice when requiring employees to sign an arbitration agreement waiving their right to pursue class and collective actions and requiring that they bring all employment-related claims through individual arbitration. The Board reasoned that these mandatory arbitration agreements constitute unlawful interference with employees' § 7 rights because they restrict employees' substantive right, established by § 7 of the act, to join together to improve their working conditions through administrative and judicial forums.

It was this holding that the Supreme Court reversed in *Epic Systems Corp. v. Lewis.*[83] In *Epic Systems*, the Court held that the term "concerted activities" in the NLRA does not include actions by employees to join together in FLSA collective litigation. The majority reasoned that "the term 'other concerted activities' [in § 7] should, like the terms that precede it, serve to protect things employees 'just do' for themselves in the course of exercising their right to free association in the workplace, rather than 'the highly regulated, courtroom-bound activities' of class and joint litigation."[84]

The reform needed is to clarify in the NLRA that the scope of § 7's right to engage in concerted activities includes joining together in collective and class action litigation, and it is unlawful for employers to require employees to waive their right to seek redress through collective and class action litigation, without regard to the unionized status of the employees involved.[85] Among other things, this will preserve the option for employees to bring

Title VII class action pattern-or-practice actions to achieve systemic changes in their conditions of employment that root out workplace discrimination.

Insulating Fair Share Agreements from State Regulation

Under the NLRA, the union, as the exclusive bargaining representative of all the employees the union represents, is legally obligated to represent all bargaining unit members equally, without regard to their membership in the union.[86] The NLRA allows unions and employers to agree that employees who are not members of the union, but benefit from a collective bargaining agreement, may be assessed a fair-share fee to support the costs of bargaining and implementing the agreement.[87] As the *NLRB v. General Motors Corp.* ruling states, "The burdens of membership upon which employment may be conditioned are expressly limited to the payment of initiation fees and monthly dues. [In other words,] '[m]embership' as a condition of employment is whittled down to its financial core."[88] In addition, in *Communications Workers of America v. Beck*,[89] the Court held that this "financial core" only includes the obligation to support union activities that are germane to collective bargaining, contract administration, and grievance adjustment.[90]

Even with these extensive limitations on NLRA unions' ability to negotiate lawful union security agreements in collective bargaining agreements, § 14(b) of the NLRA permits states to enact laws that prevent unions from requiring this "financial core" membership as a condition for employment. To date, twenty-eight states have done so.[91] State right-to-work laws create a "free rider" problem: they allow workers to join a union if they wish, but they also permit employees to not join the union and yet receive the benefits of a union contract without having to pay their share of the dues and fees needed to finance the union's ability to negotiate and administer collective bargaining agreements. In other words, right-to-work laws shift the costs of providing enhanced workplace benefits from free riders onto the shoulders of coworkers who elect to join the union and pay dues. Advocates of labor law reform have argued that regardless of state laws, unions and employers should be permitted, if they so choose, to voluntarily agree to require payment of fair-share fees to cover the costs of collective bargaining and contract administration.[92]

Epilogue
Searching for Solutions beyond the NLRA

The previous chapters of this book have documented an array of pathologies that have made our economic system since 1980 brutal for many American workers. One commentator has summarized that brutishness this way:[1]

> The years have brought wage stagnation, declining union density, widespread retaliation for organizing unions, under-resourced enforcement agencies, forced arbitration preventing access to judge and jury, a growing chasm between corporate and worker power, and the fissuring of the workplace (subcontracting, franchising, misclassification of workers, and other company practices to avoid employer status). The resulting degraded working conditions have exacerbated racial and gender disparities, as they disproportionately impact immigrant workers, Black workers, other workers of color, and women workers. On top of these problems, workers have more recently faced a devastating worldwide pandemic.

In this study, I have argued for legislative reform of the National Labor Relations Act (NLRA) as a feasible remedial strategy. Leveling the playing field by remedying the act's most oppressive dysfunctions will result in a reduction of the "representation gap," the unsatisfied demand for collective bargaining representation among the more than 50 percent of nonunion workers who state that they would vote for union representation if it were made available to them. In turn, a significant increase in collective representation will provide meaningful avenues for workers to redress many of the economic and political inequalities that have plagued the country in recent decades. Efforts to reform the NLRA legislatively, while essential, represent only part of the answer to the need for a more egalitarian distribution of wealth and enhanced levels of industrial democracy. Through a variety of other initiatives, worker activists have scored some successes in reordering labor law outside the basic framework of the NLRA.

During the several past decades, as a reaction to the NLRA's failure to facilitate collective action and keep pace with changes in the economy, and as a manifestation of the continuing demand for collective worker activism, a "process of reinvention" has begun.[2] Three strands of activism dominate efforts to add renewed dynamism to labor law without the need for legislative reform of the NLRA: private agreements resolving questions concerning representation without reliance on the representation election processes of the National Labor Relations Board (NLRB); initiatives by state and local government protecting workers; and mobilization of the use of existing protective labor legislation by local community groups to advance worker rights with and without the involvement of a traditional labor union.

Private Agreements

Through what are commonly referred to as "neutrality and card check agreements," unions and employers "establish varied sets of ground rules governing unions' and employers' conduct during organizing campaigns, procedures for registering workers' preferences on the question of collective representation and mechanisms for resolving disputes," according to Sachs (2007).[3]

Most of these private agreements regulate in some way the content of the employer's anti-union speech during a union's organizing drive among the employer's employees. Neutrality agreements typically have followed two models. The employer may agree to remain neutral during the union-organizing drive with respect to employees' decisions about whether to choose unionization. Or the employer may reserve the option to express anti-union views but agree to do so civilly, such as agreeing to limit opposition to unions to factually accurate statements.[4] In one study, 93 percent of the neutrality agreements surveyed "contained explicit neutrality language" of some type.[5]

A second concern that neutrality agreements address is the union's desire to combat delays by the employer. This often is accomplished by the employer agreeing to recognize the union once a majority of the employees sign union authorization cards. As an alternative, the employer may agree to participate in an NLRB-conducted election but commit to an obligation not to cause any delays. For example, the parties may agree to an expedited NLRB election.

Providing union access is a third focus of most neutrality agreements. The employer may agree to provide the union with enhanced access to employee names and addresses and email contact information. In addition, the private agreement may, and often does, require the employer to provide unions access to its property. The union may be granted access to the employee cafeteria or other locations throughout the workplace during nonwork time to provide the union with opportunities to communicate to employees its views on union representation. Studies have demonstrated that enhanced access correlates with subsequent union-organizing success.[6]

With the high incidence of unions' inability to obtain a first contract, one might expect that neutrality agreements typically would provide some mechanism to ensure that a union obtaining representation rights is able to obtain a first contract. Nevertheless, in the largest study of neutrality agreements conducted so far, Eaton and Kriesky (2001) found only "some examples" of neutrality agreements containing provisions designed to assist unions in achieving a first contract.[7] A plausible explanation is that unions do not need first-contract provisions in neutrality agreements. When a neutrality agreement results in recognition, which occurs most of the time when a neutrality pledge is combined with an arrangement for card check recognition, unions achieve a first contract almost 100 percent of the time. If those findings hold up over time, it is likely that unions will conclude that the key to first-contract success is a neutrality commitment coupled with card check recognition agreement. With that, no additional provision directed at achieving a first contract will be needed in the neutrality agreement.[8]

In a sense, it is correct, as one commentator has concluded, that "unions and employers are opting out of the NLRA and relying instead on varied systems of self-regulation. As they do so, labor law is evolving from a centralized federal legal regime to one defined increasingly by private ordering."[9] But to be clear, while the move toward private agreements is a significant development, this is a limited option—one that is available only when the union is in a unique position to leverage sufficient economic or political power to be able to secure such a private neutrality agreement with an employer.[10] In most situations, unions lack such leverage. In addition, the "opting out" reflected by private agreements is confined to private processes used to obtain representation rights. The resulting bargaining relationship proceeds under the umbrella of the NLRA's rules and, as the preceding chapters have demonstrated, there remains much in the NLRA, in addition to representation procedures, that requires reform if labor-management relations are to be conducted on a level playing field.

Protecting Workers through Initiatives by State and Local Governments

To fight the economic inequality caused by a widening income gap among American workers, many states, cities, and community-based groups support the adoption of innovative policies at the local level designed to protect and advance workers' rights. One initiative is a growing nationwide movement for economic justice that seeks to convert low-wage jobs into good jobs with enhanced job security. For example, in the 1990s and early 2000s, labor activists and community groups worked for enactment of living wage ordinances as a strategy for lifting low-wage workers out of poverty. A living wage is a locally mandated wage that is higher than state or federal minimum wage levels, and the living wage ordinance may also mandate or encourage firms to provide health coverage and other benefits to workers. Living wage ordinances typically require private businesses that benefit from public money to pay their workers enough income to raise a family of four above the federal poverty line. A 2002 study of Los Angeles's living wage ordinance for city employees and contractors suggests that female and Black workers were more likely to be affected by the ordinance since they make up a greater percentage of the public-sector workforce.[11] Because living wage ordinances increase pay only for workers employed by businesses that contract or receive assistance from local government, many cities have shifted strategy to address the low-wage-job problem by enacting minimum wage ordinances applicable to all employees. For example, the "Fight for $15" initiative has succeeded in many jurisdictions in setting the minimum wage at fifteen dollars per hour.

Coalitions of workers and activists of color, women, and immigrants are able to successfully advocate for adoption of local minimum wages above the federal minimum because federal law permits localities to set higher minimum wages. But such an explicit authorization in federal law permitting local options to regulate labor relations is the exception. More typically, federal labor law preemption rules sharply curtail local attempts to innovate in the field of labor law. Setting labor policy is nearly exclusively within the domain of the federal government.[12] The NLRA does not contain an explicit preemption provision. Courts nevertheless have interpreted its provisions to preempt most state or local legislative, executive, and judicial actions that regulate activity that is arguably protected or prohibited by the NLRA, as well as state or local government regulations that create the risk of "upset[ting] the balance of power between labor and management expressed in our national labor policy" by regulating conduct that Congress intended should "be controlled by the free play of economic forces."[13]

Notwithstanding the severe limits set by federal labor preemption rules, community groups and other activists have been successful in finding opportunities for state and local governments to expand and enforce worker rights. Terri Gerstein (2020) has assembled the most complete inventory of such state and local initiatives that have successfully avoided the suffocating constraints of the federal labor preemption rules.[14]

One way that state and local governments protect workers without transgressing federal labor preemption rules is through greatly expanded involvement of state attorneys general (AGs) and criminal prosecutors (including district attorneys and others) in enforcing and protecting workers' rights. For example, AGs have created dedicated units that focus on workers' rights, to wit:[15]

> These units vary in size, as some started with only one attorney, while others are more robustly staffed. They have a variety of names ("workplace rights bureau," "payroll fraud enforcement unit," "fair labor section"), but they all represent a commitment by these AGs to devote resources and institutionalize a section within their offices to focus on worker protection. State AGs have brought dozens of civil and criminal cases against predatory and exploitative employers in a range of industries with high rates of violations and workers who are low-wage, immigrants, and/or people of color. . . . They have also taken on specific employer practices, like inappropriate use of non-compete and no poach agreements and payment of wages by payroll cards. Several AGs have brought cases related to misclassification of workers as independent contractors . . . requiring [companies] to change their business practices to classify workers as employees. [Other] AG offices . . . have brought child labor cases. Some offices have pursued joint employer liability. Certain state AGs have also used their criminal jurisdiction to pursue wage theft, payroll fraud, and other violations.

State government and localities also have intervened legislatively to promote worker rights, but with mixed results. The US Supreme Court has applied *Machinists* preemption principles to bar state regulations where the Court could infer that Congress intended the subject matter to be free from state or municipal regulation. Thus, in *Golden State Transit Corp. v. Los Angeles*,[16] the Court concluded that the City of Los Angeles was preempted from conditioning the renewal of a taxicab company's operating license on the company's settling a labor dispute. By requiring the taxi company to settle to keep operating, the city effectively interfered with the company's ability to use its economic weapons to resist union bargaining demands. In *Chamber of Commerce of United States v. Brown*,[17] the Court concluded that California could not prohibit employers who received state funding from using those funds to influence support for or opposition to union organizing because the state thereby interfered with an employer's NLRA-guaranteed right to express its views on unionization. Milwaukee enacted an ordinance requiring certain employers who contract with the county to enter a "labor peace agreement" with a union seeking to represent the employer's employees. Although the requirement that the employer become a party to a labor peace agreement did not necessitate employer neutrality, but rather only regulated employer speech by banning the expression of false or misleading information about the union, the Seventh Circuit ruled that the ordinance was preempted by the NLRA.[18]

The unifying principle is that state and local jurisdictions are barred from influencing "the *process* by which an employment agreement is reached: matters touching on self-organization and collective bargaining."[19] By contrast, localities are free to enact legislation of general application that sets minimum labor standards for all employees—both union and nonunion. For example, states are free to require that employee health-care plans include certain minimum benefits, although this is a subject that otherwise might have been addressed in collective bargaining.[20] The Court also upheld a state law guaranteeing employees a severance payment in the event of a plant closing. As the Court explained, "the NLRA is concerned with ensuring an equitable bargaining process, not with the substantive terms that may emerge from such bargaining."[21]

Some local jurisdictions have adopted worker retention ordinances. Low-wage service workers are frequently displaced from their employment when their employers lose contracts. This can occur, for example, when cities that hire contractors to provide janitorial, security, and other services switch contractors, when private companies such as grocery stores or hotels change ownership, or when building service companies take over service contracts at private establishments.[22] Worker retention polices are enacted to create job stability during such transitional periods and thereby protect the welfare of working families.[23] The District of Columbia's Displaced Workers Protection Act (DWPA), enacted in 1994, is an early version and is representative of such a policy.[24] It provides that during a ninety-day transition period, employers who take over contracts for providing food, janitorial, maintenance, or nonprofessional health-care services must retain, by seniority, the predecessor employer's employees who are needed to perform the new contract.[25]

Employer groups have mounted vigorous labor preemption challenges to these worker retention policies.[26] Uniformly, courts have found no preemption, concluding that these are laws of general applicability (applicable to both unionized and nonunion employment relationships), they do not interfere with union organizing or the process of bargaining, and nothing in the *Machinists* preemption doctrine guarantees employers unfettered hiring freedom.[27]

In addition, through initiatives by workers and community organizations, often but not always with the involvement of labor unions, localities have enacted stronger laws against the misclassification of workers, particularly in the construction and hotel industries. Moreover, nonprofit organizations, including national networks, "have played a critical role in advocating for a range of new state and local laws," such as levying penalties for wage theft, banning noncompete agreements for low-wage workers, adding sexual orientation and gender identity to the protected categories under state antidiscrimination laws, and requiring paid sick days and paid family and medical leave. Activists at the community level also have succeeded in lobbying for fair workweek laws. These laws ensure predictable schedules for low-wage workers. Particularly in industries such as retail and restaurants, employees are subjected to widely varying and unpredictable schedules, combined with "on-call" shifts and insufficient work hours, all of which greatly complicate managing child care or second jobs.[28]

Finally, through a process that Professor Benjamin Sachs (2011) has described as "tripartite lawmaking," "governments act in areas of law that are entirely unrelated to labor organizing and bargaining but that are of acute interest to employers—areas such as medical malpractice rules, telecommunications policy, and zoning and permitting decisions. These governmental actions, in turn, are exchanged for private contractual agreements through which unions and employers bind themselves to new rules for organizing and bargaining." These "tripartite political exchanges" produce agreements that set organizing and bargaining rules that differ from those contained in the NLRA but can be enforced as enforceable contractual obligations.[29]

Innovative Enforcement Strategies

A third strand of the initiatives engaged in by worker activists to reorder labor law outside the basic framework of the NLRA entails innovative strategies by states and localities to deter violations of and compel compliance with existing workplace laws. These strategies take a variety of forms, including state and local workplace enforcement agencies abandoning previous approaches that emphasized reacting to the filing of complaints and instead adopting the enforcement strategy of "being proactive . . . ; focusing resources on key industries with high rates of violations; collaborating closely with community and worker organizations; use of criminal prosecutions; strategic use of publicity; using licensing to drive enforcement; and seeking up-chain joint employer liability," according to Gerstein (2020).[30] For example, a state workplace labor commissioner's office might proactively investigate or "direct sweeps . . . in collaboration with community partners and fellow government agencies, and target[] businesses with egregious violations."[31]

Through community outreach—entering into longstanding relationships with worker and community organizations—state and local agencies are better able to administer this proactive enforcement strategy. Outreach helps inform agencies of chronic violations and unlawful practices and provides agencies improved access to low-wage and immigrant workers, groups that are less likely to seek government assistance on their own. Outreach initiatives can entail funding community-based groups to educate workers regarding their rights under protective labor legislation. Such education might be provided by a nontraditional labor organization known as a "worker center," which is particularly effective in reaching immigrant workers who might otherwise be afraid of approaching the government for help.[32]

Strategic communications and publicity by government agencies augment community outreach initiatives, promote compliance, and educate workers. This communication educates workers regarding their rights and employers regarding their obligations. Multilingual websites are particularly useful for reaching the immigrant population. In addition, in jurisdictions that permit a city agency to order the temporary closure (suspension of a business license) of a chronic violator of workers' rights legislation, the jurisdiction may provide an app that allows the public to learn through their smartphones the reason for the suspension, thereby adding public pressure on the business to become more law abiding.[33]

As noted in this book, current federal labor law preemption rules greatly hobble localities from doing more to protect workers' rights. And, of course, only progressive, worker-friendly state and local governments will be motivated to adopt policies that successfully navigate preemption rules to augment the protections of the NLRA. The reality is that in many parts of the county, state and local governments lack the political will, and perhaps the desire, to enact local worker-friendly legislation and to adopt policies that serve as a countervailing force against the growing concentration of corporate power and concomitant quashing of basic labor rights. Only a robust and efficacious national labor policy can ensure the nationwide uniformity required to provide workers a meaningful ability to unionize and, through collective representation, secure an effective countervailing voice in setting their conditions of employment. Legislative reform of the NLRA is not the only strategy to enhance workers' rights, but it is the vital feature of that strategy.

Acknowledgments

It has been more than fifty years since I graduated from Cornell's New York State School of Industrial and Labor Relations (ILR). When I was an ILR student, Kurt Hanslow, having recently resigned from the legal staff of the UAW, was teaching private-sector labor relations law both at Cornell's law school and at the ILR School. Kurt was my first labor law teacher. Although his classes at the ILR School were held on Saturday mornings, throngs of students filled the auditorium to hear him. I and many others *occasionally* may have come to class blurry-eyed due to a late night the previous evening, so I am not going to say that our retention rate never suffered during some of those early Saturday-morning lectures. But Kurt's enthusiasm for the subject was infectious and instilled in many of us a love of labor-management relations law that has endured over a lifetime. I thus trace the origins of this book to those magical Saturday mornings with Kurt Hanslow.

Since the end of the 1970s, as union membership decline accelerated, a trove of scholarship has offered explanations and prescriptions. Much of my thinking about labor law reform has been shaped by this scholarship. I owe a debt to all these scholars. I dare not list the many who have helped shape my views regarding labor law reform for fear that any such list inevitably would be underinclusive. Their work fills the hundreds of notes found in this book.

I will deviate in one respect from the choice not to individually acknowledge here the scholars who have influenced my thinking. Most labor lawyers would agree, I think, that Paul Weiler's 1983 article "Promises to Keep" and his 1990 book *Governing the Workplace* set the standard for all subsequent proposals for labor law reform. Weiler was the first to strongly emphasize the value of approaching the need for labor law reform empirically and thus rely on fact-based arguments to show how contemporary labor law operates in practice to disadvantage workers. This book has attempted to follow that lead.

On a more personal note, I want to thank my colleagues on the faculty of the Columbus School of Law at the Catholic University of America, who have encouraged me. Bill Osborne, one of this country's premier labor lawyers, provided a never-ending flow of emails with snippets of recent developments, many of which found a place in this book. Bill also read the entire manuscript and provided many helpful suggestions. And my good friend Frank McDonald has been a constant source of encouragement. A special thanks goes to Emily Taber, acquisitions editor for economics, finance, and business at the MIT Press when I circulated the manuscript to prospective publishers. Emily saw the value of this book early on, offered wise counsel, provided useful suggestions for editing the manuscript, and worked diligently to bring this book to publication.

And finally, to Cathy, my scuba dive buddy, pal, copy editor extraordinaire, and wife, a very special thanks.

Appendix: Protecting the Right to Organize Act of 2021 (H.R. 842)—Section-by-Section Analysis

Source: US House of Representatives, Committee on Education and Labor (https://edlabor.house.gov/imo/media/doc/Section%20by%20Section%20-%20PRO%20Act.pdf).

Section 1. Short Title

The title of the bill is the Protecting the Right to Organize Act (PRO Act).

Title I—Amendments to the National Labor Relations Act

Section 101. Definitions of Employer, Employee, and Supervisor

(a) *Protecting employees who have multiple employers.* This section states that two or more persons shall be employers under the National Labor Relations Act (NLRA) if each codetermines or shares control over the employees' essential terms and conditions of employment. In applying this standard, the board or a court of competent jurisdiction shall consider as relevant direct control, indirect control, reserved authority to control, and control exercised in fact. The PRO Act codifies the joint employer standard the National Labor Relations Board (NLRB) enacted in its 2015 *Browning-Ferris* decision, which was overturned by the Trump NLRB in a rulemaking decision.

(b) *Ensuring that employees are not misclassified as independent contractors and denied protections of the NLRA*. The definition of "employee" under § 2(3) of the NLRA is amended to clarify that an individual performing any service is an employee and not an independent contractor unless (1) the individual is free from the employer's control in connection with the performance of the service, both under the contract for the performance of service and in fact; (2) the service is performed outside the usual course of the business of the employer; and (3) the individual is customarily engaged in an independently established trade, occupation, profession, or business of the same nature as that involved in the service performed.

(c) *Ensuring that employees are not wrongly classified as supervisors and denied the protections of the NLRA.* The definition of "supervisor" in § 2(11) of the NLRA is clarified to require that the individual's supervisory activities be executed for "a majority of the individual's worktime." The PRO Act also modifies the list of supervisory activities in § 2(11) to remove the individual's authority to "assign" and "responsibly to direct" employees.

Section 102. Reinstating the National Labor Relations Board's (NLRB) Congressional Reporting Requirement

The NLRB submitted annual reports to Congress for most of its history that detailed significant case activities and operations. The NLRB discontinued its reporting after 2009, after Congress terminated numerous federal agency reporting requirements. The PRO Act reinstates the NLRB reporting requirement to ensure that Congress has essential data on processes and procedures of the agency. This section also requires the NLRB to include in these reports information about how the members have exercised their recusal obligations pursuant to federal ethics laws.

Section 103. Allowing the National Labor Relations Board (NLRB) to Engage in Economic Analysis

The NLRA currently prohibits the NLRB from appointing any individuals for the purposes of engaging in economic analysis. Removing that prohibition would allow the NLRB to conduct economic assessments to ensure that its policies and regulations are supported by economic analysis, rather than rely on outside organizations with an interest in the outcome of the proceeding.

Section 104. Strengthening Workers' Rights to Engage in Protected Activities

(a) *Prohibiting employers from permanently replacing employees who strike.* Strikes are a last resort for workers when all other efforts to improve wages and conditions through collective bargaining are exhausted. However, current law allows employers to cripple the effectiveness of a strike by "permanently replacing" striking workers. This retaliatory tactic often deters unions from resorting to a strike. This section prohibits employers from permanently replacing striking workers and from discriminating against employees who supported or participated in a strike.

(b) *Prohibiting offensive lockouts.* Under current law, employers may offensively lock out employees by prohibiting them from returning to the worksite until they accept the employer's offer—even in the absence of a strike. This usurps workers' control over the timing and duration of any work stoppage, undercutting their bargaining power. Current law also permits employers to hire temporary replacements during offensive lockouts, and there is no limitation on the duration of an offensive lockout. The PRO Act prohibits any lockouts from occurring prior to a strike, while maintaining employers' right to respond to strikes with defensive lockouts.

(c) *Preventing the misclassification of workers.* The PRO Act clarifies that an employer violates the NLRA by misclassifying an employee. Because the NLRA protects workers only if they are employees, communicating to employees that they are not covered under the law falsely indicates that they do not have rights under the NLRA and their organizing activities are futile. This provision overturns the NLRB's August 29, 2019, decision in *Velox Express*, which held that misclassification is not a violation of the NLRA.

(d) *Removing limitations on secondary picketing and strikes.* The NLRA currently prohibits unions from engaging in "secondary" picketing, strikes, or boycotts, where workers of one company would picket, strike, or support a boycott in solidarity with another company's workers to improve wages or conditions. This section removes those prohibitions to permit unions to exercise these basic First Amendment rights.

(e) *Prohibiting captive audience meetings.* Employers often respond to union campaigns by requiring employees to attend captive audience meetings designed to persuade employees against joining the union. If an employee refuses to attend a captive audience meeting, the employer may fire him or her. This section would prohibit employers from requiring employees to attend captive audience meetings or participate in anti-union campaign activities.

(f) *Protecting collective bargaining after the first contract.* To prevent employers from declaring an impasse in bargaining and unilaterally implementing new terms or conditions of employment, the PRO Act requires employers maintain existing terms and conditions of employment pending an agreement with the union. This retains the status quo ante while bargaining is pending.

(g) *Eliminating employers' ability to unilaterally withdraw union recognition.* On July 3, 2019, the Trump NLRB issued a decision in *Johnson Controls, Inc.* that would allow an employer to announce that it will withdraw recognition of a union within a ninety-day time frame before the expiration of a collective bargaining agreement based on evidence that the union has lost majority support. The PRO Act overturns this decision by prohibiting employers from unilaterally withdrawing recognition of a union without an election to decertify the labor organization.

(h) *Facilitating initial collective bargaining agreements.* Once a union has been recognized or certified as the employees' bargaining representative, the PRO Act requires the employer and the union to commence bargaining within 10 days of the union submitting a written request. If the parties have failed to reach an agreement after 90 days of bargaining, or for additional periods as the parties may agree upon, then either party may request mediation facilitated by the Federal Mediation and Conciliation Service (FMCS). If the parties cannot reach an agreement 30 days after mediation is requested, or for additional periods as the parties may agree upon, then the FMCS shall refer the dispute to a tripartite arbitration panel. This panel will consist of one member selected by the employer, one selected by the union, and one mutually agreed to by both the employer and union; the employer and union must agree to this panel within 14 days of the referral. A majority of the panel shall render a decision settling the dispute within 120 days, absent extraordinary circumstances or an agreement between the parties. The findings of this panel shall be binding upon the parties for a period of two years, unless the parties mutually agree in writing to amend during such period.

(i) *Ending prohibitions on collective and class action litigation.* The NLRA protects workers' rights to engage in "concerted activities for the purpose of . . . mutual aid or protection." However, on May 21, 2018, the Supreme Court held in *Epic Systems Corp. v. Lewis* that, despite this explicit protection, employers may force workers into signing arbitration agreements that waive the right to pursue work-related litigation jointly, collectively, or in a class action. This section overturns that decision by explicitly stating that employers may not require employees to waive their right to collective and class action litigation, without regard to union status.

(j) *Notice-posting and transparency.* The NLRB shall promulgate regulations requiring employers to post and maintain notices to employees of their rights under the NLRA, and to notify each new employee of the information in the notice. The regulations must ensure that the notice is provided in languages spoken by the employees. The PRO Act also codifies the NLRB's 2014 Election Rule, which streamlined its election procedures, to require that employers provide unions with a list of all employees in the bargaining unit no later than two business days after the NLRB directs an election. This list must contain the employees' names, home addresses, work locations, shifts, job classifications, and, if available to the employer, personal landline and mobile telephone numbers and email addresses. This list must also be provided in a searchable electronic format.

(k) *Protecting employee concerted activity conducted electronically.* The PRO Act codifies the NLRB's 2014 decision in *Purple Communications*. This decision ensured that employees' right to engage in concerted activity, which includes discussions of wages and working conditions, is protected even when it occurs on workplace email or other employer-provided electronic communication systems. However, the Trump NLRB overturned that decision in *Caesars Entertainment* on December 17, 2019.

Section 105. Ensuring Fairness in Union Representation Elections

(a) *Preventing employers from gerrymandering union representation elections.* By codifying the NLRB's 2011 decision in *Specialty Healthcare*, the PRO Act prevents employers from gerrymandering a bargaining unit as a way to include individuals in the voting unit who have no interest in joining the union. Under the *Specialty Healthcare* standard, the Board must find that, when a union petitions to represent a unit of employees, the petitioned unit is appropriate if the union demonstrates that the employees share a community of interest unless any excluded employees share an overwhelming community of interest with the employees in the unit.

(b) *Permitting offsite union representation elections.* Under current law, NLRB elections typically occur on the premises of the employer, even if the employer is opposed to union organizing. The PRO Act allows the employees petitioning for the election to choose whether the election will be conducted electronically, through certified mail, or at another location other than the one owned or controlled by the employer, as a way to ensure that employees can cast their ballots in neutral, non-coercive environments. Electronic voting is already the norm under the Railway Labor Act (RLA), where the National Mediation Board (NMB) conducts union representation elections for railway and airline workers. During the COVID-19 pandemic, this would also allow the employees to vote in a safer manner.

(c) *Removing employer standing in representation cases.* Under current procedures before the NLRB, when employees file a petition for an election, the employer is deemed a "party" to that election, even though the employer is not on the ballot. This section would deny party status to employers in union representation proceedings, such as hearings regarding which workers should be permitted to vote. This section would harmonize the NLRB's procedures with those of the NMB, which denies standing to employers in union representation cases for workers covered under the RLA.

(d) *Remedying election interference.* If a majority of valid ballots have not been cast in favor of union representation due to election interference by the employer, and a majority of employees in the voting unit have signed authorization cards designating the union as their representative, then the NLRB shall issue an order requiring the employer to bargain with the union.

(e) *Streamlining election procedures.* This section would codify portions of the NLRB's 2014 regulations to modernize its representation election procedures. Once a union files a petition for an election, the NLRB must schedule a preelection hearing not later than eight days after notice of the hearing is served on the labor organization. When the NLRB's regional director directs an election, the agency shall transmit the notice of election at the same time as the direction of election, and the employer must post that notice within two days after it is served in a place where employees will see it. The NLRB's regional directors must schedule the election for the earliest date practicable, but not later than the twentieth business day after the direction of election. After the election, if the results are in dispute, the NLRB must schedule a postelection hearing not later than fourteen days after the filing of objections.

(f), (g), & (h) *Restoring longstanding precedent protecting collective bargaining.* These sections would codify longstanding NLRB precedent by requiring that the NLRB must dismiss a petition for a decertification or other election for certain periods of time to protect the collective bargaining process or to prevent coercion in an election. This includes the "recognition bar," which prevents elections for a reasonable time after the employer voluntarily recognizes the union, so the employer and union can focus on collective bargaining; the "successor bar," which prevents elections for a reasonable time after a successor employer begins bargaining with the union; the "remedial bargaining order bar," which prevents elections for a reasonable time after the Board issues a remedial bargaining order, so the employer and union can develop a stable bargaining relationship; the "contract bar," which prevents elections for up to the first three years of a bargaining agreement, to allow the union to focus on implementing the agreement; and the "blocking charge," which suspends the processing of any election until after the Board resolves any unfair labor practice charges, to prevent any alleged coercion from undermining the integrity of the election. However, on April 1, 2020, the Trump NLRB weakened the recognition bar and the blocking charge, and considered whether to eliminate or weaken the eighty-one-year-old contract bar. The PRO Act restores longstanding precedent to prevent employers from undermining contracts and preserving stability in collective bargaining, while allowing employees to have the right to elect a different union, or no union at all.

Section 106. Preventing Unfair Labor Practices

The PRO Act provides that, when an employee has been discharged or suffered serious economic harm in violation of the NLRA, the NLRB shall award the employee back pay (without any reduction based on the employee's interim earnings), front pay, consequential damages, and "an additional amount as liquidated damages equal to two times the amount of damages awarded." An employee cannot be denied relief under the NLRA on the basis that the employee is an unauthorized alien under the Immigration Reform and Control Act, which reverses the Supreme Court's 2002 decision in *Hoffman Plastic Compounds v. NLRB*.

Section 107. Enforcing Compliance with Orders of the Board

The NLRB's orders shall be self-enforcing, similar to orders of other federal agencies. If a party refuses to comply with an order of the Board, then it may initiate contempt proceedings in federal district court. A party that is adversely affected by an NLRB order may seek review before a federal court of appeals within thirty days of the order being issued.

Section 108. Injunctions against Unfair Labor Practices Involving Discharge or Other Serious Economic Harm

The PRO Act requires the NLRB to seek temporary injunctive relief whenever it determines that there is a reasonable basis to find that an employer unlawfully terminated an employee or significantly interfered with employees' rights under the NLRA. The district court shall grant this temporary relief for the duration of the NLRB proceedings unless the court concludes that there is no reasonable likelihood that the NLRB will succeed on the merits of its claim.

Section 109. Enacting Penalties to Strengthen Enforcement for Employees Exercising Their Rights at Work

(a) *Civil penalties for violations of the posting requirements and voter list requirements.* If an employer violates the PRO Act by failing to post a notice or to inform new employees of their rights under the NLRA, or by failing to produce the voter eligibility list on time, then the NLRB shall order the employer to provide the information to employees and impose a civil penalty not to exceed $500 for each violation.

(b) *Civil penalties to remedy violations of employees' rights.* If an employer commits a violation of employees' rights under the NLRA, then the employer shall be subject to a civil penalty not to exceed $50,000, though the NLRB may double that penalty in any case where the employer has committed another such violation in the previous five years and where such penalty involves discharge or serious economic harm. In determining the size of such a penalty, the NLRB may consider the gravity of the violation, the impact of the violation on the employee, and the size of the employer. The NLRB may, under certain circumstances, hold an officer or director of an employer personally liable and assess a civil penalty against that person.

(c) *Private right to civil action.* If the NLRB does not seek an injunction to protect an employee within sixty days of filing a charge for retaliation against the employee's right to join a union or engage in protected activity, that employee may bring a civil action in federal district court. The district court may award relief available to employees who file a charge before the NLRB.

Section 110. Clarifying the Right to Strike

The NLRA already states that nothing in the statute, unless otherwise stated, interferes with or diminishes the right to strike. The PRO Act adds that the "duration, scope, frequency, or intermittence of any strike or strikes shall not render such strike or strikes unprotected or prohibited."

Section 111. Fair Share Agreements

Under the NLRA, a union is the exclusive representative of the employees that it represents, meaning that the union must represent all workers within a bargaining unit equally and without regard to their membership in the union. The NLRA allows unions and employers to agree that employees who are not members of the union, but benefit from a collective bargaining agreement, may be assessed a fair-share fee to support the costs of bargaining and implementing the agreement. However, § 14(b) of the NLRA permits states to pass laws that prevent unions from requiring union membership as a condition for employment. Twenty-eight states have passed laws that prohibit unions and employers from requiring fair-share fees from workers who benefit from representation but are not members of the union. These laws create a free-rider problem, where individuals enjoy the benefits of representation without paying any of the costs, which shifts the costs of free riders onto the shoulders of coworkers who elect to join the union and pay dues. The PRO Act permits unions and employers to voluntarily agree to require fair-share fees, regardless of state laws, to cover the costs of collective bargaining and contract administration.

Title II—Amendments to the Labor Management Relations Act, 1947 and the Labor-Management Reporting and Disclosure Act of 1959

Section 201. Conforming Amendments to the Labor Management Relations Act (LMRA)

The PRO Act repeals a provision that provides employers with a private right of action to sue unions that conduct secondary strikes and other activity. Because the PRO Act would permit such secondary activity, the bill repeals this private right of action as extraneous.

Section 202. Amendments to the Labor-Management Reporting and Disclosure Act (LMRDA)

The PRO Act clarifies a provision in the LMRDA that requires employers to disclose arrangements that they enter into with consultants to directly or indirectly persuade employees on how to exercise their rights under the NLRA. Such arrangements may include planning or conducting employee meetings, drafting speeches or presentations to employees, training employer representatives, identifying employees for disciplinary action or targeting, and drafting employer personnel policies. This provision codifies a US Department of Labor disclosure rule clarifying reporting requirements for "indirect" activities carried out by union avoidance consultants, which was rescinded in July 2018. The PRO Act also directs the Department of Labor to make this information available through a searchable electronic format.

Title III—Other Matters

Section 301. Electronic Voting in Union Elections

This section directs the NLRB to develop a system and procedures to conduct representation elections remotely through the internet or a telephone, similar to elections conducted by the NMB for workers in the railway and airline industries.

Section 302. Government Accountability Office (GAO) Report on Sectoral Bargaining

This section directs the comptroller general to provide a report detailing the policies and procedures governing collective bargaining on the sectoral level in the countries where such bargaining occurs.

Section 303. Severability

This section states that if any provision in the PRO Act is invalidated in court, then the remainder of the PRO Act will continue to be in effect.

Section 304. Authorization of Appropriations

This section authorizes the appropriations of such sums as may be necessary to carry out the provisions of the PRO Act.

Section 305. Rule of Construction

This section states that no provision of the PRO Act shall be construed to amend § 274A of the Immigration and Nationality Act.

Section 306. Rule of Construction

This section states that the PRO Act shall not be construed to affect the jurisdictional standards of the NLRB, including any standards that measure the size of a business with respect to revenues, which are used to determine whether an industry is affecting commerce for purposes of coverage under the NLRA.

Section 307. Rule of Construction

This section states that the PRO Act shall not be construed to affect the privacy of employees with respect to the voter lists provided to labor organizations by employers pursuant to elections directed by the NLRB.

Section 308. Rule of Construction

This section states that the PRO Act shall not be construed to affect the definitions of "employer" or "employee" under the laws of any state that govern wages, work hours, workers' compensation, or unemployment insurance.

Notes

Preface

1. Labor-Management Relations (Taft-Hartley) Act, ch. 120, 61 Stat. 136 (1947) (codified as amended in scattered sections of 29 U.S.C.). Taft-Hartley was enacted by the 80th US Congress over the veto of President Harry S. Truman and became law on June 23, 1947.

2. The NLRA "announced an affirmative national policy in favor of collective bargaining and economic redistribution; worked a fundamental change in the common-law employment relationship; and promised a system of nationwide industrial democracy." Kate Andrias, "The New Labor Law," *Yale L.J.* 126, no. 1 (2016): 2–16.

3. See the discussion in chapter 1 of the "representation gap"—the unsatisfied desire of millions of workers for union representation if it were available at their workplace.

Introduction

1. In the spring of 2021, the US House of Representatives passed the Protecting the Right to Organize Act (PRO Act). H.R. 842, 117th Cong. (2021). The most transformative labor relations legislation since enactment of the 1935 National Labor Relations Act (NLRA) and the 1947 Taft-Hartley Act, the PRO Act would reform, root and branch, the rules governing American private-sector labor relations law. In the US Senate, as of mid-2022, forty-eight Democratic senators were committed to supporting the legislation, with the other two, Joe Manchin and Kyrsten Sinema, wavering. However, even if all the Democrats supported legislative labor law reform, the Senate filibuster loomed as a political reality thwarting the likelihood of passing it in 2022.

2. See Catherine L. Fisk and Deborah C. Malamud, "The NLRB in Administrative Law Exile: Problems with Its Structure and Function and Suggestions for Reform," *Duke L.J.* 58 (2009): 2013, 2015 (showing that National Labor Relations Board (NLRB) doctrine shifts in predictable ways with the shift from liberal to conservative presidential administrations); James A. Gross, *Broken Promises: The Subversion of U.S. Labor Relations*

Policy, 1947–1994 (Philadelphia: Temple University Press, 1995), 120 (observing this vacillation in the meaning of Taft-Hartley as early as the Eisenhower NLRB when it took over from the Truman NLRB).

3. See the discussion in StackExchange, "Meaning and Origin of 'That Dog Don't Hunt,'" https://english.stackexchange.com/questions/52755/meaning-and-origin-of-that-dog-dont-hunt.

4. See, for example, Cynthia L. Estlund, "The Ossification of American Labor Law," *Colum. L. Rev.* 102, no. 6 (2002): 1527–1528 (demonstrating that "private sector labor law—the law that governs workers' efforts to advance their own shared interests through self-organization and collective protest, pressure, negotiation, and agreement with employers—has shrunk in its reach and its significance, and is clearly ailing. Evidence of morbidity abounds. . . . The labor laws have failed to deliver an effective mechanism of workplace representation, and have become nearly irrelevant, to the vast majority of private sector American workers").

5. I take my lead here from Judge Stephen Reinhardt, who wrote, in an essay in the *Michigan Law Review*, "I am an optimist. I still believe that 'the arc of the moral universe is long, but it bends toward justice.'" Stephen R. Reinhardt, "The Demise of Habeas Corpus and the Rise of Qualified Immunity," *Mich. L. Rev.* 113, no. 7 (2015): 1219, 1254.

6. Sharon Block, "Go Big or Go Home: The Case for Clean Slate Labor Law Reform," *Berkeley J. Emp. & Lab. L.* 41, no. 1 (2020): 168–169 (arguing that "the status of the labor movement would [not] be all that different today if [previous labor law reform efforts] had passed. Yes, we would have had some greater success in union-organizing campaigns and some more first contracts. But I am fairly certain that we would still be having this exact conversation about the existential threat to the labor movement."). See also Julius G. Getman, *The Supreme Court on Unions: Why Labor Law Is Failing American Workers* (Ithaca, NY: Cornell/ILR Press, 2016), 197–198 (arguing that because labor law reform would be "bitterly opposed by wealthy political patrons of both parties," reform is unlikely, and even if labor law reform efforts were successful, "none would be immune to the [Supreme] Court's ability to neuter and transform pro-union legislation").

7. Lane Windham, *Knocking on Labor's Door: Union Organizing in the 1970s and the Roots of a New Economic Divide* (Chapel Hill: University of North Carolina Press, 2017), 11.

8. For a more pessimistic view, see Ellen Dannin, "At Age Seventy, Should the National Labor Relations Act Be Retired," in *Proceedings of the 2005 Annual Meeting, Association of American Law Schools Section on Labor Relations and Employment Law*, ed. Katherine Stone et al. *Emp. Rts. & Emp. Pol'y. J.* 9 (2005): 121, 125 (stating that "[s]ome have proposed new legislation, but we know that . . . [a]mending the statute is not possible").

9. See the discussion in Gross, *Broken Promises*, 122. See also Bill Fletcher, Jr. and Richard Hurd, "Beyond the Organizing Mode: The Transformation Model in Local Unions," in *Organizing to Win: New Research in Union Strategies*, ed. Kate Bronfenbrenner et al. (Ithaca, NY: Cornell/ILR Press, 1998), 37 (Arguing the need to define unionism in terms "of what [unions] stand for").

10. Joel Rogers, "Reforming U.S. Labor Relations," in *Restoring the Promise of American Labor Law*, ed. Sheldon Friedman et al. (Ithaca, NY: ILR Press, 1994), 24.

11. See Josh Eidelson, "Workers Press for Power in Rare Advance for U.S. Labor Movement," *Bloomberg Businessweek,* October 27, 2021, https://www.bloomberg.com/news/features/2021-10-27/labor-shortage-2021-workers-press-for-power-as-millions-quit-jobs-across-america.

12. Eidelson, "Workers Press for Power in Rare Advance for U.S. Labor Movement."

13. Shawn Donnan and Reade Pickert, "U.S. Unemployment Rescue Left at Least 9 Million without Help," *Bloomberg Businessweek,* June 25, 2021, https://www.bloomberg.com/news/features/2021-06-25/u-s-unemployment-at-least-9-million-americans-didn-t-receive-any-benefits.

14. See Kate Andrias, "Peril and Possibility: Strikes, Rights, and Legal Change in the Age of Trump," *Berkeley J. Emp. & Lab. L.* 40, no. 1 (2019): 135, 138–143 (covering the April 5, 2018, David E. Feller Memorial Labor Law Lecture, detailing activism among public school teachers and the "Fight for $15" movement).

15. Stephen Totilo and Megan Farokhmanesh, "Call of Duty Walkout," *Axios Gaming,* https://www.axios.com/newsletters/axios-gaming-1940f4cb-b813-4150-98a6-a5770b109201.html?chunk=1&utm_campaign=axios_app#story1 (reporting on a walkout of sixty workers at the *Call of Duty: Warzone* studio at Raven Software, owned by Activision Blizzard, demanding the reinstatement of a dozen workers from the testing department).

16. See Emma Goldberg, "Better.com's C.E.O. Is 'Taking Time Off' after Firing 900 Workers over Zoom," *New York Times,* December 10, 2021, https://www.nytimes.com/2021/12/10/business/economy/better-ceo-zoom-firing.html (also stating that the NLRB increased the termination package to two months' severance).

17. "White House Task Force on Worker Organizing and Empowerment," *Report to the President*, 12, https://www.whitehouse.gov/briefing-room/statements-releases/2022/02/07/white-house-task-force-on-worker-organizing-and-empowerment-report/.

18. Henry S. Farber et al., "Unions and Inequality over the Twentieth Century: New Evidence from Survey Data," *NBER Working Paper 24587* (2018), 42, https://www.nber.org/papers/w24587.

19. See also Katherine V. W. Stone, *From Widgets to Digits: Employment Regulation for the Changing Workplace* (New York: Cambridge University Press, 2004), 239 (arguing

that success in promoting labor law reform requires "articulat[ing] directions for reform [that] make it possible to envision legal change and to begin to build a coalition [that is] able to bring change about").

Chapter 1

1. See Bureau of Labor Statistics, US Department of Labor, "Union Members Summary," January 20, 2022, https://www.bls.gov/news.release/union2.nr0.htm.

2. See also Barry T. Hirsch, "Sluggish Institutions in a Dynamic World: Can Unions and Industrial Competition Coexist?" *J. of Econ. Perspectives* 22, no. 1 (2008): 156 (observing that as private-sector union membership fell by nearly half, "nonunion private [sector] wage and salary employment more than doubled from 47 million in 1973 to 108 in 2006").

3. The slight differences in tables 1.1 and 1.2 are explained by the fact that table 1.1 includes *all* private-sector wage and salary workers, while table 1.2 includes only non-agricultural, private-sector wage and salary workers.

4. The NLRB releases its annual election reports shortly after the fiscal year ends, which runs from October to the following September. These reports are available at https://www.nlrb.gov/reports/agency-performance/election-reports.

5. Eric Dirnbach, "State of U.S. Unions 2021," *Medium,* February 19, 2021, https://ericdirnbach.medium.com/state-of-the-u-s-unions-2021-883a2bce628.

6. Brandon Magner, "The Robb Era: A Knockdown but Not a Knockout for the NLRB," *Lab. L. Lite,* January 21, 2021, https://brandonmagner.substack.com/p/the-robb-era-a-knockdown-but-not.

7. See the discussion in Committee on Education and Labor, US House of Representatives, "Corruption, Conflicts, and Crisis: The NLRB's Assault on Worker Rights under the Trump Administration," 59–64, 7–8nn (October 2020), https://edlabor.house.gov/imo/media/doc/NLRB%20Report%20(Final).pdf; Magner, "The Robb Era."

8. Robert Combs, "Analysis: Unions Had Momentum at NLRB—Then Came Coronavirus," *Bloomberg Law,* March 24, 2020, https://news.bloomberglaw.com/bloomberg-law-analysis/analysis-unions-had-momentum-at-nlrb-then-came-coronavirus (cited at Committee on Education and Labor, "Corruption, Conflicts, and Crisis," 8n74.

9. Margaret Paydock and Celine McNicholas, "The Trump Administration's Attacks on Workplace Union Voting Rights Forewarned of the Broader Threats to Voting Rights in the Upcoming Election," *Econ Pol'y Inst.,* October 21, 2020, https://www.epi.org/publication/the-trump-administrations-attacks-on-workplace-union-voting-rights-forewarned-of-the-broader-threats-to-voting-rights-in-the-upcoming-election/.

10. Committee on Education and Labor, "Corruption, Conflicts, and Crisis," 8 (October 2020).

11. Kate Bronfenbrenner et al., "Introduction," in *Organizing to Win: New Research in Union Strategies*, ed. Kate Bronfenbrenner et al. (Ithaca, NY: Cornell/ILR Press, 1998), 6.

12. See Kate Bronfenbrenner and Robert Hickey, "Changing to Organize: A National Assessment of Union Strategies," in *Rebuilding Labor: Organizing and Organizers in the New Union Movement*, ed. Ruth Milkman and Kim Voss (Ithaca, NY: Cornell University Press, 2004), 25–27 (calculating, from a random sample of 412 elections in 1998 and 1999, that the union win rate was 44 percent in 1998 and 1999).

13. Bronfenbrenner et al., "Introduction," 3.

14. Lawrence Mishel, Lynn Rhinehart, and Lane Windham, "Explaining the Erosion of Private-Sector Unions: How Corporate Practices and Legal Changes Have Undercut the Ability of Workers to Organize and Bargain," *Econ. Pol'y Inst.*, November 18, 2020, https://www.epi.org/unequalpower/publications/private-sector-unions-corporate-legal-erosion/.

15. Benjamin I. Sachs, "Labor Law Renewal," *Harv. L. & Pol'y Rev.* 1 (2007): 375, 380.

16. During the Trump administration, the NLRB general counsel authorized the issuance of an unfair labor practice complaint against both a company and a union as a result of their entering into a neutrality agreement. See *Embassy Suites Management LLC and UNITEHERE!* Local 8, NLRB Cases 19-CA-227623, and 19-CB-227622, complaint issued July 1, 2020. See the discussion in Kauff, McGuire & Margolis, "NLRB Changes Its Stance towards Employer-Union Neutrality Agreements," February 11, 2021, https://www.kmm.com/articles-659.html.

17. 356 N.L.R.B. 256 (2010), *affirmed sub nom. Montague v. NLRB,* 698 F.3d 307 (6th Cir. 2012). In *Dana Corporation,* a union and an employer negotiated a framework agreement to govern their relationship while the union attempted to organize the employer's employees. This framework provided that the employer would remain neutral with respect to the employees' choice of whether to choose union representation. In addition, the employer agreed to recognize and bargain with the union without the need for the union to prevail in an NLRB-conducted representation election if a majority of the employees expressed a desire for union representation by signing union authorization cards (referred to as "card check" union recognition). In addition, in *Dana Corporation,* the employer agreed to permit prerecognition union contact with employees during nonwork time in nonwork areas to discuss union representation, and to provide the union with a list of employee names and addresses. The framework agreement banned strikes and lockouts prior to the negotiation of a first contract, which was to have a term of at least four years, and provided for interest arbitration to set the terms of the first contract if the parties were unable to reach agreement within six months.

18. See Unite Here Local 355 (Magic City Casino), 2011 WL 345272 (January 21, 2011) (Advice Memorandum).

19. Thomas A. Kochan, "How American Workers View Labor Unions," 102 *Monthly Lab. Rev.* 102, no. 4 (1979): 23n1 (stating that some discussion of pre-1980 opinion polls is found in Derek C. Bok and John T. Dunlop, *Labor and the American Community* (New York: Simon and Schuster, 1970), 11–19).

20. Kochan, "How American Workers View Labor Unions," 23.

21. See Richard B. Freeman and Joel Rogers, *What Workers Want* (Ithaca, NY: Cornell/ILR Press, 1999).

22. Thomas A. Kochan et al., "Worker Voice in America: Is There a Gap between What Workers Expect and What They Experience?" *Ind. & Lab. Rel. Rev.* 72, no. 2 (2019): 3, 5.

23. Freeman and Rogers, *What Workers Want.*

24. Kochan et al., "Worker Voice in America," 3.

25. Kochan et al., "Worker Voice in America," 20 (stating that the percentage was "48 percent when we limit the analysis to non-union respondents and 49 percent when we consider non-managerial, non-union respondents").

26. See the findings reported at Peter D. Hart Research Associates, *The Public View of Unions* (2005)). The economists Richard Freeman and Joel Rogers report that 87 percent of workers want some form of representation in the workplace. Freeman and Rogers, *What Workers Want,* 147.

27. White House Task Force on Worker Organizing and Empowerment," *Report to the President*, 4, 12, https://www.whitehouse.gov/briefing-room/statements-releases/2022/02/07/white-house-task-force-on-worker-organizing-and-empowerment-report/.

28. Kochan et al., "Worker Voice in America," 21 (reporting that this desire for continued union representation had been slightly higher (90%) in the 1995 survey).

29. See the discussion in Justin McCarthy, "U.S. Approval of Labor Unions at Highest Point Since 1965," Gallup, August 30, 2022, https://news.gallup.com/poll/398303/approval-labor-unions-highest-point-1965.aspx (also reporting that pay and benefits and "employee rights and representation" given as the leading reasons for joining a union).

30. Kochan et al., "Worker Voice in America," 21, 31–32. To this overall increase in interest in union representation should be added the insights added by Ruth Milkman and Kim Voss, who explain that "key population groups like immigrants and women, whose share of the workforce is growing, remain underrepresented in the ranks of organized labor—despite evidence that such workers, especially those concentrated in low-wage jobs, are especially sympathetic to unionization efforts." Ruth Milkman and Kim Voss, "Introduction," in *Rebuilding Labor: Organizing and Organizers in the New Union Movement*, ed. Ruth Milkman and Kim Voss (Ithaca, NY: Cornell University Press 2004), 1.

Chapter 2

1. See Justin McCarthy, "U.S. Approval of Labor Unions at Highest Point Since 1965," Gallup, August 30, 2022, https://news.gallup.com/poll/398303/approval-labor-unions-highest-point-1965.aspx. See also "White House Task Force on Worker Organizing and Empowerment," *Report to the President*, 12 (reporting a 68 percent approval of unions in 2021); Megan Brenan, "At 65%, Approval of Labor Unions in the U.S. Remains High," Gallup, September 3, 2020, https://news.gallup.com/poll/318980/approval-labor-unions-remains-high.aspx (reporting a 65 percent approval rating for unions in 2020). This high level of public support for unions was reflected again in 2021, in a Vox poll of 1,000 likely voters. "When asked if unions are essential to ensuring workers are compensated fairly," 57 percent of likely voters overall agreed: 74 percent of Democrats, 54 percent of independents, and 39 percent of Republicans. See Gabby Birenbaum "Poll: A Majority of Voters Support the PRO Act," *Vox Media*, June 16, 2021, https://www.vox.com/2021/6/16/22535274/poll-pro-act-unionization-majority-bipartisan.

2. Brenan, "At 65%, Approval of Labor Unions in the U.S. Remains High," 2.

3. Brenan, "At 65%, Approval of Labor Unions in the U.S. Remains High," 2.

4. Birenbaum, "Poll: A Majority of Voters Support the PRO Act."

5. Sharon Block, "Go Big or Go Home: The Case for Clean Slate Labor Law Reform," *Berkeley J. Emp. & Lab. L.* 41, no. 1 (2020): 167, 169.

6. *Report of the AFL-CIO Commission on the Future of Work and Unions*, 37 (2019), https://aflcio.org/reports/afl-cio-commission-future-work-and-unions (arguing that building a public constituency for labor law reforms requires widespread public "knowledge of the role and power of labor unions in the workplace").

7. See *Report of the AFL-CIO Commission on the Future of Work and Unions*, 37 (also reporting other evidence of nonunion workers who "had never heard of unions or had no opinion [regarding] them").

8. See *Report of the AFL-CIO Commission on the Future of Work and Unions*, 37.

9. Richard B. Morris, *Government and Labor In Early America* (New York: Columbia University Press, 1946), 206.

10. See, for example, *Commonwealth v. Pullis, Philadelphia Mayor's Court* (1806), 3; John Rogers Commons and Eugene A. Gilmore, *A Documentary History of American Industrial Society* (Norman, OK: Arthur H. Clark, 1910), 59. For a history of the events precipitating the Philadelphia Cordwainers case, the political controversy of which it was a part, and the reaction to it, see Elias Lieberman, *Unions before the Bar* (New York: Harper Bros. rev. ed. 1960), 15; Walter Nelles, "The First American Labor Case," 41 *Yale L.J.* 165 (1931).

11. The charge to the jury in the Philadelphia Cordwainers case stated, "A combination of workers to raise their wages may be considered in a two-fold point of view: One is to benefit themselves . . . the other is to injure those who do not join the society. The rule of law condemns both." See Commons and Gilmore, *Documentary History*, 233.

12. Neal W. Chamberlain, *Labor* (New York: McGraw-Hill, 1958), 18. See, for example, *Commonwealth v. Hunt*, 45 Mass. (4 Met.) 111 (1842). For a discussion of the development of this doctrine, see Edwin E. Witte, "Early American Labor Cases," *Yale L.J.* 35, no. 7 (1926): 825.

13. William Sampson, *Trial of the Journeyman Cordwainers of the City of New York* (New York: L. Riley, 1810), 6–141. See also Francis B. Sayre, "Criminal Conspiracy," *Harv. L. Rev.* 35, no. 4 (1922): 393.

14. Sampson, *Trial of the Journeyman Cordwainers*, 46–47.

15. With somewhat typical hyperbole, the counsel for the New York Cordwainers, during the 1809 criminal conspiracy trial, argued for the legitimacy of worker combinations because "like the worm that spins its bowels, and perishes in the act, so they whose hands impart to the tissue its lustre of its hue, to flatter the voluptuous and the gay, pine themselves and decay in obscurity and want." Sampson, *Trial of the Journeyman Cordwainers*, 13. Albert Gallatin, an entrepreneur and later secretary of the Treasury, also argued, in 1797, that "[t]he democratic principle on which this nation was founded should not be restricted to the political process but should be applied to the industrial operation as well." See Milton Derber, *The American Idea of Industrial Democracy, 1865–1965* (Champaign, IL: University of Illinois Press; 1970), 6. See also Clyde Summers, "Industrial Democracy: America's Unfulfilled Promise," *Clev. St. L. Rev.* 28, no. 1 (1979): 29.

16. Sampson, *Trial of the Journeyman Cordwainers*, 34, 120.

17. Sampson, *Trial of the Journeyman Cordwainers*, 26, 36.

18. See Alfred W. Blumrosen, "Group Interests in Labor Law," *Rutgers L. Rev.* 13 (1959): 432–434.

19. See Chamberlain, *Labor*, 18–20; Harry H. Wellington, *Labor and the Legal Process* (New Haven, CT: Yale University Press, 1968), 9–13.

20. William Morris Leiserson, *American Trade Union Democracy* (New York: Columbia University Press, 1959), 35.

21. See Lloyd Ulman, *The Rise of the National Trade Union* (Cambridge, MA: Harvard University Press, 1955), 3–4.

22. Chamberlain, *Labor*, 41.

23. Commons and Gilmore, *Documentary History*, 520.

24. Commons and Gilmore, *Documentary History*, 531–533. See also Foster Rhea Dulles, *Labor in America* (New York: Thomas Y. Crowell Company, 1963), 162, 184–207. Moreover, the new business unionism never fully abandoned its reforming, cooperative tradition, first developed during the nineteenth century by sponsoring educational programs, social services, and consumer cooperatives. See Chamberlain, *Labor*, 40; Dulles, *Labor in America*, 150; Leiserson, *American Trade Union Democracy*, 36, 46.

25. Summers, "Industrial Democracy: America's Unfulfilled Promise," 30.

26. Dulles, *Labor in America*, 95–96.

27. Summers, *Industrial Democracy: America's Unfulfilled Promise*, 30. See also Wilbert Ellis Moore, *Industrial Relations and the Social Order* (New York: Macmillan Company, 1946), 34–35 (explaining that "with the factory system[, the] illusion of liberty could no longer be maintained [because the] direct and insistent supervision of the laborer [closely scrutinized] [t]he quality of his work [and] his speed and general efficiency.")

28. Clyde Summers, "Individual Protection against Unjust Dismissal: Time for a Statute," *Va. L Rev.* 62, no. 3 (1976): 481, 484–485; Alfred F Delchamps III. "The Employment at Will Rule," *Ala. L. Rev.* 31 (1980): 421, 422–424, 14–15nn; J. Peter Shapiro and James F. Tune , "Implied Contract Rights to Job Security," *Stan L. Rev.*26, no. 2 (1974): 335, 341.

29. *Payne v. Western & Atl. R.R.,* 81 Tenn. 507, 519–520 (1884). *Mallard v. Boring,* 182 Cal. App. 2d 390, 394, 6 *Cal. Rptr.* 171, 174 (1960).

30. For a discussion of the employment at will doctrine and modifications by state and federal statutes that implicitly or explicitly guarantee nonunion workers protection from certain forms of discrimination or retaliation at the workplace, see William B. Gould IV, *Agenda for Reform: The Future of Employment Relationships and the Law* (Cambridge, MA: MIT Press, 1996), 63–103.

31. See Clyde Summers and Harry H. Wellington, *Labor Law: Cases and Materials* (Washington, DC: Foundation Press, 1968), 142–143, 153–154; Felix Frankfurter and Nathan Greene, *The Labor Injunction* (New York: Macmillan, 1930), 25–26.

32. Clarence E. Bonnett, "The Origin of the Labor Injunction," *S. Cal. L. Rev.* 5 (1931): 105.

33. 15 U.S.C. §§ 1–38.

34. *Loewe v. Lawlor (Danbury Hatters),* 208 U.S. 274 (1908). Seven years later, the court upheld a treble damages verdict of $252,000 assessed against the union and its members. *Lawlor v. Loewe,* 235 U.S. 522 (1915).

35. 254 U.S. 443 (1921).

36. See Clayton Act, ch. 323, § 6, 38 Stat. 730 (1914) (current version codified at 15 U.S.C. §§ 12–17).

37. *Coronado Coal Co. v. United Mine Workers*, 268 U.S. 295 (1925).

38. 208 U.S. 161 (1908).

39. Blumrosen, "Group Interests in Labor Law," 437–438. For a discussion of labor's conflict with law during the 1920s, see Irving Bernstein, *The Lean Years: A History of the American Worker, 1920–1933* (Boston: Houghton Mifflin, 1969), 190–243. See Bernstein, *The Lean Years*, 532–535nn1–17, for a bibliography of contemporary literature discussing the legal issues that arose.

40. Pub. L. No. 72–65, 47 Stat. 70 (1932) (codified at 29 U.S.C. §§ 101–115).

41. Relying on the Norris-LaGuardia Act, the Supreme Court undid the effect of *Duplex Printing* in *United States v. Hutcheson*, 312 U.S. 219 (1941).

42. Pub. L. No. 74–198, 49 Stat. 449 (1935) (codified as amended at 29 U.S.C. §§ 151–169 [hereinafter cited by section number and either NLRA or Wagner Act].

43. 310 U.S. 88 (1940).

44. *Apex Hosiery Co. v. Leader*, 310 U.S. 469 (1940). But see *Allen Bradley Co. v. Local 3, I.B.E.W.*, 325 U.S. 797 (1945) (no exemption from antitrust laws when unions combine with groups of businesspeople to restrain trade).

45. Chamberlain, *Labor*, 24–25.

46. Chamberlain, *Labor*, 25.

47. See, for example, Joseph Rosenfarb, *The National Labor Policy* (New York: Harper & Bros., 1940), 23–24; Summers and Wellington, *Labor Law*, 99; Clyde Summers, "American Legislation for Union Democracy," *Mod L. Rev.* 25, no. 3 (1962): 273, 275n10 (collecting commentary).

48. Bernstein, *The Lean Years*, 145–146.

49. Bernstein, *The Lean Years*, 146–189. See Derber, *The American Idea of Industrial Democracy, 1865–1965*, 3 (discussing of the struggle between welfare capitalism and labor unionism).

50. Bernstein, *The Lean Years*, 173, 186–189.

51. Irving Bernstein, *Turbulent Years: A History of the American Worker, 1933–1941* (Boston: Houghton Mifflin, 1971), 333; Summers, "Industrial Democracy: America's Unfulfilled Promise," 33.

52. Rosenfarb, *The National Labor Policy*, 21–35; Wellington, *Labor and the Legal Process*, 26–28, 40–42. See also Dulles, *Labor in America*, 287.

53. For instance, see Bernstein, *Turbulent Years*, 331–332; Rosenfarb, *The National Labor Policy*, 33–35; Wellington, *Labor and the Legal Process*, 27, 340n36.

54. 75 *Cong. Rec.* 4918 (1932).

55. 7 *Cong. Rec.* 7571 (1935).

56. Bernstein, *Turbulent Years,* 333.

57. Bernstein, *Turbulent Years,* 209. The Supreme Court, in *American Steel Foundries v. Tri-City Cent. Trades Council,* 257 U.S. 184 (1921), had recognized explicitly that unions "were organized out of the necessities of the situation. A single employee was helpless in dealing with an employer."

58. Bernstein, *Turbulent Years,* 331.

59. Wagner Act, § 1.

60. *J.I. Case Co. v. NLRB,* 321 U.S. 332, 338 (1944). *Barrentine v. Arkansas-Best Freight Sys.,* 450 U.S. 728 (1981).

61. Wagner Act, § 1.

62. 301 U.S. 1, 42 (1937).

63. See Bernstein, *Turbulent Years,* 332. American communists recognized this goal of the Wagner Act. They saw it as a cynical conspiracy of the capitalist–New Dealer nexus inevitably serving the interests of employers at the expense of a militant working class. For this reason, they joined conservative business interests in opposing the Wagner bill. Many noncommunist leftists also opposed it, arguing that it threatened to lull militant labor organizations into a false sense of security and reliance on government, and that it would be accompanied inevitably by other government actions detrimental to the union movement. See Cletus E. Daniel, *The ACLU and the Wagner Act: An Inquiry into the Depression-Era Crisis of American Liberalism* (Ithaca, NY: Cornell/ILR Press, 1980). See also Bernstein, *Turbulent Years,* 820n4.

64. James B. Atleson, *Values and Assumption s in American Labor Law* (Amherst: University of Massachusetts Press, 1983), 2. See also Bernstein, *Turbulent Years,* 769, 787–788. Between 1935 and 1945, the NLRB conducted 24,000 representation elections involving six million workers. In all but 16.1 percent of the elections, employees chose union representation. Dulles, *Labor in America,* 280.

65. Between 1935 and 1945, the NLRB disestablished approximately 2,000 company unions. Dulles, *Labor in America,* 280. See also Derber, *The American Idea of Industrial Democracy, 1865–1965,* 4.

66. Bernstein, *Turbulent Years,* 770, 772–774.

67. Dulles, *Labor in America,* 312. See generally Bernstein, *Turbulent Years,* 776–783.

68. Dulles, *Labor in America,* 276–279.

69. Bernstein, *Turbulent Years,* 515, 639, 646.

70. *NLRB v. Jones & Laughlin Steel Corp.,* 301 U.S. 1 (1937).

71. Between 1935 and 1945 in cases involving employer discrimination, the NLRB ordered 300,000 employees to be reinstated with back pay totaling nine million dollars. Dulles, *Labor in America*, 280.

72. Bernstein, *Turbulent Years*, 663–664, 666–671.

73. See Gould, *Agenda for Reform*, 11, 63, 122.

74. Atleson, *Values and Assumption s in American Labor Law*, 108–109, 120 (stating that "20 percent of all workers under agreement, or over three million workers, were covered by maintenance of membership clauses").

75. Atleson, *Values and Assumption s in American Labor Law*, 120.

76. Atleson, *Values and Assumption s in American Labor Law*, 1 (emphasis in the original).

77. During 1946, a pattern of strikes seriously disrupted the national economy. In late November 1945, a total of 500,000 workers were on strike and by January 1946, almost two million workers were simultaneously on strike. During the twelve months following V-J Day, the nation experienced 4,630 work stoppages and more than five million workers had gone on strike, causing a total of 120 million worker-days of lost production. Dulles, *Labor in America*, 358–367.

78. Labor-Management Relations (Taft-Hartley) Act, ch. 120, 61 Stat. 136 (1947) (codified as amended in scattered sections of 29 U.S.C.).

79. Taft-Hartley Act, §§ 7, 8(b)(1)(A).

80. Taft-Hartley Act, §§ 8(a)(3), 8(b)(2), 14(b).

81. Taft-Hartley Act, § 9(e)(1). The requirement of union shop authorization elections was repealed on October 22, 1951, primarily because in 97.1 percent of the 46,146 union authorization elections that were held, the union shop was approved, and 85.7 percent of the over 5.5 million workers who cast ballots gave such approval. Philip Taft, "Internal Affairs of Union and the Taft-Hartley Act," *Indus. & Lab. Rel. Rev.* 11, no. 3 (1958): 352, 354–355.

82. Taft-Hartley Act, § 9(c)(1)(A)(ii).

83. Taft-Hartley Act, §§ 9(b)(1) & (2), 9(c)(5). See also *Emporium Capwell Co. v. Western Addition Community Org.*, 420 U.S. 50, 64 (1975) (shaping appropriate bargaining units combines employees with a sufficient commonality of interest "to ensure against the submergence of a minority with distinctively different interests in the terms and conditions of their employment").

84. Few in 1947 saw Taft-Hartley as the first installment of the prediction advanced thirty years earlier by the dissenters on the Commission of Industrial Relations of 1916, that "if the State recognized any particular union by requiring the employer to

recognize it, the State must necessarily guarantee the union to the extent that it must strip it of any abuses that it may practice." *Final Report of the Commn. on Indus. Rel.* S. Doc. No. 415, 64th Cong., 1st Sess. 212 (1916). See Summers and Wellington, *Labor Law*, 19.

85. See the discussion in Benjamin Aaron, "Amending the Taft-Hartley Act: A Decade of Frustration," *Indus. & Lab. Rel. Rev.* 11, no. 3 (1958): 327; Gerald Pomper, "Labor Legislation: The Revision of Taft-Hartley in 1953–54," *Lab. Hist.* 6, no. 2 (1965): 143.

86. Wellington, *Labor and the Legal Process*, 198.

87. 105 Cong. Rec. 6471–6472 (1959).

88. See S. Rep. No. 187, 86th Cong., 1st Sess. 6–7 (1959).

89. S. Rep. No. 187, 86th Cong., 1st Sess. 6–7 (1959), at 7–8; H.R. Rep. No. 741, 86th Cong., 1st Sess. 7–8 (1959).

90. Alexander Hertel-Fernandez, William Kimball, and Thomas Kochan, "What Forms of Representation Do American Workers Want? Implications for Theory, Policy, and Practice," *Indus. & Lab. Rel. Rev.* 75, no. 2 (2020): 1, 12.

91. Thomas A. Kochan, *Contemporary Views of American Workers toward Trade Unions* (Alexandria, VA: National Technical Information Service (US Department of Commerce), 1978), 4–5, 8.

92. Thomas A. Kochan et al., "Worker Voice in America: Is There a Gap between What Workers Expect and What They Experience?" *Indus. & Lab. Rel. Rev.* 72, no. 1 (2019): 3, 5.

93. Kochan et al., "Worker Voice in America," 31–33.

94. Hertel-Fernandez et al., "What Forms of Representation Do American Workers Want?" 12–13.

95. See, for example, Hertel-Fernandez et al., "What Forms of Representation Do American Workers Want?," 4–6 (collecting authority); Sharon Block, "Go Big or Go Home: The Case for Clean Slate Labor Law Reform," *Berkeley J. Emp. & Lab. L.* 41, no. 1 (2020): 182 (arguing for amending federal law to provide for a "flipping of the default [to require] that all workplaces must have some channel of collective worker voice, be it a union or something more like a works council"). For an excellent discussion of European-model works councils, "an in-house procedure through which the employees at local work sites address and help resolve a range of employment issues," see Paul C. Weiler, *Governing the Workplace: The Future of Labor and Employment Law* (Cambridge, MA: Harvard University Press, 1990), 284–296.

96. See Hertel-Fernandez et al., "What Forms of Representation Do American Workers Want?" 5, 11–13, 21 (also finding that workers are enthusiastic about models of union representation "in which they could keep their [union] membership if they

changed or left their jobs" and also strongly desired "portable health insurance and retirement savings coverage . . . that workers could continue using even if they switched employers").

97. Henry S. Farber, et al., "Unions and Inequality over the Twentieth Century: New Evidence from Survey Data," NBER Working Paper 24587 (2018), at i, https://www.nber.org/papers/w24587.

98. Chad Stone et al., "A Guide to Statistics on Historical Trends in Income Inequality," *Center on Budget and Policy Priorities*, last updated January 13, 2020, https://www.cbpp.org/research/poverty-and-inequality/a-guide-to-statistics-on-historical-trends-in-income-inequality.

99. Lane Windham, *Knocking on Labor's Door: Union Organizing in the 1970s and the Roots of a New Economic Divide* (Chapel Hill: University of North Carolina Press, 2017), 5 (outlining economic data showing a growing income gap).

100. Mark Price and Estelle Sommelier, "The New Gilded Age? It's Everywhere," *AM Prospect*, August 14, 2018, http://prospect.org/article/new-gilded-age-its-everywhere.

101. Stone et al., "A Guide to Statistics on Historical Trends."

102. See the discussion in Neil Irwin, "Report Questions the Conventional Wisdom on Interest Rates and Inequality," *Washington Post*, September 7, 2021, B6 (reporting the findings of Atif Mian, Ludwig Straub, and Amir Sufi). Also see Thomas Piketty and Emmanuel Saez, "Income Inequality in the United States, 1913–1998," *Q.J. Econ.* 118, no. 1 (2003): 11.

103. Kate Andrias, "Peril and Possibility: Strikes, Rights, and Legal Change in the Age of Trump," *Berkeley J. Emp. & Lab. L.* 40, no. 1 (2019): 135, (April 5, 2018 David E. Feller Memorial Labor Law Lecture) (citing Estelle Sommeiller et al., *Econ Policy Inst.*, "Income Inequality in the U.S. by State, Metropolitan Area and County" 2, 7 (2016), http://www.epi.org/files/pdf/107100.pdf (discussing the gap between the top 1 percent and bottom 99 percent)).

104. On wage stagnation, see Lawrence Mishel et al., *Econ. Pol'y Inst.*, "Wage Stagnation in Nine Charts" (2015), http://www.epi.org/files/2013/wage-stagnation-in-nine-charts.pdf. On the rise in executive pay, see Callie Holtermann, "Are C.E.O.s Paid Too Much?" *New York Times*, May 11, 2020, https://www.nytimes.com/2021/05/11/learning/are-ceos-paid-too-much.html (concluding that "[c]hief executives of big companies now make, on average, 320 times as much as their typical worker, according to the Economic Policy Institute. In 1989, that ratio was 61 to 1. From 1978 to 2019, compensation grew 14 percent for typical workers. It rose 1,167 percent for C.E.O.s").

105. See, for example, Richard Freeman, "How Much Has De-unionization Contributed to the Rise in Male Earnings Inequality?" in *Uneven Tides: Rising Inequality in America*, ed. Sheldon Danziger and Peter Gottschalk (New York: Russell Sage

Foundation, 1993), 133–163; John DiNardo et al., "Labor Market Institutions and the Distribution of Wages, 1973–1992: A Semiparametric Approach," *Econometrica* 64 (1996): 1001–1044.

106. Nicole M. Fortin et al., "Labor Market Institutions and the Distribution of Wages: The Role of Spillover Effects," NBER Working Paper 28375 (2021), 42, https://www.nber.org/papers/w28375 (citing authority).

107. Farber et al., "Unions and Inequality over the Twentieth Century."

108. Fortin et al., Labor Market Institutions and the Distribution of Wages," 1.

109. Lawrence Mishel, "Report: the Enormous Impact of Eroded Collective Bargaining on Wages," *Econ. Pol'y. Inst.*, April 8, 2021, https://www.epi.org/publication/eroded-collective-bargaining/ (citing authority) (also noting that "[u]nions disproportionately benefit those with low and moderate wages, those with lower levels of education, and nonwhites, and this has been the case since the birth of the modern labor movement in the New Deal. The erosion of collective bargaining, correspondingly, has therefore increased wage inequality.).

110. Julius G. Getman, *The Supreme Court on Unions: Why Labor Law Is Failing American Workers* (Ithaca, NY: Cornell/ILR Press, 2016), 12 and n.38. See also White House Task Force on Worker Organizing and Empowerment, *Report to the President*. 3, concluding that "today's union households earn up to 20% more than non-union households, with an even greater union advantage for workers with less formal education and workers of color").

111. Kate Bronfenbrenner et al., "Introduction," in *Organizing to Win: New Research in Union Strategies*, ed. Kate Bronfenbrenner et al. (Ithaca, NY: Cornell/ILR Press, 1998), 6.

112. Mishel, "Report: the Enormous Impact of Eroded Collective Bargaining on Wages."

113. See, for example, Fortin et al., "Labor Market Institutions and the Distribution of Wages," 1–2. See also Windham, *Knocking on Labor's Door*, 20 (stating that "[o]ne business school professor studied twenty-six nonunion companies over thirty years and found that they followed organized companies in setting wage and benefit rates up through the early 1980s").

114. See Michael Podgursky, "Unions, Establishment Size, and Intraindustry Threat Effects," *Indus & Lab. Rel. Rev.* 39, no. 2 (1986): 277–284; Jake Rosenfeld et al., "Union Decline Lowers Wages of Nonunion Workers," *Econ. Pol'y. Inst.* (2016); Mathieu Taschereau-Dumouchel, "The Union Threat," *Rev of Econ. Stud.* 87, no. 6 (2020): 2859–2892.

115. Mishel, "Report: the Enormous Impact of Eroded Collective Bargaining on Wages."

116. See the discussion in Mishel, "Report: the Enormous Impact of Eroded Collective Bargaining on Wages" (citing Jake Rosenfeld, Patrick Denice, and Jennifer Laird, "Union Decline Lowers Wages of Nonunion Workers: The Overlooked Reason Why Wages Are Stuck and Inequality Is Growing," *Econ. Pol'y Inst.*, 2016); Patrick Denice and Jake Rosenfeld, "Unions and Nonunion Pay in the United States, 1977–2015," *Soc. Sci.* 5 (2018): 541, http://dx.doi.org/10.15195/v5.a23.

117. Farber et al., "Unions and Inequality over the Twentieth Century," 41. Also see Getman, *The Supreme Court on Unions*, 189 (concluding that "[b]y the mid-1960s . . . [c]ollective bargaining had taken root in most major industries [and] had achieved high wages and decent working conditions for millions of workers, and had indirectly affected the wages of millions more, as nonunion employers paid a premium to remain nonunion").

118. Windham, *Knocking on Labor's Door*, 5 (explaining that vigorous union-organizing efforts during the 1970s proved ineffective in avoiding a crisis for American workers).

119. Hedrick Smith, *Who Stole the American Dream?* (New York: Random House, 2012), 73 (citing Lawrence Mishel, Joshua Bivens, and Heidi Shierholz, *The State of Working America, 2012–2013* (Ithaca, NY: Cornell University Press, 2012) (figure 4U).

120. Eli Saslow, "The Death Spiral of an American Family," *Washington Post*, at A1, A7, March 21, 2022, https://www.washingtonpost.com/nation/2022/03/20/intergenerational-wealth-middle-class-spiral/.

121. Katherine V. W. Stone, *From Widgets to Digits: Employment Regulation for the Changing Workplace* (New York: Cambridge University Press, 2004), 258.

122. See Smith, *Who Stole the American Dream?* xii–xvii (citing the conservative sociologist Charles Murray and the conservative radio commentator Rush Limbaugh as being in agreement on this point with the liberal economist Alan Krueger and the former AFL-CIO president Richard Trumka).

123. Smith, *Who Stole the American Dream*," xxiii (citing Pew Research Center, January 11, 2012, http://www.pewresearch.org).

124. Smith, *Who Stole the American Dream?*" xvi, xxiv. See also Thomas I. Palley, "America's Exhausted Paradigm: Macroeconomic Causes of the Financial Crisis and Great Recession," *New American Contract* (Washington, DC: New America Foundation, 2009), http://www.newamerica.net (explaining the role of robust consumer spending, and its erosion, to the health of the US economy).

125. Katherine Stone has reviewed the literature evaluating theories of the causes of income inequality, and particularly the claim that skill-biased technological change is to blame, That claim is that with technological change, some failed to obtain the skills needed to succeed economically in the new economy, resulting in their poverty,

So the solution is to provide education and training for the ill equipped. Stone shows that "a growing chorus of economists [have demonstrated] that skill-biased technological change cannot be the sole [or even the dominant] explanation for dramatically growing income dispersion." Nor can the shift from manufacturing to service industries explain this development. *See* Stone, *From Widgets to Digits*, 261–265 (collecting authority).

126. Paul C. Weiler, "A Principled Reshaping of Labor Law for the Twenty-first Century," *U. Pa. J. Lab. & Emp. L.* 3, no. 2 (2001): 177, 185.

127. See Jake Rosenfeld, *What Unions No Longer Do* (Cambridge, MA: Harvard University Press, 2014), 109; Windham, *Knocking on Labor's Door*, 16–17.

128. Weiler, "A Principled Reshaping of Labor Law," 186 (quoting the University of Chicago economist and Republican leader George Shultz).

129. Getman, *The Supreme Court on Unions*, 13 (explaining how seniority provides workers an enforceable claim for benefits acquired through their labor).

130. In the modern era, nearly all collective bargaining agreements have contained grievance-arbitration provisions to resolve contract disputes. See Getman, *The Supreme Court on Unions*, 189–190 (stating that "labor arbitration . . . replaced strikes, conflict and formal litigation with a system of private rules"). Implicitly or explicitly, the vast majority of collective bargaining agreements limit the employer's power to discharge. Summers, "Individual Protection against Unjust Dismissal," 481, 499n104.

131. Archibald Cox, "The Role of Law in Preserving Union Democracy," *Harv. L. Rev.* 72, no. 4 (1959): 609, 610.

132. See Stone, *From Widgets to Digits*, 197 (explaining how labor contract provisions have freed millions of workers from the whims of arbitrary superiors).

133. See Karl Frieden, "Workplace Democracy and Productivity," National Center for Economic Alternatives (1980), 19, 33–36, 40–41, 73. For contemporary use of self-managed worker teams, see Stone, *From Widgets to Digits*, 106, 167, 200–202.

134. Kochan et al., "Worker Voice in America," 31

135. Leiserson, *American Trade Union Democracy* 53.

136. Gus Tyler, "The Role of Trade Unions in a Democratic Society," *N.Y.U. Ann. Conf. on Lab.* 14 (1961): 277, 282.

137. See Chamberlain, *Labor*, 75.

138. See Bernstein, *Turbulent Years*, 446.

139. J. Goldstein, *The Government of British Trade Unions* (London: Allen & Unwin, 1952), 32, quoted in Peter Magrath, "Democracy in Overalls: The Futile Quest for Union Democracy," 12 *Indus. & Lab. Rel. Rev.* 12, no. 4 (1959): 503, 509.

140. Bronfenbrenner et al., "Introduction," 7.

141. Leonard R. Sayles and George. Strauss, *The Local Union: Its Place in the Industrial Plant* (New York: Harper & Bros., 1953), 7; Moore, *Industrial Relations and the Social Order*, 312; Hirschel Kasper, "The Size of the Bargaining Unit and the Locus of Union Power," *Q. Rev. Econ. & Bus.* 6 (1966): 59.

142. 397 U.S. 99 (1970).

143. See 397 U.S. 99 (1970), at 103–104. Also see *First Nat'l. Maint. Corp. v. NLRB*, 452 U.S. 666, 678 (1981) (collective bargaining "is premised on the belief that collective decisions backed by the parties' economic weapons will result in decisions that are better for both management and labor and for society as a whole.").

144. Wellington, *Labor and the Legal Process*, 28–29; Harry H. Wellington, "Union Democracy and Fair Representation: Federal Responsibility in a Federal System," *Yale L. J.* 67, no. 8 (1958): 1327, 1355–1356 n.146, 1358n159.

145. Clyde Summers, "Internal Relations between Trade Unions and Their Members," *Intl. Lab. Rev.* 91 (1965): 175, 177.

146. Bok and Dunlop, *Labor and the American Community*, 464–465 (also arguing that a union presence "helps to gain general acceptance for the rates of pay and . . . help[s] to persuade the worker that the conditions under which he labors are tolerably fair").

147. William Gomberg, "Government Participation in Union Regulation and Collective Bargaining," *Lab. L.J.* 13 (1962): 941.

148. Paul R. Hays, "The Union and Its Members," *N.Y.U. Ann. Conf. on Lab.* 11 (1958): 35, 44.

149. Gould, *Agenda for Reform*, 34 (making a case for private ordering of working conditions).

150. Seymour Martin Lipset, Martin Trow, and James S. Coleman, *Union Democracy: The Internal Politics of the International Typographical Union* (New York: Doubleday Anchor, 1956), 411–412. See also M. W. Reder, "Job Scarcity and the Nature of Union Power," *Indus. & Lab. Rel. Rev.* 13, no. 3 (1960): 361.

151. Stone, *From Widgets to Digits*, 197 (explaining the essential role of unions both at the workplace and in the political process).

152. Leiserson, *American Trade Union Democracy*, 315.

153. Moore, *Industrial Relations and the Social Order*, 315.

154. Bok and Dunlop, *Labor and the American Community*, 82; Jack Barbash, "Union Response to the 'Hard Line'," *Indus. Rel.* 1, no. 1 (1961): 25, 31.

155. For a review of labor's role in US presidential election campaigns, see Walter Galenson and Robert S. Smith, "The United States," in *Labor in the Twentieth Century*, ed. John T. Dunlop and Walter Galenson (Amsterdam: Elsevier, 1978), 50–57.

156. For a summary of these and other methods of union political action and education, see Bok and Dunlop, *Labor and the American Community*, 384–427, 465; Chamberlain, *Labor*, 117–125. For a discussion of unions' role in increasing members' political knowledge and generally fostering a more politically informed electorate, see David Macdonald, "How Labor Unions Increase Political Knowledge: Evidence from the United States," *Political Behavior* 43 (2019): 1.

157. See, for example, Walter Reuther, "The United Automobile Workers: Past, Present, and Future," *Va. L. Rev.* 50, no. 1 (1964): 58, 78.

158. Barbash, "Union Response to the 'Hard Line'," 25, 31. See also Chamberlain, *Labor*, 74–75. For a discussion of the proposition that unions are drawn inexorably to an economywide role of helping sever the connections between the inflation dynamic and such things as crises in energy and the environment, full or high employment, and high levels of consumer spending brought on by an affluent society, see Jack Barbash, "Labor Movement Theory and the Institutional Setting," *Monthly Lab. Rev.* 104, no. 9 (1981): 34.

159. *United States v. CIO*, 335 U.S. 106, 144 (1948) (concurring opinion).

160. Lipset et al., *Union Democracy*, 15. See Walter Galenson, "Communists and Trade Union Democracy," *Indus. Rel.* 13, no. 3 (1974): 228, 232.

161. Tyler, "The Role of Trade Unions in a Democratic Society," 287.

162. Blumrosen, "Group Interests in Labor Law," 432.

163. Daniel Bell, *The End of Ideology: On the Exhaustion of Political Ideas in the Fifties*, 208–221 (Cambridge, MA: Harvard University Press, 1960); Reuther, "The United Automobile Workers: Past, Present, and Future," 78.

164. See, for example, Gould, *Agenda for Reform*, 34.

165. See, for example, Bronfenbrenner et al., "Introduction," 7; Gould, *Agenda for reform*, 57–58; Stone, *From Widgets to Digits*, 123.

166. Penn Kemble, "Rediscovering American Labor," *Commentary* (April 1971), 45, 49.

167. See the discussion in Senator Brian Schatz, "Labor Unions," https://www.schatz.senate.gov/coronavirus/labor-unions.

168. Jack T. Conway, "New Challenges to Union Leadership," *Monthly Lab. Rev.* 92 (1969): 56.

169. Bronfenbrenner et al., "Introduction," 7 (discussing attempts by conservative legislators to roll back longstanding protective provisions of the Occupational Safety

and Health Act (OSHA), the Davis-Bacon Act, state workers' compensation laws, and the NLRA's ban on company unions).

170. Thomas Byrne Edsall, *The New Politics of Inequality* (New York: W. W. Norton & Co., 1984), 177.

171. See Bok and Dunlop, *Labor and the American Community*, 24.

172. "Labor Outlook," *Opinion Outlook*, February 23, 1981), 3, table 2.

173. Hertel-Fernandez et al., "What Forms of Representation Do American Workers Want?" 14–15 (emphasis added).

174. A. H. Raskin, "Management's Hard Line: 'Class War' or Labor's Chance to Reform?" *Monthly Lab. Rev.* 102, no. 2 (1979): 34, 36.

Chapter 3

1. This chapter title was inspired by Hedrick Smith, *Who Stole the American Dream?* (New York: Random House, 2012), 6. The phrase comprising the chapter title originates in the work of Ted Nace, *Gangs of America: The Risa of Corporate Power and the Disabling of Democracy* (San Francisco: Berrett-Koehler, 2002) and is used to describe the early 1970s political revolt by corporate America's leaders to put the US on a new political track that would be more favorable to business.

2. James A. Gross, *Broken Promises: The Subversion of U.S. Labor Relations Policy, 1947–1994* (Philadelphia: Temple University Press, 1995), 234 (blaming excessive government regulation and intervention for slow economic growth, diminished productivity increases, unemployment, inadequate savings and investment, and international trade problems).

3. Thomas Byrne Edsall, *The New Politics of Inequality* (New York: W. W. Norton, 1984), 107.

4. See the discussion in Smith, *Who Stole the American Dream?* xiii–xiv, 6–11; David Vogel, *Fluctuating Fortunes: The Political Power of Business in America* (New York: Basic Books, 1989; see chapter 8).

5. Edsall, *The New Politics of Inequality*, 117 (stating that these business-funded think tanks "functioned to lay the scholarly and theoretical groundwork for a major shift in public policy favoring business and higher-bracket taxpayers"); Smith, *Who Stole the American Dream?* 133 (stating that of the $3.5 billion spent on lobbying between 2009 to 2010, 67 percent was spent by business interests and that as early as 2006, business lobbyists outnumbered labor lobbyists 30:1).

6. Gross, *Broken Promises*, 196, 234–241.

7. Gross, *Broken Promises*, 204–205.

8. Edsall, *The New Politics of Inequality*, 120–121.

9. For the specifics of the LLRG's proposed amendments, see Lane Windham, *Knocking on Labor's Door: Union Organizing in the 1970s and the Roots of a New Economic Divide* (Chapel Hill: University of North Carolina Press, 2017), 61–65.

10. Gross, *Broken Promises*, 218. The 1974 midterm elections raised the Democratic margin in the House from 243–192 to 291–144 and in the Senate from 57–43 to 62–38, and these margins held through the 1976 election of President Jimmy Carter. Edsall, *The New Politics of Inequality*, 36.

11. The following discussion of the PR effort of the LLRG and its long-lasting effects is taken from Gross, *Broken Promises*, 201, 205–216, 235–236.

12. Windham, *Knocking on Labor's Door*, 63 (explaining that the PR firm drafted anti-union memos to newspaper editors and women's clubs and gathered research material for use in an investigative report).

13. Gross, *Broken Promises*, 214–216, 237 (also showing that in 1976, in opposing union proposals for labor law reform, "[t]he business lobbyists' campaign concentrated on public portrayals of the bill as the creation of power-grabbing union bosses").

14. Gross, *Broken Promises*, 216.

15. Gross, *Broken Promises*, 236 (also stating that this success in besmirching the labor movement accounts for the failure of labor law reform efforts in Congress over the years).

16. See Neil Ulman, "Companies Fight Harder against Labor Attempts to Organize Employees," *Wall Street Journal*, January 19, 1966, 1.

17. Cynthia L. Estlund, "The Ossification of American Labor Law," *Columbia L. Rev* 102, no. 6 (2002): 1527, 1529–1530.

18. See Katherine V. W. Stone, *From Widgets to Digits: Employment Regulation for the Changing Workplace* (New York: Cambridge University Press, 2004), 260. In addition, some scholars have pointed to the difficulty of organizing recent immigrants from Asia and Central and South America, and also highly technical workers, due to lack of expertise among unions to effectively organize high-tech workers. See, for example, William B. Gould IV, *Agenda for Reform: The Future of Employment Relationships and the Law* (Cambridge, MA: MIT Press, 1996), 18–19.

19. See a discussion of the industrial production system that was dominant through most of the twentieth century in Stone, *From Widgets to Digits*, 5, 47–48, 52–53, 62, 70.

20. Gould *Agenda for Reform*, 12–13, 35.

21. Edsall, *The New Politics of Inequality*, 143–144. See also Julius G. Getman, *The Supreme Court on Unions: Why Labor Law Is Failing American Workers* (Ithaca, NY: Cornell/ILR Press, 2016), 194–195.

22. Michael Goldfield and Amy Bromsen, "The Changing Landscape of U.S. Unions in Historical and Theoretical Perspective," *Annual Rev. of Pol. Sci.* 16 (2013): 231, 234, https://doi.org/10.1146/annurev-polisci-032211-214003. See also Michael Goldfield, *The Decline of Organized Labor in the United States* (Chicago: University of Chicago Press, 1987) (showing that changes in the labor force structure account for a small fraction of union decline).

23. Windham, *Knocking on Labor's Door*, 58–59 (noting, for example, that "[a] new breed of container ship . . . increased cargo capacity fivefold over the 1970s and brought competitors to newly expanded U.S. ports").

24. The following discussion of the abandonment of "internal labor markets" and the substitution of a more flexible digital workplace relies extensively on Stone, *From Widgets to Digits*, ix, 4–6, 47–48, 51–53, 67–116.

25. Stone, *From Widgets to Digits*, 86 (explaining the primary cause of changes in the contemporary employment relationship).

26. See Arne L. Kalleberg, *Good Jobs, Bad Jobs: The Rise of Polarized and Precarious Employment Systems in the United States, 1970s to 2000s* (New York: Russel Sage Foundation, 2011).

27. David Weil, *The Fissured Workplace: Why Work Became So Bad for So Many and What Can Be Done to Improve It* (Cambridge, MA: Harvard University Press, 2014). He defines "fissuring" as corporations splitting off certain core functions that previously had been managed internally. Weil, *The Fissured Workplace,* at 3–4.

28. Nonstandard working arrangements such as freelance and contract work, sometimes are referred to as the "gig economy." See Emily Hong, "Making It Work: A Closer Look at the Gig Economy," *Pac. Standard,* October 23, 2015 https://psmag.com/economics/making-it-work-a-closer-look-at-the-gig-economy.

29. See Erin Elizabeth Hatton, *The Temp Economy: From Kelly Girls to Permatemps in Postwar America* (Philadelphia: Temple University Press, 2011).

30. Katherine V. W. Stone, *From Widgets to Digits: Employment Regulation for the Changing Workplace* (New York: Cambridge University Press, 2004), 68.

31. US Gov't Accountability Office, GAO-15–168R, "Contingent Workforce: Size, Characteristics, Earnings, and Benefits" (2015), https://www.gao.gov/assets/670/669899.pdf.

32. Matthew Ginsburg, "Nothing New under the Sun: 'The New Labor Law' Must Still Grapple with the Traditional Challenges of Firm-Based Organizing and Building Self-sustainable Worker Organizations," *Yale L.J. Forum* 126 (2017): 488, citing Anthony Caruso, US Census Bureau, "Statistics of U.S. Businesses Employment and Payroll Summary: 2012," 1 (2015), http://www.census.gov/content/dam/Census/library/publications/2015/econ/g12-susb.pdf, which states that 51.6 percent of employees worked for large enterprises in 2012, a figure that has increased steadily since 2004.

33. See Windham, *Knocking on Labor's Door*, 81 (explaining that with the advent of global competition, US employers "believed that they needed to deflect [the] surge in union organizing in order . . . to gain more control in a rapidly changing economy").

34. This is not to suggest that unions themselves have not contributed to their own decline. The corruption among some in the union movement in the 1950s has had a lingering negative effect on the public opinion of unions. See, for example, Gould, *Agenda for Reform*, 31 (also noting that the "tardy adherence to civil rights" by some unions), and Getman, *The Supreme Court on Unions*, 11. And, although many unions during and after the 1970s vigorously attempted to organize, some unions during the critical decade of the 1980s and 1990s became complacent, but by the end of the 1990s, organizing again became a priority for most unions. See the discussion in Windham, *Knocking on Labor's Door*, 6, 25–26. Thomas Edsall makes a convincing case that labor was unprepared for the attack by business that began in the mid-1970s. The "thirty-year entente cordiale" of cooperative dealings with business prior to the mid-1970s had lulled union leaders into a false sense of security that the era of hostile labor-management relations had ended. These union leaders were slow to realize that "a raft of chief executives from the Fortune 500—men whom the unions had come to think of almost as allies"—had joined with the traditionally virulently anti-union corporations in an all-out assault undermining the base of organized labor. By 1980, the AFL-CIO, "working with twenty-nine member unions, put together [a] $1 million [organizing campaign, and] in 1982 the AFL-CIO set up the Labor Institute of Public Affairs with an annual budget of $2 million, which in 1983 began producing prolabor television programs . . . designed, in part, to counter the proliferation of business-financed [television programming]." See Edsall, *The New Politics of Inequality*, 155–156, 168.

35. Stone, *From Widgets to Digits*, 291 (explaining why, in the digital era, "unions are more necessary than ever").

Chapter 4

1. This and subsequent chapters begin by listing the labor law reforms needed to address the deficiencies in the current law that the chapter discusses. Each chapter begins by providing citations to the sections of the Protecting the Right to Organize Act (PRO Act), pending before Congress as of the beginning of 2023, that provides for that reform. The chapter's focus is on the reform needed; the reference to the PRO Act is for the convenience of readers who might want to look at the discussion of the needed reform to examples of specific legislative language that provides that reform. The bill has not yet been enacted, but President Joe Biden, in his State of the Union address on February 7, 2023, urged Congress to do so.

2. NLRA §§ 1 & 2 (29 U.S.C. §§ 151 & 152(3)).

3. See NLRA § 2(3), 29 U.S.C. 152(3).

4. See Charley Richardson, "The Role of Technology in Undermining Union Strength," in *Restoring the Promise of American Labor Law*, ed. Sheldon Friedman et al. (Ithaca, NY: ILR Press, 1994), 233.

5. See, for example, *Meyers Industries (Meyers II)*, 281 N.L.R.B. 882 (1986), *aff'd sub nom Prill v. NLRB*, 835 F.2d 1481 (D.C. Cir. 1987) (holding that an activity, whether by unionized or nonunion employees, is concerted when an employee acts "with or on the authority of other employees, and not solely by and on behalf of the employee himself").

6. *Epilepsy Found. of N. Ohio v. NLRB*, 268 F.3d 1095, 1096 (D.C. Cir. 2001).

7. See, for example, Lafe E. Solomon, "Report of the Acting General Counsel Concerning Social Media Cases," General Counsel Memorandum No. 11–74 (Aug. 18, 2011) (concluding that a "conversation [on Facebook] among coworkers about job performance and staffing level issues was . . . concerted activity").

8. See Julius G. Getman, *The Supreme Court on Unions: Why Labor Law Is Failing American Workers* (Ithaca, NY: Cornell /ILR Press, 2016), 137; Tanya Goldman and David Weil, "Who's Responsible Here? Establishing Legal Responsibility in the Fissured Workplace," *Berkeley J. Emp. & Lab. L.* 42 (2021): 55, 72n86 (citing Ira Katznelson, *Fear Itself: The New Deal and the Origins of Our Time* (New York: Liveright, 2014).

9. See Terri Gerstein, "State and Local Workers' Rights' Innovations: New Players, New Laws, New Methods of Enforcement," *St. Louis U. L.J.* 65, no. 1 (2020): 45, 47 (citing *inter alia* David Cooper, "Workers of Color Are Far More Likely to Be Paid Poverty-Level Wages than White Workers" *Econ. Pol'y Inst.*, June 21, 2018, https://www.epi.org/blog/workers-of-color-are-far-more-likely-to-be-paid-poverty-level-wages-than-white-workers/; Annette Bernhardt et al., "Broken Laws, Unprotected Workers: Violations of Employment and Labor Laws in America's Cities," *Nat'l Emp. L. Project*, September 21, 2009, https://www.nelp.org/wp-content/uploads/2015/03/BrokenLawsReport2009.pdf; Tsedeye Gebreselassie and Laura Huizar, "What a $15 Minimum Wage Means for Women and Workers of Color," *Nat'l Emp. L. Project*, December 13, 2016, https://www.nelp.org/wp-content/uploads/Policy-Brief-15-Minimum-Wage-Women-Workers-of-Color.pdf).

10. Benjamin I. Sachs, "Labor Law Renewal," *Harv. L. & Pol'y Rev.* 1 (2007): 375, 383–384.

11. Sachs, "Labor Law Renewal," 384.

12. These amendments reversed the results of two Supreme Court decisions, *NLRB v. Hearst Publications*, 322 U.S. 111 (1944), which held that "employee" status was to be determined by an inquiry into a worker's economic dependency on the employer, not by application of common-law standards for the status of "employee" versus "independent contractor"; and *Packard v. NLRB*, 330 U.S. 485 (1947), which held that

supervisors (foremen) were "employees," and accordingly had the right to demand that the employer recognize and bargain with a union representing them.

13. Sachs, "Labor Law Renewal," 384.

14. Investigations by both federal and state governmental agencies have demonstrated the significant incidence of misclassification of workers. See, for example, US Government Accountability Office, "Employee Misclassification: Improved Coordination, Outreach, and Targeting Could Ensure Detection and Prevention" (August 2009), https://www.gao.gov/assets/300/293679.pdf; Francoise Carré, "Independent Contractor Misclassification," *Econ. Pol'y. Inst.*, 1–2 (June 8, 2015), https://files.epi.org/pdf/87595.pdf (citing state-level data substantiating misclassification estimates in the range of 10 percent to 20 percent of employers that misclassify at least once and an even higher incidence in the construction industry, where misclassification is most profitable due to cost savings from avoiding payment of high worker compensation premiums because workers are independent contractors rather than employees).

15. Lance Compa, "Report Unfair Advantage: Workers' Freedom of Association in the United States under International Human Rights Standards," *Human Rights Watch* (2000); see the text accompanying notes 11 and 12, https://www.hrw.org/reports/2000/uslabor/index.htm#TopOfPage.

16. See *Velox Express, Inc.*, 368 N.L.R.B. No. 61 (August 29, 2019). In 2021, the general counsel of the NLRB indicated an intent to request that the Board reconsider its decision in *Velox*. As of now, *Velox* remains the controlling precedent. See *Memorandum GC 21–04*, 2021 WL 3662454 (N.L.R.B.G.C.). However, it is widely anticipated that sometime in 2023, the NLRB is likely to reverse the decision and rule that independent contractor misclassification, by itself, is an unfair labor practice. See Todd Lebowitz, "Who Is My Employee? Exploring Issues of Independent Contractor Misclassification & Joint Employment Issues (December 27, 2022), https://whoismyemployee.com/.

17. The following facts can be found at *SuperShuttle DFW, Inc. (Amalgamated Transit Union, Local No. 1338)*, 367 N.L.R.B. No. 75 (2019).

18. See, for example, Goldman and Weil, "Who's Responsible Here? Establishing Legal Responsibility," 57–58 (summarizing the conversion of employees to independent contractors by Dynamex, a nationwide courier and delivery service "offering on-demand pickup and delivery to individual and businesses such as Office Depot and Home Depot").

19. See the discussion in *SuperShuttle DFW, Inc. (Amalgamated Transit Union, Local No. 1338)*, 367 N.L.R.B. No. 75, at *26–27 (member McFerran, dissenting).

20. See *SuperShuttle DFW, Inc. (Amalgamated Transit Union, Local No. 1338)*, 367 N.L.R.B. No. 75, at *6.

21. See *SuperShuttle DFW, Inc. (Amalgamated Transit Union, Local No. 1338)*, 367 N.L.R.B. No. 75, at *27 (member McFerran, dissenting).

22. See *SuperShuttle DFW, Inc. (Amalgamated Transit Union, Local No. 1338)*, 367 N.L.R.B. No. 75, at *19.

23. See *SuperShuttle DFW, Inc. (Amalgamated Transit Union, Local No. 1338)*, 367 N.L.R.B. No. 75, at *28 (member McFerran, dissenting).

24. Goldman and Weil, "Who's Responsible Here? Establishing Legal Responsibility," 58.

25. David Weil, "Understanding the Present and Future of Work in the Fissured Workplace Context," *RSF: The Russell Sage Foundation J. Soc. Sciences* 5, no. 5 (2019): 149.

26. See *SuperShuttle DFW, Inc. (Amalgamated Transit Union, Local No. 1338)*, 367 N.L.R.B. No. 75 (2019).

27. Karen Kosanovich, "Workers in Alternative Employment Arrangements," US Bureau of Labor Statistics (November 2018), 2, https://www.bls.gov/spotlight/2018/workers-in-alternative-employment-arrangements/home.htm.

28. Weil, "Understanding the Present and Future of Work," 149. See Jonathan P. Hiatt, "Policy Issues Concerning the Contingent Work Force," *Wash. & Lee L. Rev.* 52, no. 3 (1995): 739, 749 (explaining that misclassification of employees as independent contractors benefits employers by permitting them to avoid both payment of "benefits and worker compensation premiums" and payment of the Federal Insurance Contributions Act and other tax contributions on behalf of its employees).

29. See Weil, "Understanding the Present and Future of Work," 149–151.

30. See Weil, "Understanding the Present and Future of Work," 147–165.

31. David Weil, *The Fissured Workplace: Why Work Became So Bad for So Many and What Can Be Done to Improve It* (Cambridge, MA: Harvard University Press, 2014), 3–4.

32. Weil, "Understanding the Present and Future of Work," 148.

33. Weil, "Understanding the Present and Future of Work," 148.

34. See the discussion in Hiatt, "Policy Issues Concerning the Contingent Work Force," 742; Lance Compa, *Unfair Advantage: Workers' Freedom of Association in the United States under International Human Rights Standards* (Ithaca, NY: Cornell University Press, 2000), 164–175; see the text accompanying note 15, http://www.jstor.org/stable/10.7591/j.ctv3mt98x.4.

35. Matthew Dey, Susan N. Houseman, and Anne Elise Polivka, "What Do We Know about Contracting Out in the United States? Evidence from Household and Establishment Surveys," in *Labor in the New Economy*, ed. Katharine Abraham et al. (Chicago: University of Chicago Press, 2010), 267.

36. See Sanjukta Paul, "Fissuring and the Firm Exemption," *Law & Contemp. Probs.* 82, no. 2 (2019): 65, 76 (explaining that today, trucking companies "buy truck-driving services from individuals whom they characterize as independent contractors, and they sell trucking services to their customers [and while] they typically have a few administrative employees, . . . their core product is not only made by independent contractors, it is the very service performed by those individuals [and] other than obtaining contracts with customers and bargaining those contracts, such a firm usually does not do much else"). For a discussion of the delivery of goods by independent contractors from ports to warehouses, see Compa, "Report: Unfair Advantage," the text accompanying note 17.

37. Compa, "Report: Unfair Advantage"; see the text accompanying note 21 (also reporting that "[c]argo firms have reacted to truckers' efforts to improve pay and conditions by renewed organizing and bargaining with refusals to bargain, blacklisting, and discrimination against organizing leaders. Excluded from coverage by the NLRA, these workers have no recourse. Employers even threaten to sue the workers under antitrust laws, accusing them of price-fixing for their services.").

38. Brishen Rogers, "Employment Rights in the Platform Economy: Getting Back to Basics," *Harv. L. & Pol'y Rev.* 10 (2016): 479, 480 (citing "The Rise of the Platform Enterprise: A Global Survey, Ctr. For Global Enterprise," January 7, 2016, https://thecge.net/the-center-for-global-enterprise-releases-first-globalplatformsurvey-valuing-platform-based-companies-at-4-3-trillion/ [https://perma.cc/QBS7-A8UZ] (outlining the global growth of the "platform economy")).

39. See, for example, *FedEx Home Delivery v. NLRB*, 563 F.3d 492 (D.C. Cir. 2009) (refusal to bargain by a company with the International Brotherhood of Teamsters claiming that drivers are independent contractors, where the NLRB held that they were employees, but the D.C. Circuit Court of Appeals held that they were independent contractors).

40. See the discussion in Weil, "Understanding the Present and Future of Work," 154–155.

41. Weil, "Understanding the Present and Future of Work," 155 (reporting that other investigators have found a wage penalty as a result of a subcontracting of 4 percent to 7 percent for janitors and 8 percent to 24 percent for security guards).

42. See *NLRB v. United Ins. Co.*, 390 U.S. 254, 256; See also *St. Joseph News Press*, 345 N.L.R.B. 474, 478 (2005) ("Supreme Court precedent 'teaches us not only that the common law of agency is the standard to measure employee status but also that we have no authority to change it.'") (quoting Dial-A-Mattress Operating Corp., 326 N.L.R.B. 884, 894 (1998)). Prior to the 1947 Taft-Hartley amendments to the NLRA, the Supreme Court had upheld the NLRB's view that newsboys who sold newspapers for the Hearst Corporation were "employees" because they were "economically dependent" on Hearst, rejecting the court of appeals view that "employee"

was to be determined by application of factors found in the common law and that, applying those standards, the newsboys were independent contractors. See *NLRB v. Hearst Publications*, 322 U.S. 111, 117 (1944).

43. The applicable factors include (1) the extent of control that the employing entity exercises over the details of the work; (2) whether the individual is engaged in a distinct occupation or work; (3) the kind of occupation, including whether, in the locality in question, the work is usually done under the employer's direction or by a specialist without supervision; (4) the skill required in the particular occupation (with low-skilled work suggesting the status of "employee" rather than "independent contractor"); (5) whether the employer or the individual supplies the instrumentalities, tools, and place of work for the worker; (6) the length of time that the individual is employed (increased duration suggesting employee status); (7) the method of payment, whether by the time or by the job; (8) whether the work in question is part of the employer's regular business (including whether the worker has an independent business other than providing work for the lead company); (9) whether the parties believe they are creating an employment relationship; and (10) whether the principal itself is in business. See *Restatement (Second) of Agency* § 220(2).

44. See the discussion in Stephen F. Befort, "Revisiting the Black Hole of Workplace Regulation: A Historical and Comparative Perspective of Contingent Work," *J. Emp. & Lab. L.* 24 (2003): 153, 166, 168.

45. Goldman and Weil, "Who's Responsible Here? Establishing Legal Responsibility," 73 (summarizing some of the criticisms of the common law test for "independent contractor" status as "insufficiently predictive, an improper proxy, under-inclusive, and evaluating the wrong factors in the working relationship [to identify] which workers are so economically dependent on their employers that they require the protections of labor and employment law").

46. *FedEx Home Delivery v. NLRB*, 563 F.3d 492 (D.C. Cir. 2009).

47. *FedEx Home Delivery v. NLRB*, 563 F.3d at 497 (emphasis added).

48. *FedEx Home Delivery v. NLRB*, 563 F.3d at 503 (emphasis added).

49. *FedEx Home Delivery*, 361 N.L.R.B. 610, 620 (2014) (emphasis added).

50. *FedEx Home Delivery v. NLRB*, 849 F.3d 1123 (D.C. Cir. 2017).

51. 765 F.3d 981 (9th Cir. 2014) (applying California common law).

52. 367 N.L.R.B. No. 75 (2019).

53. *SuperShuttle DFW*, 367 N.L.R.B. No. 75, at 3, fn. 4 (emphasis added). But see Hunter Igoe, "I Know It When I See It," 38 *Hofstra Lab. & Empl. L. J.* 285, 310 (2021) (stating that just months after *SuperShuttle*, in *Velox Express*, "the Board . . . resurrected entrepreneurial opportunity . . . not merely . . . as a factor, but instead used it as a 'prism' to

view all the other factors [and concluding that using] entrepreneurial opportunity in this way has no practical difference than using it as an "animating" principle").

54. As the dissent explained, through the nonnegotiable franchise agreement, SuperShuttle prohibited the drivers from working for other transportation companies, and even with respect to their own work for SuperShuttle, the drivers may not arrange for a substitute or surrogate without SuperShuttle's approval, and "[a]t the time of the hearing, only 1 of 88 drivers employed a relief driver. SuperShuttle DFW, 367 N.L.R.B. No. 75, at 3, fn. 4.

55. 371 N.L.R.B. No. 45 (2021).

56. Goldman and Weil, "Who's Responsible Here? Establishing Legal Responsibility," 78.

57. Robert Sprague, "Updating Legal Norms for a Precarious Workforce," *ABA J. Lab. & Emp. L.* 35 (2020): 85, 101n83.

58. See, for example, *Athol Daily News v. Bd. of Div. of Emp. & Training*, 786 N.E.2d 365, 369–370 (Mass 2003) ("The employer bears the burden of proof, and, because the conditions are conjunctive, its failure to demonstrate any one of the criteria set forth in subsections [A, B, or C], suffices to establish that the services in question constitute 'employment'").

59. See Assemb. Bill 5, § 2, 2019–2020 Sess. (Cal. 2019) (codified at Cal. Lab. Code § 2750.3; effective January 1, 2020). Subsequently, by referendum, California voters in November 2020, exempted some ride-share drivers, resulting in Uber and Lyft drivers in California remaining contractors. But see "Time Is Money: A Quick Wage-Hour Tip on . . . Independent Contractor Classification," *Nat. L. Rev.*, 11, December 2, 2021 (reporting that "[i]n August 2021, a California state court found the law unconstitutional, and a coalition of the companies that funded Prop 22 planned an appeal). See the discussion in Goldman and Weil, "Who's Responsible Here? Establishing Legal Responsibility," 78.

60. Goldman and Weil, "Who's Responsible Here? Establishing Legal Responsibility," 103.

61. Sprague, "Updating Legal Norms for a Precarious Workforce," 102.

62. *People of the State of California v. Uber Techs., Inc. & Lyft, Inc.*, Case No. CGC-20–584402 (S.F. Sup. Ct. August 11, 2020); *People v. Uber Techs., Inc.*, 56 Cal. App. 5th 266 (October 22, 2020) (affirming trial court's order preliminarily enjoining the defendant from classifying drivers as independent contractors and violating any provisions of the Labor Code). See also *Cunningham v. Lyft, Inc.*, No. 1:19-cv-11974-IT, 2020 WL 2616302 (D. Mass. May 22, 2020) (focusing on whether drivers' services were integral to the employer's usual course of business for the purposes of part B of the ABC test, and stating that courts are to reject a company's "self-labeling" and instead inquire into the

realities of the business; and, doing that with respect to Lyft, concluding that where riders pay Lyft for rides, the business encompasses the transportation of riders). The lower court's preliminary injunction was stayed pending appeal. See Appellate Courts Case Information, *California v. Uber Techs., Inc.,* No. A160706, Order Filed August 20, 2020, https://appellatecases.courtinfo.ca.gov/search/case/dockets.cfm?dist=1&doc_id=2325037&doc_no=A160706&request_token=NiIwLSEmXkw3WyApSCM9SExJQDw6UVxfJSJeWzpS%3D%3D.

63. Order on People's Motion for Preliminary Injunction and Related Motions, *California v. Uber Techs., Inc.,* at 23–26. See also the discussion in Sprague, "Updating Legal Norms for a Precarious Workforce," 102.

64. See Goldman and Weil, "Who's Responsible Here? Establishing Legal Responsibility," 111 (pointing out that the ABC test can in some cases be overinclusive in designating persons as employees rather than independent contractors, especially where one operates a truly independent business, such as a barber who works on the premises of another person by renting a chair in a barber shop, has her own customers who will move with her should she rent a chair on a different premises, but might be viewed as performing services that are integral to the normal operations of the enterprise that owns the barber shop. Accordingly, the California legislature addressed this by enacting legislation containing carve-outs excluding certain professions and occupations from application of the ABC test—Cal. Lab. Code §§ 2750.3(a)-(b) (West 2020).). The NLRB could create similar carve-outs, either by decision or regulation.

65. NLRA § 2(11), 29 U.S.C. 152(11). Section 2(11) defines a "supervisor" as "any individual having authority, in the interest of the employer, to hire, transfer, suspend, lay off, recall, promote, discharge, *assign*, reward, discipline other employees, or *responsibly to direct them*, or to adjust their grievance, or effectivity to recommend such action, if in connection with the foregoing the exercise of such authority is not of a merely routine or clerical nature, but requires the use of independent judgment" (emphasis added).

66. NLRA § 2(11), 29 U.S.C. 152(11) (emphasis added).

67. The PRO Act, for example, proposes each of these changes. See PRO Act, § 101(c).

68. See the discussion in *NLRB v. Kentucky River Community Care, Inc. (Kentucky River),* 532 U.S. 706, 718 (2001). See also *Douglas Aircraft Co.,* 50 N.L.R.B. 784, 787 (1943) (stating the pre-1947 test of "supervisor").

69. *Kentucky River,* 532 U.S. at 718.

70. Craig Becker and Diana Orantes Ceresi, "Toward a Rational Interpretation of the Term 'Supervisor' after Kentucky River," *Lab. Law.* 18 (2003): 385.

71. Richardson, "The Role of Technology in Undermining Union Strength," 234.

72. *Holly Farms Corp. v. NLRB,* 517 U.S. 392, 399 (1996) (cited in Becker and Ceresi, "Toward a Rational Interpretation of the Term 'Supervisor,'" 386).

73. NLRB, *Legislative History of the Labor-Management Relations Act, 1947* 410 (1985) (Senate Committee Report).

74. See *NLRB v. Health Care & Retirement Corp. of America*, 511 U.S. 571, 579–580 (1994).

75. See *Kentucky River*, 532 U.S. at 708.

76. Getman, *The Supreme Court on Unions*, 143 (describing the Court's understanding of the nursing profession as an "unsustainable vision of reality").

77. *Oakwood Health Care*, 348 N.L.R.B. 686, 687 (2006).

78. Ronald Meisburg, "Memorandum Concerning *Oakwood Healthcare, Inc.*, 34 NLRB No. 37 (2006), and Related Cases," *Memorandum GC 07–05*, 2007 WL 1108896. (N.L.R.B.G.C.).

79. Meisburg, Memorandum Concerning *Oakwood Healthcare, Inc.*, 9.

80. See Getman, *The Supreme Court on Unions*, 145 (stating that the NLRB majority in *Oakland Health Care* refused to consider the consequences of its decision in terms of the many nurses the decision excluded from the act's protections).

81. *Oakwood Health Care*, 348 N.L.R.B. 686, 700 (2006) (members Liebman and Walsh dissenting in part and concurring in part on the result).

82. American Association of Colleges of Nursing, "Nursing Fact Sheet" (last updated September 2022), https://www.aacnnursing.org/news-Information/fact-sheets/nursing-fact-sheet.

83. Tera Rowland, "The Pros and Cons of Nursing Unions," *Soliant Blog,* August 26, 2020, https://blog.soliant.com/nursing/the-pros-and-cons-of-nursing-unions/.

84. Scott Silverman, "The Impact of Recent NLRB Decisions on Supervisory Status," *Lab. Law.* 23, no. 1 (2007): 11, 17.

85. Compa, "Report: Unfair Advantage"; see the text accompanying note 24.

86. *Ten Broeck Commons*, 320 N.L.R.B. 806, 809–810 (1996).

87. Hiba Hafiza, "Structural Labor Rights," *Mich. L. Rev.* 119, no. 4 (2021): 651, 679.

88. *Velox Express, Inc.*, 368 N.L.R.B. No. 61 (2019).

89. See, for example, *American Freightways Co.*, 124 N.L.R.B. 146, 147 (1959) ("[I]nterference, restraint, and coercion under Section 8(a)(1) of the Act does not turn on the employer's motive or on whether the coercion succeeded or failed. The test is whether the employer engaged in conduct which, it may reasonably be said, tends to interfere with the free exercise of employee rights under the Act").

90. See *Sisters' Camelot*, 363 N.L.R.B 162, 167 (2015).

91. See *Parexel International, LLC*, 356 N.L.R.B. 516, 518–519 (2011).

92. *Velox Express, Inc.*, 368 N.L.R.B. No. 61, at *7.

93. *Velox Express, Inc.*, 368 N.L.R.B. No. 61 (member McFerran dissenting).

94. See, for example, Julia H. Weaver, "Two Sides of the Same Coin: Examining the Misclassification of Workers as Independent Contractors," *Ga. L. Rev.* 55, no. 3 (2021): 1355 (arguing that misclassification should be viewed as a violation of § 8(a)(1) of the NLRA).

95. See, for example, § 104 (c) of the PRO Act.

96. 362 N.L.R.B. 1599 (2015), *enfd. in part, Browning-Ferris Indus. of Cal. v. N.L.R.B.*, 911 F.3d 1195, 1211, 1216 (D.C. Cir. 2018).

97. NLRB Employer Status under the National Labor Relations Act, 85 Fed. Reg. 111, 84 (February 26, 2020) (codified at 29 C.F.R. pt. 103); see also 29 C.F.R. § 103.40 (2020).

98. See Michael Grabell, "The Expendables: How the Temps Who Power Corporate Giants Are Getting Crushed," *Propublica: Temp Land,* June 27, 2013, https://www.propublica.org/article/the-expendables-how-the-temps-who-power-corporate-giants-are-getting-crushe (citing many instances. of supposedly "temporary" employees who have worked for the same employer for long periods of time).

99. US Bureau of Labor Statistics, "What Happened to Temps? Changes since the Great Recession," *Monthly Lab. Rev.* (February 2021) (table 2), https://www.bls.gov/opub/mlr/2021/article/temp-help.htm.

100. Grabell, "The Expendables" (explaining that "[i]n some lines of work, huge numbers of full-time workers have been replaced by temps. One in five manual laborers who move and pack merchandise is now a temp. As is one in six assemblers who work in a team, such as those at auto plants").

101. US Bureau of Labor Statistics, "What Happened to Temps?"

102. *Boire v. Greyhound Corp.*, 376 U.S. 473, 481 (1964) (concluding that a putative joint employer must "possess[] sufficient control over the work of the employees to qualify as a joint employer[stressing that this inquiry] is essentially factual, and is not controlled by the fact that one putative employer is an independent contractor of another" (internal quotation marks omitted)).

103. See, for example, *Bethlehem-Fairfield Shipyard, Inc.*, 53 N.L.R.B. 1428, 1428–1431 (1943). (A restaurant company that managed cafeterias within a shipyard operated by Bethlehem-Fairfield found to be a joint with Bethlehem, where restaurant company supervised cafeteria workers and controlled their conditions of employment and "in practice, [the employees were] not controlled or supervised by Bethlehem." but joint employer status found based on powers found the contract between Bethlehem and restaurant company permitting Bethlehem to control restaurant workers' conditions of employment, such as insisting on the discharge of any employee and the power to

approve the employees' wage rates, even though Bethlehem had never actually exercised these powers).

104. *Airborne Express*, 338 N.L.R.B. 597, 597 n.1 (2002).

105. 362 N.L.R.B. 1599 (2015).

106. James van Wagtendonk, "Is There an Employer in the House? Evaluating the National Labor Relations Board's Joint-Employer Standard in the Fissured Health Care Workplace," *B.U. L. Rev.* 98, no. 4 (2018): 1105, 1113, 1116.

107. Van Wagtendonk, "Is There an Employer in the House?" 1117.

108. The NLRB during President Barack Obama's administration announced its intention to review the joint-employer standard and requested comments and amici briefs on the subject. *Browning-Ferris Industries of California, Inc.*, 362 N.L.R.B. 1599, 1599 (2015).

109. *Browning-Ferris Industries. of California, Inc. v. N.L.R.B.*, 911 F.3d 1195, 1211, 1213–1218, 1222–1223 (D.C. Cir. 2018) (but denying enforcement with respect to "the Board's articulation and application of the indirect-control element in this case to the extent that it failed to distinguish between indirect control that the common law of agency considers intrinsic to ordinary third-party contracting relationships, and indirect control over the essential terms and conditions of employment," and recognizing that *Browning-Ferris* did not present the issue of whether either indirect control or a contractually reserved but unexercised right to control can be dispositive of joint-employer status absent evidence of exercised direct and immediate control).

110. *Browning-Ferris Industries. of California, Inc. v. N.L.R.B.*, 911 F.3d, at 1216.

111. Savannah Warner, "Employers Now Liable for Acts of Sub-contractors," *Corp. Couns. Rev.* 38 (2019): 161, 162.

112. 365 N.L.R.B. No. 156 (2017), *vacated* 366 N.L.R.B. No. 26 (2018) (concluding that "indirect control or contractually-reserved (but [un]exercised) authority is probative of joint-employer status only to the extent that it supplements and reinforces evidence of direct control).

113. *Hy-Brand Industrial Contractor's, LTD.*, 366 N.L.R.B. No. 26 (2018).

114. NLRB Employer Status Under the National Labor Relations Act, 85 Fed. Reg. 111, 84 (February 26, 2020) (codified at 29 C.F.R. pt. 103); see also 29 C.F.R. § 103.40 (2020). The Trump NLRB's final administrative regulation establishes the standards for determining whether two employers are a joint employer under the NLRA. Under this final rule, "an entity may be considered a joint employer of a separate employer's employees only if the two share or codetermine the employees' essential terms and conditions of employment, which are exclusively defined as wages, benefits, hours of work, hiring, discharge, discipline, supervision, and direction."

115. See NLRB, Standard for Determining Joint-Employer Status, 87 FR 54641 (September 6, 2022, codified at 29 CFR Part 103). To further confuse matters, in the summer of 2022, the D.C. Circuit reconfirmed its view that "the *failure* to consider reserved or indirect control is inconsistent with the common law of agency," suggesting that perhaps the court disagrees with the board's 2020 joint employer standard as set forth through agency rulemaking. See *Sanitary Truck Drivers and Helpers Local 50, Intl. Bhd. of Teamsters v. NLRB*, 2022 WL 3008026 (July 29, 2022), at * 7 (emphasis added).

116. The joint employer question also arises in franchising. A strong case can be made that in some circumstances, the NLRB should hold franchisors and their franchisees to be joint employers. See, for example, Ruben Alan Garcia, "Modern Accountability for a Modern Workplace: Reevaluating the National Labor Relation Board's Joint Employer Standard," *George Wash. L. Rev.* 4 (2016): 741. The joint employer status of franchisors and franchisees has been the subject of renewed scrutiny at the NLRB. In 2014, the NLRB Office of the General Counsel issued complaints against McDonald's franchisees and their franchisor, McDonald's USA, LLC, as joint employers. The complaints allege that McDonald's USA, LLC and certain franchisees violated the rights of employees working at McDonald's restaurants at various locations around the country by, among other things, making statements and taking actions against them for engaging in activities aimed at improving their wages and working conditions. See NLRB, "McDonald's Fact Sheet," https://www.nlrb.gov/news-outreach/fact-sheets/mcdonalds-fact-sheet; https://web.archive.org/web/20151017205049/https://www.nlrb.gov/news-outreach/fact-sheets/mcdonalds-fact-sheet.

117. Even when two employers, such a staffing agency and a host employer, are ruled to be joint employers, there remains a lingering hurdle to a union's ability to file a valid union representation petition seeking to represent nontraditional employees such as temps and include them in collective bargaining units along with regular employees of a host company by naming the host employer and the staffing agency as joint employers. Beginning in 1990, the NLRB held that temporary workers could not be represented by a union in a bargaining unit with employees of the host employer unless both the staffing agency and its client, the host employer, consented. Under this view, the rules creating multiemployer bargaining units controlled. See, for example, *Lee Hospital*, 300 N.L.R.B. 947 (1990). The Board overruled *Lee Hospital* in *M. B. Sturgis, Inc.*, 331 N.L.R.B. 1298 (2000), holding that consent is unnecessary if two conditions are satisfied: (1) the staffing agency and the host company are determined to be joint employers; and (2) the temporary employees share a community of interest with the user company's regular workforce. Four years later, *Sturgis* was overruled by *H.S. Care L.L.C.*, 343 N.L.R.B. 659 (2004), restoring consent as a necessary condition in these types of cases. In turn, *H.S. Clare* was overruled in 2016 by *Miller & Anderson, Inc.*, 364 N.L.R.B. No. 39 (2016), returning to the rule that consent is not required. As of the spring of 2023, *Miller & Anderson, Inc.*, with its rule that consent is not required, is the controlling case.

118. Sheldon Friedman et al., "Introduction: The Context of Reform of Labor Law," in *Restoring the Promise of American Labor Law*, ed. Sheldon Friedman et al. (Ithaca, NY: ILR Press, 1994), 4.

Chapter 5

1. See the PRO Act §§ 104 (j); 105 (a)—(c) & (e); 109; 301; and 307.

2. Joel Rogers, "Reforming U.S. Labor Relations," in *Restoring the Promise of American Labor Law*, ed. Sheldon Friedman et al. (Ithaca, NY: ILR Press, 1994), 18.

3. Richard Hurd and Joseph B. Uehlein, "Patterned Responses to Organizing: Case Studies of the Union-Busting Convention," in *Restoring the Promise of American Labor*, ed. Sheldon Friedman et al. (Ithaca, NY: ILR Press, 1994), 62.

4. Lane Windham, *Knocking on Labor's Door: Union Organizing in the 1970s and the Roots of a New Economic Divide* (Chapel Hill: University of North Carolina Press, 2017), 57, 69 (stating that by 1979, the estimate reported to Congress was that "a full 70 percent of all [antiunion] campaigns involved some sort of management consultant or outside legal counsel"). Also see Kate L. Bronfenbrenner, "Employer Behavior in Certification Elections and First-Contract Campaigns: Implications for Labor Law Reform, in *Restoring the Promise of American Labor Law*, ed. Sheldon Friedman et al. (Ithaca, NY: ILR Press, 1994), 80 (finding in a study of a random sample of 261 NLRB certification elections that took place between July 1986 and June 1987 that "seventy-one percent of the employers in the sample utilized a management consultant during their election campaigns").

5. Windham, *Knocking on Labor's Door*, 67 and 68, and Figure 3.2.

6. Windham, *Knocking on Labor's Door*, 67. It has been reported that during the five years between 2014–2018, employers spent on average $340 million per year on "union avoidance" consultants. As recently as 2021, faced with union-organizing drives at some of its warehouses, Amazon is reported to have paid antiunion consultants roughly $4.3 million during just one year in an effort to combat union-organizing campaigns. Dave Jamieson, "Amazon Spent $4.3 Million on Anti-Union Consultants Last Year," *Huffington Post*, March 21, 2022, https://www.huffpost.com/entry/amazon-anti-union-consultants_n_62449258e4b0742dfa5a74fb; Gordon Lafer and Lola Loustaunau, "Fear at Work," *Econ. Pol'y Inst.*, July 23, 2020, https://www.epi.org/publication/fear-at-work-how-employers-scare-workers-out-of-unionizing/.

7. Windham, *Knocking on Labor's Door*, 70 (reporting that: "[c]onsultants tapped the fears that resided in the hearts of [management]" and that one management consulting firm used tactics "to 'awaken within the mostly white supervisor corps a hatred of blacks . . . contempt for women and mistrust of the poor.'").

8. Windham, *Knocking on Labor's Door*, 71–72nn70–74.

9. Windham, *Knocking on Labor's Door*, 73 (outlining the many opportunities for delay built into the current NLRA representation election procedures).

10. Hurd and Uehlein, "Patterned Responses to Organizing," 62.

11. See, for example, *Esso Standard Oil Co.*, 124 N.L.R.B. 1383 (1959).

12. In the Board's decision in *Munro Co.*, 217 N.L.R.B. 1011 (1975), it found no violation when the plant superintendent stated, "Don't sign any union cards as this can be fatal," and a manager told employees that he could "show you why signing their cards could be fatal" to the company." The Board cited its earlier decision in *Airporter Inn Hotel*, 215 N.L.R.B. 824 (1974).

13. Windham, *Knocking on Labor's Door*, 73–74 (reporting advice given by a consultant to management, as recorded clandestinely and introduced at a congressional hearing).

14. Windham, *Knocking on Labor's Door*, 74–75 (citing Alan Kistler, "Union Organizing: New Challenges and Prospects," *Annuls Am. Acad. of Pol. & Soc. Sci.* 473 (1984): 96, 101 (1984)).

15. Kate Bronfenbrenner and Robert Hickey, "Changing to Organize: A National Assessment of Union Strategies," in *Rebuilding Labor: Organizing and Organizers in the New Union Movement*, ed. Ruth Milkman and Kim Voss (Ithaca, NY: Cornell University Press, 2004), 25.

16. In *NLRB v. Gissel Packing Co.*, 395 U.S. 575 (1969), the Supreme Court held that in appropriate circumstances, the NLRB may remedy employer unfair labor practices by issuing a bargaining order, normally in circumstances where the union had obtained evidence of majority support through authorization cards. To reach this conclusion, the Court had to confront a decision by the Fourth Circuit that authorization cards are an inherently unreliable indicator of employee preferences concerning unionization. The Court held that the cards are a reliable indicator of employee sentiment, stating that in most cases, the employer is aware of the ongoing union effort to obtain signatures and thus has an adequate opportunity to express its views on unionization during that period. *Gissel*, 395 U.S. at 615. Julius Getman states that at an organizing campaign's early stages, the union makes no effort to conceal the fact that it is organizing and concludes that "[i]n fact, . . . employers typically find out about the organizing drive based on observations from supervisors or reports from antiunion employees"); Julius G. Getman, *The Supreme Court on Unions: Why Labor Law Is Failing American Workers* (Ithaca, NY: Cornell/ILR Press, 2016), 32.

17. Bronfenbrenner, "Employer Behavior in Certification Elections" (finding in a study of a random sample of 261 NLRB certification elections that took place between July 1986 and June 1987 that "in more than 73 percent of the campaigns studied, unions signed up a majority of the unit on cards before the election [and] in more than 84 percent of the campaigns, the unions got within 5 percent of a majority"); Getman, *The Supreme Court on Unions*, 15 (stating that "[i]n actuality, unions do not

seek elections until they have authorization cards signed by at least a majority of employees in the desired bargaining unit").

18. These expedited procedures are adopted by § 105 (e) of the PRO Act.

19. See U.S. Chamber of Commerce, Employment Policy Division, "Labor's Litany of Dangerous Ideas: The PRO Act 2021 Update" (referring to proposals to streamline union representation procedures as "Preserving Ambush Elections"), https://www.uschamber.com/sites/default/files/024112_emp_pro_act_report_2021_update.pdf.

20. Robert A. Penney, "Workers against Unions: Union Organizing and Anti-union Countermobilizations," in *Rebuilding Labor: Organizing and Organizers in the New Union Movement*, ed. Ruth Milkman and Kim Voss (Ithaca, NY: Cornell University Press, 2004), 93n6.

21. See, for example, *Motz Poultry Co.*, 244 N.L.R.B. 573 (1979).

22. See, for example, *B.L.K. Steel, Inc.*, 245 N.L.R.B. 1347 (1980) (to be eligible to vote, a person must be actively employed on the eligibility date).

23. Windham, *Knocking on Labor's Door*, 74.

24. Hurd and Uehlein, "Pattern Responses to Organizing," 63–64.

25. Penney, "Workers against Unions," 92–93.

26. Penney, "Workers against Unions," 95.

27. *NLRB v. Exchange Parts Co.*, 375 U.S. 405 (1964).

28. Penney, "Workers against Unions," 93.

29. A discussion of the "carrot and stick" components of the typical anti-union campaign cited here in this chapter can be found in Penney, "Workers against Unions," 94–96.

30. See, for example, *NLRB v. Gissel Packing Co.*, 395 U.S. 575 (1969); *General Indus. Elec. Co.*, 146 N.L.R.B. 1139, 1141 (1964) (finding unlawful interference with employees' free choice in employer statements that "it was futile for [employees] to select the [union, and] that selection . . . could only bring strikes, violence, and loss of jobs").

31. *NLRB v. Gissel Packing Co.*, 395 U.S. 575, 618 (1969) (emphasis added).

32. See, for example, *Crown Cork & Seal Co.*, 255 N.L.R.B. 14 (1981) (unlawful to predict that unionization would result in plant closure due to wage rates increasing 30 to 40 percent, in accordance with the union's master agreement where the union had not yet stated its bargaining position and the employer lacked objective basis for the prediction).

33. See, for example, *River Bend Health & Rehabilitation Service*, 350 N.L.R.B. 184 (2007).

34. See *Reeves Bros.*, 320 N.L.R.B. 1082 (1996) (stating that the employer "probably" would need to reduce production to three days a week because two customers had sent letters stating that they "would consider" withdrawing their business if the employer's employees unionized was unlawful because the employer had no basis for communicating a certainty that it would lose two clients in the event of unionization).

35. 148 N.L.R.B. 577, 578–580 (1964) (emphasis added).

36. For an example of the NLRB distinguishing between "will" and "could," see *UXB Intl.*, 321 N.L.R.B. 446 (1996) (unlawful for employer to state that plant "will" or "would" close but same statements would have been permissible had employer said plant "could" close).

37. See the study results at Larry Cohen and Richard W. Hurd, "Fear, Conflict, and Union Organizing," in *Organizing to Win*, ed. Kate Bronfenbrenner et al. (Ithaca, NY: ILR Press, 1998), 182–190.

38. Cohen and Hurd, "Fear, Conflict, and Union Organizing," 193.

39. See *Sears, Roebuck & Co.*, 305 N.L.R.B. 193 (1991).

40. See, for example, *NLRB v. Almet, Inc.*, 987 F.2d 445 (7th Cir. 1993).

41. *Greensboro Hosiery Mills*, 162 N.L.R.B. 1275, 1276 (1967) (emphasis added).

42. *Midland National Life Insurance*, 263 N.L.R.B. 127 (1982) (noting an exception "where a party has used forged documents which render the voters unable to recognize propaganda for what it is").

43. See *Taylor Chair Co.*, 292 N.L.R.B. 658 (1989) (unlawful to express the futility of choosing unionization by stating that employer will not sign a collective bargaining agreement). See also *Dayton Newspapers, Inc. v. NLRB*, 402 F.3d 651, 660 (6th Cir. 2005) (unlawful for an employer to express the futility of choosing unionization by stating that a certain ongoing conflict could not be resolved so long as the union continued to represent them).

44. See *Fern Terrace Lodge of Bowling Green*, 297 N.L.R.B. 8 (1989).

45. *General Elec. Co.*, 332 N.L.R.B. 919 (2000).

46. Phil Comstock and Maier B. Fox, "Employer Tactics and Labor Law Reform," in *Restoring the Promise of American Labor Law*, ed. Sheldon Friedman et al. (Ithaca, NY: ILR Press, 1994): 98–99, 101 (also reporting that "[w]omen are more likely to feel coerced by employer tactics during union-organizing campaigns than are men").

47. Comstock and Fox, "Employer Tactics and Labor Law Reform," 93.

48. Peter G. Bruce, "On the Status of Workers' Rights to Organize in the United States and Canada," in *Restoring the Promise of American Labor Law*, ed. Sheldon Friedman et al. (Ithaca, NY: ILR Press, 1994): 273.

49. Roy Adams, "Union Certification as an Instrument of Labor Policy: A Comparative Perspective," in *Restoring the Promise of American Labor Law*, ed. Sheldon Friedman et al. (Ithaca, NY: ILR Press, 1994): 265.

50. This was the proposal advanced by Paul Weiler twenty years ago. See Paul C. Weiler, "A Principled Reshaping of Labor Law for the Twenty-first Century," *U. Pa. J. Lab. & Emp. L.* 3, no. 2 (2001): 177, 190–191.

51. See the discussion in Hurd and Uehlein, "Patterned Responses to Organizing," 63.

52. Bronfenbrenner, "Employer Behavior in Certification Elections and First-Contract Campaigns," 78 and 79, table 5.1.

53. William B. Gould IV, *Agenda for Reform: The Future of Employment Relationships and the Law* (Cambridge, MA: MIT Press, 1996), 158.

54. For the standard charge of denial of due process, see US Chamber of Commerce, "Labor's Litany of Dangerous Ideas," https://www.uschamber.com/employment-law/unions/labors-litany-of-dangerous-ideas-the-pro-act.

55. Comstock and Fox, "Employer Tactics and Labor Law Reform," 102.

56. James A. Gross, "The Demise of National Labor Policy: A Question of Social Justice," in *Restoring the Promise of American Labor Law*, by Sheldon Friedman et al. (Ithaca, NY: ILR Press, 1994): 56.

57. 45 U.S.C. § 152 Ninth (emphasis added).

58. *Railway Labor Executives' Ass'n v. National Mediation Bd.*, 29 F.3d 655, 664–668 (DC Cir. 1994).

59. Weiler explains that employees' selection of "representatives of their own choosing" might be likened to one choosing which law firm should be retained to represent an employee in a workplace dispute with an employer, such as a workplace safety or sexual harassment dispute. No one would suggest, he argues, that in the process of an employee choosing such legal counsel, the employer should have standing to intervene and "campaign against the employee's decision about whether to hire a law firm (and if so, which one)." See Weiler, "A Principled Reshaping of Labor Law," 190–191.

60. See, for example, the PRO Act, § 105(d) (obligation of the NLRB to immediately issue an order to bargain when union prevails in the election); PRO Act § 107 (provision stating that the NLRB's orders shall be self-enforcing and that a party that is adversely affected by an NLRB order may seek review before federal court of appeals within thirty days of the order being issued). Prior to the election, the employer provides the list of those it believes are eligible to vote and the NLRB agent conducting the election is required to challenge anyone seeking to vote who is not on that eligibility list. Those challenged are provided an envelope that identifies the voter and the reason for the challenge. The marked ballot is placed inside the envelope, and the

voter casts the sealed envelope in the ballot box. At the time of the count, challenged ballots are segregated and impounded, and thus preserved to be ruled on after the election if there are sufficient challenged ballots to affect the outcome of the election. To ensure finality, the eligibility of voters must be challenged "prior to the actual casting of ballots." *NLRB v. A. J. Tower Co.*, 329 U.S. 324 (1946).

61. See the discussion of statistics derived from NLRB report in Jeffrey M. Hirsh, "NLRB Elections: Ambush or Anticlimax?," *Emory L.J.* 64 (2015): 1647, 1652–1653nn24–25.

62. Eric Dirnbach, "The NLRB Will Eliminate Faster Union Elections. How Much Does It Matter?" December 27, 2019, https://ericdirnbach.medium.com/the-nlrb-will-eliminate-faster-union-elections-how-much-does-it-matter-fd62060a1b3e (but also noting that reduced delay resulted in only a modest 3 percent increase in the union win rate).

63. See "Trump-era NLRB Union Election Rule up for Debate at D.C. Circuit, *Bloomberg Law,* May 14, 2021, https://news.bloomberglaw.com/daily-labor-report/trump-era-nlrb-union-election-rule-up-for-debate-at-d-c-circuit.

64. 85 Fed. Reg. 17500 (March 30, 2020).

65. *AFL-CIO v. NLRB*, Civ. No. 20-CV-0675 (D.D.C. 2020). This order was appealed to the D.C. Circuit and the remainder of the challenge to the NLRB's 2019 rule was put on hold pending resolution of that appeal. See "AFL-CIO Challenge to Labor Board Election Rule Put on Hold," *Bloomberg Law,* October 23, 2020, https://news.bloomberglaw.com/daily-labor-report/afl-cio-challenge-to-labor-board-election-rule-put-on-hold?context=article-related.

66. For a discussion of the 2019 changes that were not enjoined but created more delay than would have been permitted by the NLRB's 2014 final rule, see Peter B. Robb, "Guidance Memorandum on Representation Case Procedure Changes," *Memorandum GC 20–07*, 2020 WL 2945327 (N.L.R.B.G.C.).

67. NLRB Office of Public Affairs, "NLRB Establishes Standards for Mail- and Manual-Ballot Representation Elections during the COVID-19 Pandemic," *NLRB News and Publications*, https://www.nlrb.gov/news-outreach/news-story/nlrb-establishes-standards-for-mail-and-manual-ballot-representation.

68. 18-RC-263185, 370 N.L.R.B. No. 45 (2020).

69. 370 N.L.R.B. No. 45, at *13-*15 (member McFerran, concurring).

70. See, for example, Stephen Smith and Reid Carron, "NLRB: Is Electronic Voting on the Horizon?" *Littler Mendelson's Daily News and Analysis*, June 24, 2010, https://www.littler.com/publication-press/publication/nlrb-electronic-voting-horizon (arguing that "turnout" is problematic with e-voting, and stating that with mail balloting, "elections have low employee participation rates compared to manual ballot elections [and] unions tend to fare better in 'low turnout' elections").

71. See Chad M. Horton, "E-Voting in Union Elections at the NLRB?" *Labor Law & Workplace Trends*, July 22, 2021, https://www.laboremploymentreport.com/2021/07/22/e-voting-in-union-elections-at-the-nlrb/.

72. For an example of sample language, see the PRO Act, § 105(b).

73. See the discussion in Gould, *Agenda for Reform*, 159.

74. *PCC Structurals, Inc.*, 365 N.L.R.B. No. 160 (2017). A recent example of an employer insisting on a bargaining unit larger than the one that the union proposes is the 2021 union-organizing drive at Amazon's Bessemer, Alabama, fulfillment center. The union sought a unit of 1,500 full-time and part-time workers, but Amazon demanded a pre-election hearing to litigate its demand that the unit be expanded almost fourfold to include 5,800 employees. Lynn Rhinehart, "How Amazon Gerrymandered the Union Vote—and Won," *Econ. Pol'y Inst., Working Economics Blog*, April 15, 2021, https://www.epi.org/blog/how-amazon-gerrymandered-the-union-vote-and-won/.

75. See, for example, Henry S. Farber, "Union Success in Representation Elections: Why Does Unit Size Matter?" *Ind. & Lab. Rel. Rev.* 54 (2001): 329, 332 (stating that "[i]t is uniformly true that union win rates decline with election size"). See also Rhinehart, "How Amazon Gerrymandered the Union Vote" (stating that "[t]ypically, employers will argue that the voting bloc/bargaining unit should be larger than the one sought by workers, because employers know they can dilute the union's support by adding workers who haven't previously been involved in the organizing drive").

76. This traditional community-of-interest analysis states: "[W]hether the employees are organized into a separate department; have distinct skills and training; have distinct job functions and perform distinct work, including inquiry into the amount and type of job overlap between classifications; are functionally integrated with the Employer's other employees; have frequent contact with other employees; interchange with other employees; have distinct terms and conditions of employment; and are separately supervised." *Specialty Healthcare & Rehabilitation Center of Mobile*, 357 N.L.R.B 934, 942–943, 945 (2011) (quoting United Operations, Inc., 338 N.L.R.B 123, 123 (2002)).

77. This is what occurred during the 2021 union-organizing drive at Amazon's Bessemer fulfillment center. After the employer insisted on modifying the proposed bargaining unit of 1,500 by expanded it to 5,800, the union agreed in order to avoid weeks or months of delay, and it subsequently lost the election. See Rhinehart, "How Amazon Gerrymandered the Union Vote—and Won," *Econ. Pol'y Inst.*, April 15, 2021, https://www.epi.org/blog/how-amazon-gerrymandered-the-union-vote-and-won/.

78. 357 N.L.R.B. 934 (2011), *enfd. sub nom, Kindred Nursing Centers East, LLC v. NLRB*, 727 F.3d 552 (6th Cir. 2013).

79. The NLRB's approach to unit determinations in *Specialty Healthcare*, thus, entails a two-step test. *NLRB v. FedEx Freight, Inc.*, 832 F.3d 432, 440 (3d Cir. 2016). First, applying the traditional criteria, the Board must determine if the petitioned-for employees

share a community of interest. If yes, then if the employer claims that a petitioned-for unit is nevertheless inappropriate because it does not contain additional employees, the burden is on the employer to demonstrate that the excluded employees share an overwhelming community of interest with the included employees. *Specialty Healthcare*, 357 N.L.R.B., at 934.

80. See *PCC Structurals, Inc.*, 365 N.L.R.B No. 160, at *17 (2017) (members Pearce AND McFerran, dissenting) (listing cases).

81. *PCC Structurals, Inc.*, 365 N.L.R.B No. 160 (2017).

82. *PCC Structurals, Inc.*, 365 N.L.R.B. No. 160, at *17 (members Pearce and McFerran, dissenting) (also observing that "of course, the extent of employees' freedom of association (which, by definition, includes the freedom not to associate) is not a matter for employers to decide. As the Supreme Court has made clear, the Board is entitled to "giv[e] a short leash to the employer as vindicator of its employees' organizational freedom." *Auciello Iron Works, Inc. v. N.L.R.B.*, 517 U.S. 781, 790 (1996)").

83. *Am. Hosp. Ass'n v. NLRB*, 499 U.S. 606, 610 (1991). Also see *FedEx Freight, Inc. v. NLRB*, 816 F.3d 515, 523 (8th Cir. 2016).

84. *Overnite Transportation Co.*, 322 N.L.R.B. 723, 723 (1996).

85. This is the proposal contained in § 105(a) of the PRO Act.

86. See Jason R. Stanevich and Marie Duarte, "NLRB Final Rule Signals More Balanced and Efficient Elections Ahead," *Littler Mendelson's Daily News & Analysis*, December 17, 2019, https://www.littler.com/publication-press/publication/nlrb-final-election-rule-signals-more-balanced-and-efficient-elections.

Chapter 6

1. See the PRO Act, §§ 106, 107, 108, 109(b) & (c), and 202.

2. Richard Hurd and Joseph B. Uehlein, "Patterned Responses to Organizing: Case Studies of the Union-Busting Convention," in *Restoring the Promise of American Labor Law*, ed. Sheldon Friedman et al. (Ithaca, NY: ILR Press, 1994), 64.

3. See Kate L Bronfenbrenner, "Employer Behavior in Certification Elections and First-Contract Campaigns: Implications for Labor Law Reform," in *Restoring the Promise of American Labor Law*, ed. Sheldon Friedman et al. (Ithaca, NY: ILR Press, 1994), 81.

4. Celine McNicholas et al., "Unlawful: U.S. Employers Are Charged with Violating Federal Law in 41.5% of All Union Election Campaigns," *Econ. Pol'y Inst.* (December 2019), https://www.epi.org/publication/unlawful-employer-opposition-to-union-election-campaigns/ (stating that calculations based on information provided online by the NLRB for FY 2017 actually "understate the extent of employer aggression against unions, as they cannot capture the full extent of all illegal or coercive

behavior by employers in opposing worker organizing efforts. For example, many union-organizing efforts are thwarted by employers before making it to the [unfair labor practice] filing stage. In addition, many anti-union violations go unreported").

5. Kate Bronfenbrenner, "No Holds Barred: the Intensification of Employer Opposition to Organizing," *Econ. Pol'y. Inst.* (May 2009), https://files.epi.org/page/-/pdf/bp235.pdf.

6. See, for example, John Schmitt and Ben Zipperer. "Dropping the Axe: Illegal Firings during Union Organizing Campaigns, 1951–2007," *Center for Economic and Policy Research*, Washington, DC (2009) (using aggregate data on all elections and discharges from NLRB annual reports and finding that employers discharged workers for union activity in 26.0% of NLRB elections between 2001 and 2007), https://cepr.net/documents/publications/dropping-the-ax-update-2009-03.pdf.

7. John T. Dunlop, "Fact Finding Report: Commission on the Future of Worker-Management Relations" (May 1994), 84 & Exhibit III-4 ("Discriminatory Discharges during NLRB Election"), https://ecommons.cornell.edu/handle/1813/79171.

8. Paul Weiler, "Promises to Keep: Securing Workers' Rights to Self-organization under the NLRA," *Harv. L. Rev.* 96, no. 8 (1983): 1769, 1780–1781.

9. In FY 2021 (October 1, 2020–September 30, 2021), the NLRB recovered $53,878,300 in back pay and 6,307 victims of discrimination were offered reinstatement to jobs from which they had been unlawfully discharged. These results represent a dramatic increase from FY 2020, both in the amount of back pay awarded and the number of employees reinstated. See NLRB, "The NLRB Recovered Over $56 Million and 6,307 Workers Were Offered Reinstatement in Fiscal Year 2021," https://www.nlrb.gov/news-outreach/news-story/the-nlrb-recovered-over-56-million-and-6307-workers-were-offered.

10. The following examples are drawn from Hurd and Uehlein, "Patterned Responses to Organizing," 62–70.

11. In November 2021, in *Thyrv, Inc.*, 371 N.L.R.B. No. 37 (2021), the NLRB invited the parties and interested amici to brief whether the Board should award consequential damages to make employees whole for economic losses and under what circumstances. The Board requested that interested parties brief the following questions:

- Should the board modify its traditional make-whole remedy in all pending and future cases to include relief for consequential damages, where these damages are a direct and foreseeable result of a respondent's unfair labor practice?
- Alternatively, should the make-whole remedy include relief for consequential damages only upon findings of egregious violations by a respondent?
- If consequential damages are to be included in make-whole relief, how should they be proved, and what would be required to demonstrate that they are a direct and foreseeable result of an employer's unfair labor practice?

- What considerations support making the proposed change to the board's traditional make-whole remedies?
- What considerations support retaining the board's traditional exclusion of consequential damages from its make-whole remedies?

12. Morris M. Kleiner, "What Will It Take? Establishing the Economic Costs to Management of Noncompliance with the NLRA," in *Restoring the Promise of American Labor Law*, ed. by Sheldon Friedman et al. (Ithaca, NY: ILR Press, 1994), 139.

13. James A. Gross, "The Demise of National Labor Policy: A Question of Social Justice," in *Restoring the Promise of American Labor Law*, ed. by Sheldon Friedman et al. (Ithaca, NY: ILR Press, 1994), 57.

14. Kleiner, "What Will It Take?" 139.

15. See the discussion in Phil Comstock and Maier B. Fox, "Employer Tactics and Labor Law Reform," in *Restoring the Promise of American Labor Law*, ed. by Sheldon Friedman et al. (Ithaca, NY: ILR Press, 1994), 98.

16. In one study of 261 certification elections, the NLRB ordered reinstatement before the election in only 34 percent of the campaigns in which there were illegal discharges for union activity. Bronfenbrenner, "Employer Behavior in Certification Elections and First-Contract Campaigns," 81.

17. Bronfenbrenner, "Employer Behavior in Certification Elections and First-Contract Campaigns," 81.

18. Paul C. Weiler, "A Principled Reshaping of Labor Law for the Twenty-first Century," *U. Pa. J. Lab. & Emp. L.* 3, no. 2 (2001): 177, 188 (also concluding that "[b]y th[e] time [the NLRB orders reinstatement], only one in three of the reinstated employees will exercise their right to return to work with the firm that fired them, and of those who do return, four out of five will feel compelled by management to leave that job within a year).

19. Bronfenbrenner, "Employer Behavior in Certification Elections and First-Contract Campaigns," 81.

20. Kleiner, "What Will It Take?" 140–141, 145.

21. Kleiner, "What Will It Take?" 145.

22. For an example of reform proposals that incorporate these four changes, see PRO Act §§ 106–108 and 109(b) & (c).

23. In addition, labor law reform should provide that an employee cannot be denied relief under the NLRA on the basis that the employee suffering a violation of NLRA rights is an unauthorized alien under the Immigration Reform and Control Act, which would reverse the Supreme Court's 2002 decision in *Hoffman Plastic Compounds v. NLRB*, 535 U.S. 137 (2002).

24. Lynn Rhinehart and Celine McNicholas, "Shortchanged—Weak Anti-retaliation Provisions in the National Labor Relations Act Cost Workers Billions," *Econ. Pol'y. Inst.*, April 22, 2021 (emphasis in original). (also arguing that "this estimate is low, because the NLRB's practice is to make deductions for interim earnings that the worker earned or could have earned, but the PRO Act provides for back pay and liquidated damages without these deductions"), https://www.epi.org/publication/shortchanged-weak-anti-retaliation-provisions-in-the-national-labor-relations-act-cost-workers-billions/.

25. The NLRB general counsel Jennifer Abruzzo has recognized the present need for the NLRB to "do a better job of really looking at 'consequential' damages," such as fees and penalties charged to an unlawfully discharged employee needing to take out 401(k) money to be able to pay for living expenses, credit card late fees, training for new certifications, or medical insurance while on discharge status. See the interview with Abruzzo in Josh Eidelson, "Biden's Top Labor Lawyer Will Use Her Whole Enforcement Arsenal," *Bloomberg Businessweek*, December 14, 2021, https://www.bloomberg.com/news/articles/2021-12-14/biden-labor-lawyer-jennifer-abruzzo-to-fully-use-nlrb-power-to-protect-workers.

26. Amending the NLRA to provide that NLRB orders are self-enforcing also could decrease the number of cases brought to the circuit courts of appeal to review because the party adversely affected by the order must seek judicial review within thirty days. Some have advanced the view that a reduction in judicial review of Board decisions would be a positive development on the ground that Supreme Court and circuit court of appeals review of NLRB decisions is the "core" of the reason that employee rights under the NLRA have eroded. See Ellen Dannin, "At Age Seventy, Should the National Labor Relations Act Be Retired?" in *Proceedings of the 2005 Annual Meeting, Association of American Law Schools Section on Labor Relations and Employment Law*, ed. Katherine Stone et al., *Emp. Rts. & Emp. Pol'y. J.* 9 (2005): 126 (asserting that "[i]t's class bias" and stating, "To me, the key is that what unions don't like, by and large, about the NLRA is what I call judicial amendments [and citing several Supreme Court cases that eroded employee rights under the NLRA]").

27. William B. Gould IV, *Agenda for Reform: The Future of Employment Relationships and the Law* (Cambridge, MA: MIT Press, 1996), 160–161 and table 5.3 (listing § 10(j) requests and Board authorizations of § 10(j) relief between 1982–1991).

28. In determining the size of such a penalty, the NLRB would consider the gravity of the violation, the impact of the violation on the employee, and the size of the employer.

29. See *Consolidated Edison Co. v. NLRB*, 305 U.S. 197, 236 (1938) (holding that the Board's power to remedy unfair labor practices was "remedial, not punitive," and it must be exercised as "a means of removing or avoiding the consequences of violation"—not to deter violations). Also see *Phelps Dodge Corp. v. NLRB*, 313 U.S. 177, 197–198 (1941) and *Republic Steel Corp. v. NLRB*, 311 U.S. 7, 9–12 (1940). Scholars have

argued that limiting "[t]he Court's prohibition [to] deterrence finds scant support in the statutory language, which authorizes the Board to order violators 'to cease and desist from such unfair labor practice, and to take such affirmative action including reinstatement of employees with or without back pay, as will effectuate the policies of this [act].'" James Gray Pope, "How American Workers Lost the Right to Strike, and Other Tales," *Mich. L. Rev.* 103, no. 3 (2004): 518, 535.

30. For example, Rhinehart and McNicholas have pointed out that that the "Department of Labor . . . announced an award of $290,000, including $150,000 in punitive damages, for a worker who faced illegal retaliation under the Federal Railroad Safety Act [and] [i]n another case, the Department of Labor ordered an employer to pay $23,000 in back wages and $70,000 in punitive damages under the anti-retaliation provisions of the Surface Transportation Assistance Act to two employees who were illegally fired for refusing to operate unsafe trucks." Rhinehart and McNicholas, "Shortchanged."

31. This interpretation appeared in a technical assistance publication for employers, US Department of Labor, Bureau of Labor Management Reports, "Technical Assistance Aid No. 4: Guide for Employer Reporting" (1960), at 18. See the discussion in US Department of Labor, Office of Labor Management Standards, "Rescission of Rule Interpreting 'Advice' Exemption in Section 203(c) of the Labor-Management Reporting and Disclosure Act," effective August 17, 2018, 83 FR 33826–01 (2018 WL 3437183(F.R.) ("Recission of Persuader Rule"), at *33828.

32. Due to dissatisfaction with the categorical reporting exemption of consultants who had no direct contact with employees, the Department of Labor altered its interpretation of § 203(c), expanding the scope of reportable activities by focusing on whether an activity has persuasion of employees as an object, rather than categorically exempting activities in which a consultant has no direct contact with employees. See 66 FR 2782 (January 11, 2001). However, later that year, that interpretation was rescinded and the Department of Labor returned to its prior view. See 66 FR 18864 (April 11, 2001).

33. See 81 FR 15924 (March 24, 2016).

34. See 2016 Persuader Rule, at 15925.

35. *Associated Builders & Contractors of Arkansas v. Perez* (E.D. Ark. 4:16-cv-169) (September 26, 2018); *Labnet, Inc. v. U.S. Dep't. of Labor*, 197 F. Supp. 3d 1159 (D. Minn. 2016); *Nat'l. Fed'n. of Indep. Bus. v. Perez*, 2016 WL 3766121 (N.D. Tex.).

36. *Nat'l. Fed'n of Indep. Bus. v. Perez*, 2016 WL 3766121 (N.D. Tex.), at *46. Previously, the federal district court in Minnesota found that the plaintiffs were likely to establish that the Persuader Rule violated the LMRDA in at least some of its applications, but it denied their request for preliminary relief on the ground that plaintiffs had not shown the threat of irreparable harm. *Labnet, Inc. v. U.S. Dep't. of Labor*, 197 F. Supp. 3d at 1175–1176.

37. See *Nat'l. Fed'n of Indep. Bus. v. Perez*, Dkt. No. 16-66 (N.D. Texas, June 27, 2016). The other two court cases also were stayed. For a discussion of the litigation surrounding the 2016 Persuader Rule, see 2018 "Recission of the Persuader Rule," at 33828.

38. Section 202 of the PRO Act reinstates the 2016 Persuader Rule by amending the LMRDA.

39. For a discussion of the claim that the 2016 Persuader Rule violated the attorney-client relationship and the response to that argument, see the 2018 Recission of the Persuader Rule at 33831–33833. Section 102 of the PRO Act includes an additional reporting obligation—reinstatement of the NLRB's Congressional Reporting Requirement. For many years, the NLRB submitted annual reports to Congress detailing case activities and operations. The NLRB discontinued its reporting after 2009. The PRO Act reinstates the NLRB reporting requirement that now includes information about how the Board members have exercised their recusal obligations pursuant to federal ethics law.

Chapter 7

1. See the PRO Act, §§ 104 (e) & (k).

2. Charles L. Black, Jr., "He Cannot Choose but Hear: The Plight of the Captive Auditor," *Colum. L. Rev.* 53, no. 7 (1953): 960, 966–967.

3. See Labor Relations Institute, Inc., "Anti-Union Campaign Tips—How Many Meetings," https://lrionline.com/anti-union-campaign-tips-how-many (stating that "[t]he captive audience meeting is management's most important weapon in a[n] [anti-union] campaign"); Julius G. Getman, Stephen Goldberg, and Jeanne B. Herman, *Union Representation Elections: Law and Reality* (New York: Russell Sage Foundation, 1976), 90–92 (reporting that in a sample of union representation elections conducted by the NLRB in 1972–1973, the captive audience meeting was a fixture of the employer's anti-union strategy, and employees were far more likely to attend such meetings than union meetings held off the property).

4. Kate Bronfenbrenner, *Uneasy Terrain: The Impact of Capital Mobility on Workers, Wages, and Union Organizing: Report Submitted to the U.S. Trade Deficit Review Commission: Causes, Consequences, and Recommendations for Action* (Washington, DC: US Trade Deficit Review Commission, 2000), 8, table 8,https://ecommons.cornell.edu/bitstream/handle/1813/74284/Bronfenbrenner_24_Uneasy_Terrain_2000.pdf?sequence=1. (finding that employers held captive audience meetings in 92 percent of 400 NLRB-conducted union representation elections conducted between January 1, 1998, and December 31, 1999); Kate Bronfenbrenner, "No Holds Barred: The Intensification of Employer Opposition to Organizing," *Econ. Pol'y. Inst.* (May 2009), https://www.epi.org/publication/bp235/ (reporting the incidence of one-on-one meetings with supervisors).

5. Larry Cohen and Richard W. Hurd, "Fear, Conflict, and Union Organizing," in *Organizing to Win*, ed. Kate Bronfenbrenner et al. (Ithaca, NY: Cornell/ILR Press, 1998), 185.

6. See Alfred DeMaria, *How Management Wins Union Organizing Campaigns* (Hoboken, NJ: Prentice-Hall, 1980), xvii (viewpoint from the perspective of an employers' labor consultant); See also *Pub. Utils. Comm'n v. Pollak*, 343 U.S. 451, 469 (1952) (Douglas, J., dissenting) ("When we force people to listen to another's ideas, we give the propagandist a powerful weapon").

7. See DeMaria, *How Management Wins Union Organizing Campaigns*, xvii. Employer access to employees through the captive audience meeting and denial of union access both result in a disproportionate percentage of employees who become familiar with the tenets of the employer's campaign arguments but are far less familiar with the union's. This gives employers a "measurable advantage in conveying the message to the employees, an advantage that leads employees to vote against union representation." Julius G. Getman, *The Supreme Court on Unions: Why Labor Law Is Failing American Workers* (Ithaca, NY: Cornell/ILR Press, 2016), 192.

8. *Livingston Shirt Corp.*, 107 N.L.R.B. 400, 406 (1953).

9. See "Anti-Union Campaign Tips" (concluding that "[i]f you hope to win your NLRB election, you must conduct a minimum of 5 captive audience meetings [and that] the odds of a company victory increase with each captive audience meeting held"); and "Uneasy Terrain," 73, table 8 (showing that of the 400 union representation elections studied, the overall union win rate was 63 percent, but in those where employers held captive audience meetings, the union win rate was 43 percent).

10. See DeMaria, *How Management Wins Union Organizing Campaigns*, xvii, 9–10 (advising employer-clients to schedule captive audience meetings soon after discovering union-organizing efforts); William T. Dickens, "The Effect of Company Campaigns on Certification Elections: Law and Reality Once Again," *Indus. & Lab. Rel. Rev.* 36, no. 4 (1983): 560, 570–571 (showing correlation between conducting captive audience meetings and anti-union outcomes in representation elections).

11. Kate Bronfenbrenner, "Employer Behavior in Certification Elections and First-Contract Campaigns: Implications for Labor Law Reform," in *Restoring the Promise of American Labor Law*, ed. by Sheldon Friedman et al. (Ithaca, NY: ILR Press, 1994), 78, table 5.1, 82.

12. See, for example, *Litton Sys., Inc.*, 173 N.L.R.B. 1024, 1030 (1968) (holding that an employer may discipline an employee who leaves a captive audience meeting).

13. *NLRB v. Prescott Indus. Prod. Co.*, 500 F.2d 6, 11 (8th Cir. 1974) (holding that an employer may discipline an employee attempting to interject questions during captive audience meetings); *J.P. Stevens & Co., Inc.*, 219 N.L.R.B. 850 (1975), *aff'd in part, J. P. Stevens & Co. v. Textile Workers Union*, 547 F.2d 792 (4th Cir. 1976) (upholding

discharge of employees who asked or sought to ask questions during a captive audience speech or stood silently during an anti-union speech). The NLRB view is that the employer may refuse to permit employee questions and may discipline those who ask questions if the Board concludes that the intent of seeking to raise questions was to disrupt the meeting. *Prescott Indus. Prod. Co.*, 205 N.L.R.B. 51, 52 (1973). Compare *Howell Metal Co.*, 243 N.L.R.B. 1136, 1137 (1979) (stating that "the Board has held consistently that discipline for having the 'temerity to ask questions' during such meetings violates the Act, except when there is a scheme or plan to disrupt the meeting") with *Hicks Ponder Co.*, 168 N.L.R.B. 806, 814 (1967) (discipline is lawful when employees in concert engage in a course of conduct designed to disrupt a captive audience meeting).

14. See *F.W. Woolworth Co.*, 251 N.L.R.B. 1111, 1113 (1980).

15. See *Bonwit Teller, Inc.* 96 N.L.R.B. 608, 622 (1951) (employer locked exits and physically restrained some employees attempting to leave the premises during a captive audience meeting).

16. See, for example, *Am. Freightways Co.*, 124 N.L.R.B. 146, 147 (1959).

17. *Clark Bros. Co.*, 70 N.L.R.B. 802, *enfd as modified, NLRB v. Clark Bros. Co.*, 163 F.2d 373 (2d Cir. 1947).

18. *Clark Bros. Co.*, at 805. The Board has long recognized that "the rights guaranteed to employees by the Act include the full freedom to receive aid, advice, and information from others, concerning [the right to self-organization]. . . . Such freedom is meaningless, however, unless the employees are also free to determine whether or not to receive such aid, advice, and information. To force employees to receive such aid, advice, and information impairs that freedom; it is calculated to, and does, interfere with the selection of a representative of the employees' choice. And this is wholly apart from the fact that the [content of the] speech itself may be privileged under the Constitution." *Clark Bros. Co.*, at 805 & 805n4 (citing *Matter of Harlan Fuel Co.*, 8 N.L.R.B. 25, 32 (1938)).

19. *Clark Bros. Co.*, at 805. In *Thomas v. Collins*, 323 U.S. 516, 543 (Douglas, J., concurring), Justice William O. Douglas, joined by Justices Hugo Black and Frank Murphy, argued that "no one may be required to obtain a license to speak. But once he uses the economic power which he has over other men and their jobs to influence their action, he is doing more than exercising the freedom of speech protected by the First Amendment."). The Second Circuit enforced the NLRB's order in *Clark Brothers*. See *Clark Bros. Co.*, 163 F.2d at 376 (2d Cir. 1947). Declining to hold that employers may *never* hold captive audience meetings, the court agreed with the Board on these facts because the employer had refused union representatives a comparable opportunity to address employees.

20. David J. Doorey, "The Medium and the 'Anti-Union' Message: 'Forced Listening' and Captive Audience Meetings in Canadian Labor Law, *Comp. Lab. L. & Pol'y J.* 29,

no. 2 (2008): 79, 80 (discussing how the Canadian Labor Relations Board bans the use of captive audience meetings on the theory that employer exploitation of its economic power over employees to force listening interferes with legislatively guaranteed employee freedom of association and free choice whether to support unionization).

21. National Labor Relations Act, § 158(c).

22. See S. Rep. No. 105, at 23–24 (1947) (Senate Report), reprinted in NLRB, *Legislative History of the Labor Management Relations Act*, 1947 429–430 (1948); *H.R. Rep. No. 510*, at 45 (1947) (Conference Report).

23. 77 N.L.R.B. 577, 578 (1948).

24. Initially, the NLRB held that the employer owes the union no such "equal opportunity" duty. See *S. & S. Corrugated Paper Mach. Co.*, 89 N.L.R.B. 1363, 1364 (1950). That view soon gave way in *Bonwit Teller, Inc.*, 96 N.L.R.B. 608, 612 (1951), and *Biltmore Mfg. Co.*, 97 N.L.R.B. 905, 907 (1952), that together established the rule that the employer cannot campaign against the union by holding a captive audience meeting and then deny a union's request to address employees under similar circumstances. In *Livingston Shirt Corp.*, 107 N.L.R.B. 400 (1953) the Board returned to the no-equal-opportunity rule in most cases.

25. 107 N.L.R.B. 400 (1953).

26. The general rule is that "[n]o restriction may be placed on the employees' right to discuss self-organization among themselves, unless the employer can demonstrate that a restriction is necessary to maintain production or discipline." *NLRB v. Babcock & Wilcox Co.*, 351 U.S. 105, 113 (1956). As applied, the NLRB normally permits employers to ban solicitation only during work time. See, for example, *Peyton Packing Co.*, 49 N.L.R.B. 828, 843 (1943). In unusual cases, an employer may choose to avail itself of the privilege of promulgating and enforcing what is referred to as a "broad but privileged" no-solicitation rule. See *May Dep't Stores*, 136 N.L.R.B. 797, 800 (1962). These are permitted upon the employer's demonstration of special circumstances that necessitate the promulgation and enforcement of a rule that bans solicitation, even during nonwork time, in certain work areas of the employer's premises, such as selling areas of the store, to avoid customer confusion. See, for example, *Marshall Field & Co. v. NLRB*, 200 F.2d 375 (7th Cir. 1952); *May Dep't. Stores, Co.*, 59 N.L.R.B. 976 (1944), *enfd.*, 154 F.2d 533 (8th Cir. 1946).

27. In 1958, the Supreme Court decided two consolidated cases collectively known as the "*Nutone* case"—*NLRB v. Steelworkers (Nutone, Inc.)* and *NLRB v. Avondale Mills*, 357 U.S. 357 (1958). Neither raised the issue of the free-speech-protected nature of the captive audience meeting per se, but both did address the question of whether an employer may ban pro-union speech at the workplace while itself engaging in workplace anti-union speech. The Court held that the employer's expression of an anti-union viewpoint to employees during work time creates no NLRA duty to provide

employees or the union an equal workplace opportunity to express pro-union views unless the confluence of the employer's speech and the denial of an equal opportunity to express a contrary viewpoint "create[s] an imbalance in the opportunities for organizational communication." 357 U.S. at 362. Following *Nutone*, the NLRB reaffirmed its *Livingston Shirt* doctrine as striking a proper balance that, in its view, was consistent with the rule in *Nutone*. See *May Dep't. Stores Co.*, 136 N.L.R.B. 797 (1962) (establishing a violation when the employer enforces a broad but privileged no-solicitation rule, conducts a captive audience meeting, and denies the union a similar opportunity to reply), *enf. denied*, 316 F.2d 797 (6th Cir. 1963); also see *Montgomery Ward & Co.*, 145 N.L.R.B. 846 (1964), *enfd. as modified*, 339 F.2d 889 (6th Cir. 1989).

28. Julius G. Getman, *The Supreme Court on Unions* (Ithaca, NY: Cornell/ILR Press, 2016), 30.

29. *NLRB v. Babcock & Wilcox Co.*, 351 U.S. 105, 113 (1956).

30. 502 U.S. 527 (1992).

31. 502 U.S., at 540.

32. See, for example, *Cedar Point Nursery v. Hasid*, 141 S.Ct. 2063 (2021) (holding that a California regulation granting union organizers access to private agricultural property "for up to three hours per day, 120 days per year" was a physical appropriation of property, constituting a per se "taking").

33. See, for example, *Texas v. Johnson*, 491 U.S. 397 (1989) (holding that the court's "most exacting [judicial] scrutiny" is reserved for regulations where the government's interest in regulating is "the suppression of expression"); *Boos v. Barry*, 485 U.S. 312 (1988) (ban on signs near foreign embassies that tend to bring a foreign government into "public odium" evaluated under strict judicial scrutiny because the government's interest is related to the suppression of the content of expression, not just the time and place of its dissemination).

34. See, for example, *Ward v. Rock Against Racism*, 491 U.S. 781 (1989). Also see *Clark v. Community for Creative Nonviolence*, 468 U.S. 288 (1984) (bans on overnight sleeping in tents during the winter to communicate the plight of the homeless constitutional using the three-prong test); *Renton v. Playtime Theatres, Inc.*, 475 U.S. 41 (1986) (the same, regarding a zoning ban on adult motion picture theaters within 1,000 feet of any residential zone); *Heffron v. Intl. Soc. For Krishna Consciousness*, 452 U.S. 640 (1981) (the same, regarding ban on distribution of printed material or the solicitation of funds at a state fair except from a duly licensed booth at the fairgrounds).

35. See *Ward v. Rock Against Racism*, 491 U.S. 781, 791 (1989) (holding that "[t]he principal inquiry in determining content neutrality, in speech cases generally and in time, place, or manner cases in particular, is whether the government has adopted a regulation of speech because of disagreement with the message it conveys"). Neither does a ban on captive audience meetings constitute unconstitutional content regulation

because the ban applies to speech regarding unionization and does not ban all other coerced listening, such as an employer's views on the economy. In *Virginia v. Black*, 538 U.S. 343, 344–345 (2003), the Court held that Virginia may ban only cross burnings done with the intent to intimidate, and need not prohibit all intimidating messages, just as a state need not ban all obscenity, but rather may regulate only that obscenity that the state considers the most obscene due to its prurient content. The operative principle is that a state may single out for opprobrium a subset of a class of proscribable speech where the subset regulated is chosen because it is particularly virulent, in the sense that it is most likely to create the very problem that justifies regulating the class of speech—the loathsomeness of being coerced into ideological listening with respect to a choice that federal law reserves exclusively for each individual worker.

36. *Hill v. Colorado*, 530 U.S. 703, 718 (2000) (citing *Lehman v. Shaker Heights*, 418 U.S. 298 (1974) and *Erznoznik v. Jacksonville*, 422 U.S. 205, 209 (1975)).

37. *Rowan v. U.S. Post Office Dep't.*, 397 U.S. 728, 738 (1970).

38. *Memorandum GC 22–04*, 2022 WL 1078095 (N.L.R.B.G.C.).

39. See *Burnett Specialists v. Abruzzo*, E.D. Tex., No. 4:22-cv-00605, complaint filed July 18, 2022, discussed in Robert Iafolla, "NLRB Top Attorney Sued Over 'Captive Audience' Meeting Guidance," *Bloomberg Law*, July 20, 2022, https://news.bloomberglaw.com/daily-labor-report/nlrb-top-attorney-sued-over-captive-audience-meeting-guidance.

40. See Josh Eidelson, "Amazon Anti-union Confabs Deemed Illegal by Labor Officials," *Bloomberg Law*, May 6, 2022, https://news.bloomberglaw.com/daily-labor-report/amazon-anti-union-nyc-meetings-deemed-illegal-by-labor-board.

41. *Register Guard*, 351 N.L.R.B. 1110 (2007).

42. *Purple Communications, Inc.*, 361 N.L.R.B. 1050 (2014).

43. 368 N.L.R.B. No. 143 (2019).

44. *Caesar's Entertainment*, 368 N.L.R.B. No. 143, at *9n56.

45. *Caesar's Entertainment*, 368 N.L.R.B. No. 143, at *9.

46. 324 U.S. 793 (1945).

47. See, for example, *Peyton Packing Co.*, 49 N.L.R.B. 828, 843 (1943), *enfd.* 142 F.2d 1009 (5th Cir. 1944) (oral solicitation); *Stoddard-Quirk Manufacturing Co.*, 138 NLRB 615, 620 (1962) (distribution of literature).

48. *NLRB v. Babcock & Wilcox Co.*, 351 U.S. 105, 113 (1956) (citing *Republic Aviation*, 324 U.S. at 803).

49. *Caesar's Entertainment*, 368 N.L.R.B. No. 143, at *12.

50. *Caesar's Entertainment*, 368 N.L.R.B No. 143, at *6.

51. Benjamin Sachs, "Privileging Property in the NLRB Email Case," *OnLabor*, December 19, 2019, https://onlabor.org/privileging-property-in-the-nlrb-email-case/.

Chapter 8

1. See the PRO Act, §§ 103, 104(h) & 105(d).

2. See the discussion in Richard Hurd and Joseph B. Uehlein, "Patterned Responses to Organizing: Case Studies of the Union-Busting Convention," in *Restoring the Promise of American Labor Law*, ed. Sheldon Friedman et al. (Ithaca, NY: ILR Press, 1994), 62.

3. NLRB Rules and Regulations, Rules § 102.69(c)(1).

4. Objections to conduct affecting the results of the election are the most recurring type of postelection objection. These focus mostly on misconduct during the election campaign that warrant setting aside the election because the conduct interfered with employees' free choice. But in addition, and occurring less frequently, there are postelection objections that are termed "objections to the conduct of the election," which object to the conduct of the NLRB agent, or others, at the election itself.

5. *Howard Johnson Co.*, 242 N.L.R.B. 1284 (1979).

6. *American Federation of Labor v. NLRB*, 308 U.S.401 (1940).

7. Kate Bronfenbrenner, "Employer Behavior in Certification Elections and First-Contract Campaigns: Implications for Labor Law Reform," in *Restoring the Promise of American Labor Law*, ed. by Sheldon Friedman et al. (Ithaca, NY: ILR Press, 1994): 86, table 5.2.

8. See the discussion in William B. Gould IV, *Agenda for Reform: The Future of Employment Relationships and the Law* (Cambridge, MA: MIT Press, 1996), 169.

9. The language of the PRO Act does not provide for an automatic stay of the NLRB's bargaining order during an appeal to a circuit court of appeals. Thus, if the employer does not immediately begin to bargain in good faith, it likely would be subject to contempt proceedings during the appeal. Presumably, the employer could seek a stay from the court of appeals. But a stay would be counterproductive, for the whole point of the PRO Act amendments is that these appeals seldom are meritorious, and thus an appeal to the courts should not delay the commencement of bargaining.

10. Section 109(b) of the PRO Act provides that for the doubling of the $50,000 fine provision to take effect, it would be necessary for the NLRB to establish that a second refusal to bargain within five years caused "serious economic harm" to the employees. This might prove difficult to do because how would one show that the union would have obtained some economically advantageous clause in the collective bargaining

agreement "but for" the employer's bad-faith bargaining? In *Ex-Cell-O Corporation*, 185 N.L.R.B. 107 (1970), the Board held that the principle that the NLRA precludes it from imposing contract terms on the parties also precluded it from fashioning a "make whole" order to remedy bad-faith bargaining—an order providing damages paid to employees that makes them whole for wages and benefits that would have been negotiated in the collective bargaining agreement but for the employer's unlawful conduct of engaging in bad-faith bargaining. The PRO Act's provision imposing a civil fine is different. The doubling of the $50,000 fine is a civil penalty paid to the federal government, and its imposition does not entail, as in the *Ex-Cell-O* case, indirectly imposing a contract term on the employer in the guise of a make-whole damage remedy.

11. This is what occurred following the union's loss in the representation election held in 2021 at Amazon's warehouse in Bessemer, Alabama. The NLRB regional director found that Amazon management had engaged in conduct interfering with the conduct of a free election and ordered that a rerun election be held. Julia Love and Jeffrey Dastin, "U.S. Labor Board Official Orders Amazon to Redo Union Vote at Alabama Warehouse," *Reuters,* November 29, 2021, https://www.reuters.com/business/amazon-alabama-facility-ordered-re-run-union-election-us-labor-board-2021-11-29/.

12. Gould, *Agenda for Reform,* 162 (also noting that in Canada, union majority status can be established where unions obtain authorization cards from 55 percent or more of the workers).

13. *Joy Silk Mills, Inc.*, 85 N.L.R.B. 1263, 1264 (1949), *enfd,* 185 F.2d 732 (D.C. Cir. 1950).

14. See Brian J. Petruska, "Adding Joy Silk to Labor's Reform Agenda," *Santa Clara L. Rev.* 57, no. 1 (2017): 97, 108–111 (explaining that the associate general counsel misstated controlling NLRB law regarding the *Joy Silk* doctrine at oral argument in the *Gissel* case).

15. *NLRB v. Gissel Packing Co.*, 395 U.S. 575, 614–615. (1969).

16. See the discussion of "hallmark" violations that will support the issuance of a bargaining order in most cases at *NLRB v. Jamaica Towing Co.*, 632 F.2d 208, 212 (2d Cir. 1980).

17. In 2022, the NLRB general counsel Jennifer Abruzzo filed a brief urging the Board to reinstate its *Joy Silk* doctrine "with the employer bearing the burden to demonstrate its good faith doubt as to majority status without requiring an increased threshold of "substantial unfair labor practices." See Brief in Support of General Counsel's Exceptions to the Administrative Law Judge's Decision at 36, *Cemex Const. Materials Pacific, LLC (International Brotherhood of Teamsters),* No. 28-CA-230115 (NLRB April 11, 2022).

18. Cf. *Gourmet Foods, Inc.*, 270 N.L.R.B. 578 (1984). (Even though the Supreme Court stated in *Gissel,* in dicta, that nonmajority bargaining orders are valid when there is no other way to remedy extreme and outrageous employer unfair labor practices, and

although the NLRB had issued nonmajority bargaining orders in the past, the decision here held that it no longer would do so.)

19. See, for example, Gordon R. Pavy, "Winning NLRB Elections and Establishing Collective Bargaining Relationships," in *Restoring the Promise of American Labor Law*, ed. by Sheldon Friedman et al. (Ithaca, NY: ILR Press, 1994): 110 (reporting the results of a 1985 study by William Cook of a random sample of 500 NLRB elations held during 1979–1980 that concluded that 28 percent of the unions that won elections were unable to obtain a first contract); Congressional Research Service, "The National Labor Relations Act (NLRA): Union Representation Procedures and Dispute Resolution" (hereinafter "CRS Report"), table 2, December 11, 2013 (showing no-first-contract rates in the 1970s averaging approximately 30 percent), https://www.everycrsreport.com/reports/RL32930.html#_Ref219693732.

20. See "CRS Report," at table 2 (estimates published in US Departments of Labor and Commerce, "Fact Finding Report: Commission on the Future of Worker-Management Relations," May 1994, 73, 87, http://digitalcommons.ilr.cornell.edu/cgi/viewcontent.cgi?article=1279&context=key_workplace). This report also states that obtaining a first contract could be lower (33 percent) due to some first contracts having been executed when the FMCS was not contacted to assist.

21. John-Paul Ferguson, "The Eyes of the Needles: A Sequential Model of Union Organizing Drives, 1999–2004," *Ind. & Lab. Rel. Rev.* 62, no. 1 (October 2008), 3–6. See also "CRS Report," at table 2.

22. Joel Rogers, "Reforming U.S. Labor Relations," in *Restoring the Promise of American Labor Law*, ed. by Sheldon Friedman et al. (Ithaca, NY: ILR Press, 1994): 19.

23. Pavy, "Winning NLRB Elections," 111.

24. Pavy, "Winning NLRB Elections," 113–114, table 7.2 (concluding that "the results for all three years, spanning two decades, show that despite a clear expression by employees for union representation, unions have a difficult time getting employers to sign collective bargaining agreements. In fact, unions that won elections in 1982 and 1987 had a considerably more difficult time establishing normal labor relations with employers than did unions that won elections in 1970").

25. NLRA § 8(d) states that the "obligation [to bargain in good faith] does not compel either party to agree to a proposal or require the making of a concession." NLRA § 8(d), 29 U.S.C. § 158(d).

26. *H. K. Porter Co. v. NLRB*, 397 U.S. 99 (1970) (NLRB lacks the remedial authority to require a party to agree to a specific bargaining proposal).

27. Pavy, "Winning NLRB Elections," 114–115.

28. See Richard Hurd and Joseph B. Uehlein, "Patterned Responses to Organizing: Case Studies of the Union-Busting Convention," in *Restoring the Promise of American*

Labor, ed. by Sheldon Friedman et al. (Ithaca, NY: ILR Press, 1994): 62. The NLRB has held that there does come a point where an employer's bargaining proposals are so "unusually harsh or vindictive or so unreasonable as to warrant the conclusion that they were proffered in bad faith." See *Chevron Chemical Co.*, 261 N.L.R.B. 44 (1982), *enfd.* 701 F.2d 172 (5th Cir. 1983).

29. *General Electric Co.*, 150 N.L.R.B. 192, 194 (1964).

30. Hurd and Uehlein, "Patterned Responses to Organizing," 71.

31. Hurd and Uehlein, "Patterned Responses to Organizing," 72. Also see Julius G. Getman, *The Supreme Court on Unions: Why Labor Law Is Failing American Workers* (Ithaca, NY: Cornell/ILR Press, 2016), 36–37 (concluding that "[i]f a union cannot strike effectively and cannot negotiate an agreement, it is likely to become moribund and fade away [and in this way, the employer] can use the process of bargaining for a first contract to rid itself of the union").

32. Hurd and Uehlein, "Patterned Responses to Organizing," 72 (on the employer's right to permanently replace economic strikers, see the discussion in chapter 10 of the reform proposal to ban the practice).

33. Getman, *The Supreme Court on Unions*, 36 (concluding that "[t]he nature of the bargaining process is such that it is almost impossible for the board to distinguish between tough bargaining and bargaining in bad faith [especially] in evaluating first contract negotiations"); Gould, *Agenda for Reform*, 167 (arguing that "in practice, unlawful intent [not to consummate an agreement] or conduct from which the intent can be inferred is difficult to prove").

34. Getman, *The Supreme Court on Unions*, 193 (discussing dragging negotiations out for more than a year as a means to undermine support for the union).

35. In addition, to remedy employer bad-faith bargaining, the NLRB has, infrequently, required the employer to reimburse the union for its bargaining expenses and members of the union bargaining committee for lost wages due to attendance at bad-faith bargaining sessions. See *Wellman Indus.*, 248 N.L.R.B. 325 (1980) (union expenses); *M. F. A. Milling Co.*, 170 N.L.R.B.1079 (1968) (lost wages of employee-members of union bargaining committee). But these are minor costs compared to the benefit that the employer receives from eliminating the union.

36. See Gould, *Agenda for Reform*, 168–169 (the "inability of the union to produce anything for the rank and file . . . is virtually the same as decertification or lack of certification during the organizing campaign [and the] delay in unfair labor practice litigation, even if unsuccessful from the employer's perspective, erodes support").

37. See also Getman, *The Supreme Court on Unions*, 33n55 (discussion of studies showing that unions that receive *Gissel* bargaining orders seldom are able to create productive bargaining relationships).

38. Gary N. Chaison and Joseph B. Rose, "The Canadian Perspective on Workers' Rights to Form a Union and Bargain Collectively," in *Restoring the Promise of American Labor Law*, ed. by Sheldon Friedman et al. (Ithaca, NY: ILR Press, 1994): 245; Gould, *Agenda for Reform*, 222.

39. See Steven H. Lopez, "Overcoming Legacies of Business Unionism," in *Rebuilding Labor: Organizing and Organizers in the New Union Movement*, ed. Ruth Milkman and Kim Voss (Ithaca, NY: Cornell/ILR Press, 2004), 124–125, 129.

40. Gould, *Agenda for Reform*, 169, 223.

41. Gould, *Agenda for Reform*, 169 (explaining that "[t]he idea here is to keep the parties in a state of uncertainty by precluding any arbitral compromise and then require the arbitrator to accept one side or the other's last position [the goal being to] induce both sides to be more flexible and reasonable as they approach the bargaining table").

42. Gould, *Agenda for Reform*, 196–198 (also outlining many challenges and problems that final-offer arbitration can generate, including how the system can be manipulated, and proposing solutions).

43. Section 103 of the PRO Act changes the current bar on the NLRB appointing any individuals for the purposes of engaging in economic analysis. Permitting the board to conduct economic assessments will help ensure that its policies and regulations are factually supported by economic analysis rather than relying on outside organizations with an interest in the outcome of the proceeding. Having the benefit of reliable data to assist in filling the interstices in the PRO Act's first-contract arbitration provisions is a good example of the value that economic analysis could bring to the work of the Board.

Chapter 9

1. See the PRO Act §§ 104(a), (b), (f), & (g) and 105(f), (g), & (h).

2. NLRA § 1, 29 U.S.C. § 151.

3. The bargaining duty can continue during the term of an existing agreement. The leading case is *NLRB v. Jacobs Mfg. Co.*, 196 F.2d 680 (2d Cir. 1952) (duty to bargain during the term of an existing agreement over mandatory subjects of bargaining that were neither discussed nor embodied in any of the terms and conditions of an existing contract).

4. 369 U.S. 736 (1962). Even following impasse, the employer is barred from making a unilateral change that is greater than that offered to the union, *NLRB v. Crompton-Highland Mills*, 337 U.S. 217 (1949).

5. Ellen Dannin, "From Dictator Game to Ultimatum Game . . . and Back Again: The Judicial Impasse Amendments," *U. Pa. J. Lab. & Emp. L.* 6, no. 2 (2004): 241, 255.

6. See *American Shipbuilding v. NLRB*, 380 U.S. 300 (1965) (offensive lockout is lawful after impasse, absent union animus and if the employer is not engaging in it to advance bad faith bargaining by the employer). See *Graphic Communications Local 458–3M (Chicago) v. NLRB*, 206 F.3d22 (D.C. Cir. 2000) (offensive lockout is lawful because the employer's bargaining position was regressive, but not constituting bad-faith bargaining). See also *Darling & Co.*, 171 N.L.R.B. 801 (1968) (preimpasse offensive lockout is lawful, assuming that no motive to discourage union activity or to evade bargaining obligation is proved).

7. *Harter Equipment*, 280 N.L.R.B. 597 (1986).

8. See *Ancor Concepts*, 323 N.L.R.B. 742 (1997) (lawful lockout is initiated when employer communicated to striking workers that employer would refuse to offer reinstatement until a new agreement was reached).

9. Julius G. Getman, *The Supreme Court on Unions: Why Labor Law Is Failing American Workers* (Ithaca, NY: Cornell/ILR Press, 2016), 194–195.

10. *NLRB v. Mackay Radio & Tel. Co.*, 304 U.S. 333 (1938).

11. See *Laidlow Corp.*, 171 N.L.R.B. 1366 (1968).

12. Getman, *The Supreme Court on Unions*, 195 (discussing the likelihood of striker replacements, "supported by disheartened former strikers," voting to decertify the union).

13. See the discussion in William B. Gould IV, *Agenda for Reform: The Future of Employment Relationships and the Law* (Cambridge, MA: MIT Press, 1996), 190.

14. *Levitz Furniture Co. of the Pacific, Inc.*, 333 N.L.R.B. 717 (2001). See *Wurtland Nursing & Rehabilitation Center*, 351 N.L.R.B. 817 (2007) (employer may withdraw recognition based on a decertification petition that demonstrates union's loss of majority support by a preponderance of the evidence.) Cf. *Remington Lodging Hospitality*, LLC, 359 N.L.R.B. 803, 806 (2013) (unlawful for an employer to assist, support, encourage, or otherwise advance an employee decertification effort, any resulting petition is tainted, and withdrawal of recognition based on such a tainted decertification petition is unlawful).

15. See PRO Act § 104(f).

16. 368 N.L.R.B. No. 20 (2019).

17. *Levitz Furniture Co. of the Pacific, Inc.*

18. For an example of reversing the process, see PRO Act § 104(g).

19. In this regard, see also PRO Act §§ 105(f), (g). & (h).

20. See, for example, *Chelsea Indus.*, 331 N.L.R.B. 1648 (2000).

21. The only difference is that the election bar forbids an election within one year but permits the filing for an election prior to one year, whereas the certification bar forbids the filling of a petition during a union's certification year.

22. *Brooks v. NLRB*, 348 U.S. 96 (1954).

23. Under the decision of *Keller Plastics*, 157 N.L.R.B. 583 (1966), once the parties consummate a valid voluntary recognition agreement, it operates as an election bar—but is called the "voluntary recognition bar"—by foreclosing an election in that bargaining unit for a reasonable time to permit the parties to negotiate a first collective bargaining contract. For example, the recognition bar will bar a decertification petition supported by a 30 percent showing of interest. *Baseball Club of Seattle Mariners*, 335 N.L.R.B., 563 (2001). Cf. *Rollins Transp. Sys.*, 296 N.L.R.B. 793 (1989) (no bar exists when voluntary recognition occurs in the context of two unions competing for recognition in the same bargaining unit). And during the period that the recognition bar is in effect, an irrebuttable presumption of majority status arises barring the withdrawal of recognition until the recognition bar lapses. See *Americold Logistics, LLC*, 362 N.L.R.B. 493 (2015).

24. See *St. Elizabeth's Manor*, 329 N.L.R.B. 341 (1999) (recognition bar not limited to initial organization of employees but applies also to a successor employer extending recognition to an incumbent union). Also see *UGL-UNICCO Service Co.*, 357 N.L.R.B. 801 (2011) (reinstating the successor bar previously rejected in *MV Transportation*, 337 N.L.R.B. 770 (2002).

25. See, for example, *Lee Lumber & Bldg. Material Corp. v. NLRB*, 117 F.3d 1454, 1463 (D.C. Cir. 1997) (holding that "it was also rational for the Board to conclude that requiring an employer to bargain with the union for a reasonable time in order to cure the taint of its unlawful refusal to bargain 'removes from the employer the temptation to avoid its bargaining duties in the hope that delay will undermine employee support for the union").

26. A union enjoys an irrebuttable presumption of majority support while a collective bargaining agreement is in effect. *Auciello Iron Works, Inc. v. NLRB*, 517 U.S. 781 (1996); Belcon, Inc., 257 N.L.R.B. 1341, 1346–1347 (1981). After the contract expires, the presumption becomes rebuttable. *Guerdon Indus., Inc.*, 218 N.L.R.B. 658, 659 (1975). Under the NLRB's current application of the contract-bar doctrine, a valid collective-bargaining agreement ordinarily is a bar to a representation petition during the term of the agreement, but for no longer than three years. *General Cable Corp.*, 139 N.L.R.B. 1123, 1125 (1962). During this contract bar period, the Board will dismiss all representation petitions unless they are filed during the thirty-day period that begins ninety days and ends sixty days before the agreement expires. See *Leonard Wholesale Meats, Inc.*, 136 N.L.R.B. 1000, 1001 (1962). In other words, there is a thirty-day period—customarily known as the "window period"—during which a petition may be properly filed while the agreement is still in effect. The subsequent

sixty-day period immediately preceding and including the expiration date of an existing agreement is customarily known as the "insulated period" because, during that time, no timely petition may be filed. See *Deluxe Metal Furniture Co.*, 121 N.L.R.B. 995, 1000 (1958).

27. Unless the charging party requests that the NLRB proceed with a pending election, the Board generally will refuse to direct an election during the pendency of unfair labor practice charges that, if valid, interfere with the ability of employees to make a free and fair choice concerning representation while the charges remain unresolved. This NLRB-created rule, including unblocking the election when the charging party requests the Board to proceed, has been upheld in the courts. See, for example, *NLRB v. Tri-City Linen Supply*, 579 F.2d 51 (9th Cir. 1978).

28. "Representation—Case Procedures: Election Bars; Proof of Majority Support in Construction-Industry Collective-Bargaining Relationships," effective June 1, 2020, 85 FR 18366–01.

29. If a complaint issues with respect to the charge at any time prior to expiration of that sixty-day postelection period, then the ballots shall continue to be impounded until there is a final determination regarding the charge and its effect, if any, on the election petition.

30. See *United States Coal & Coke Co.*, 3 N.L.R.B. 398 (1937).

31. A third amendment, in the Trump NLRB's April 2020 Final Rule, but not redressed by the PRO Act, provides that contract language cannot establish the existence of a § 9(a) majority-based bargaining relationship for parties in the construction industry, rather than a relationship under § 8(f), the second proviso of which prohibits any election bar. To prove the establishment of a § 9(a) relationship in the construction industry, the new rule requires extrinsic evidence, in the form of employee signatures on union authorization cards that recognition was based on a contemporaneous showing of majority employee support. In 2022, the NLRB decided *Enright Seeding, Inc. (International Union of Operating Engineers, Local 150)*, 371 N.L.R.B. No. 127 (2022). There, the Board agreed that contract language *alone* cannot create a § 9(a) bargaining relationship, but a § 9(a) relationship was found to have been established by a construction industry union and employer when the parties' collective bargaining agreement provided that the employer recognizes the union as the exclusive bargaining representative and that the "employer was presented and reviewed valid written evidence of the Union's exclusive designation as bargaining representative by the majority of appropriate bargaining unit employees of Employer." In reaching this conclusion, the Board reaffirmed its 1978 ruling in *John Deklewa & Sons*, 282 NLRB 1375 (1987), *enfd. sub nom. Iron Workers Local 3 v. NLRB*, 843 F.2d 770 (3d Cir. 1988), that NLRA § 9(a) has the same application in the construction industry as elsewhere, and that includes the NLRA § 10(b) six-month time limitations for challenging the validity of § 9(a) recognition.

32. See Robert Iafolla, "Labor Board Proposes Bringing Back 'Blocking Charge' Policy," *Bloomberg Law,* November 3, 2022, https://news.bloomberglaw.com/daily-labor-report/nlrb-proposes-to-reverse-trump-era-blocking-charge-regulation.

33. On June 23, 2020, in *Mountaire Farms, Inc.*, 370 N.L.R.B. No. 110 (Case 05-RD-256888) (April 21, 2021), the NLRB granted the union's request for review of a regional director's decision that found that the collective-bargaining agreement between the employer and the union does not bar a decertification petition because the agreement contains an unlawful union-security clause. The Board used this request for review to "undertake a general review of its contract-bar doctrine." On July 7, 2020, it issued a Notice and Invitation to File Briefs, inviting the parties and interested amici curiae to file briefs addressing whether the Board should rescind, retain, or modify the contract-bar doctrine. In addition to briefs by the parties, seventeen amicus briefs were filed. In *Mountaire Farms,* the NLRB "decided not to modify the doctrine *at this time*" (emphasis added).

Chapter 10

1. See the PRO Act, §§ 104(a), (b), (d) & (i); 110, 111.

2. *NLRB v. Mackay Radio & Tel. Co.,* 304 U.S. 333 (1938).

3. Ahmed White, "Its Own Dubious Battle: The Impossible Defense of an Effective Right to Strike," *Wis. L. Rev.* 1261 (2018): 1065, 1126.

4. Paul C. Weiler, "A Principled Reshaping of Labor Law for the Twenty-first Century," *U. Pa. J. Lab. & Emp. L.* 3, no. 2 (2001): 177, 201.

5. NLRA § 13, 29 U.S.C. § 163 (emphasis added).

6. Weiler, "A Principled Reshaping of Labor Law," 201.

7. White, "Its Own Dubious Battle," 1065. See, for example, William B. Gould IV, *Agenda for Reform: The Future of Employment Relationships and the Law* (Cambridge, MA: MIT Press, 1996), 202. (reasoning that "[t]he lawfulness of the permanent replacement tactic is a factor in the erosion of the strike and the labor movement itself. [We ought to] reassess the compatibility of job loss as a price for the strike's exercise and the ideal of a civilized and democratic society"), 2.

8. Weiler, "A Principled Reshaping of Labor Law," 201.

9. Gould, *Agenda for Reform,* 190.

10. White, "Its Own Dubious Battle," 1068.

11. See Bureau of Labor Statistics, press release, "Major Work Stoppages (Annual) News Release" (February 19, 2021), https://www.bls.gov/news.release/archives/wkstp_02192021.htm. See also White, "Its Own Dubious Battle," 1067–1068 (stating that

"[f]rom 1947 through 1976, the government documented an average of just over 300 "major work stoppages" (strikes and lockouts involving at least 1000 workers) every year; over the last decade, the annual average was only 14," citing Bureau of Labor Statistics, "Major Work Stoppages in 2016," https://www.bls.gov/news.release/archives /wkstp_02092017.pdf.).

12. See the discussion in Gould, *Agenda for Reform*, 182–183 (listing at table 6.1 and figure 6 statistics demonstrating that striking has "plummeted dramatically").

13. White, "Its Own Dubious Battle," 1093.

14. Julius G. Getman, *The Supreme Court on Unions: Why Labor Law Is Failing American Workers* (Ithaca, NY: Cornell/ILR Press, 2016), 56, 66, 194; Jonathan Hiatt, "At Age Seventy, Should the National Labor Relations Act Be Retired?" in *Proceedings of the 2005 Annual Meeting, Association of American Law Schools Section on Labor Relations and Employment Law*, ed. Katherine Stone et al., *Emp. Rts. & Empl. Pol'y. J.* 9 (2005): 121, 139 (noting that it was the "major destigmatizing of the use of permanent replacements [following the PATCO strike in 1981] that led private sector employers to start making use of this tactic much more than before"). The report of the Senate Committee on Labor and Human Resources on the striker replacement bill makes this case most fully. See Workplace Fairness Act, S Rep No 102–111, 102d Cong, 1st Sess. 6–16 (1991) (employers only began to hire permanent replacements routinely in the 1980s).

15. See the testimony before Congress by William B. Gould IV, described in Gould, *Agenda for Reform*, 186.

16. *NLRB v. Insurance Agents Intl. Union*, 361 U.S. 477, 489 (1960) (stating that "[t]he presence of economic weapons in reserve, and their actual exercise on occasion by the parties, is part and parcel of the system that the Wagner and Taft-Hartley Acts have recognized").

17. White, "Its Own Dubious Battle," 1068, 1082–1083. See the discussion in chapter 2 of this book of the economic and social costs associated with the demise of collective bargaining and a healthy labor movement.

18. See Weiler, "A Principled Reshaping of Labor Law," 202 (arguing that "[t]he demonstrated ability of many employers to recruit temporary replacements in both strikes and lockouts provides tangible evidence that offering permanent status is not crucial to employers seeking to bring in replacements in our ever-increasingly 'contingent' work force," and explaining that hiring temporary replacements permits the employer to continue operations and "eventually forces the employees to give up [or compromise] and return to work.").

19. White, "Its Own Dubious Battle," 1072. See also Gould, *Agenda for Reform*, 185, 261 (remarking on the "imperviousness of the new workforce—particularly part-timers, two and more income families who may have family responsibilities—to the

clarion call not to cross the picket line . . . as a result of their own vulnerable employment situation").

20. 473 U.S. 95 (1985) (it is an unfair labor practice for a union to place limits on the right to resign during a strike and enforce those limits through fines and other union discipline).

21. 489 US 426, 432–434, 436–439 (1989) (case arising under the RLA, but understood to be equally applicable under the NLRA).

22. See White, "Its Own Dubious Battle," 1093, 1115, 1116.

23. NLRA § 13, 29 U.S.C. § 163 (emphasis added).

24. See PRO Act, § 110.

25. See, for example, *Local 1229, Electrical Workers v. NLRB*, 202 F.2d 186 (D.C. Cir. 1952) (jurisdictional strikes and secondary boycotts); *Claremont Polychemical Corp.*, 196 N.L.R.B. 613 (1972) (recognition picketing).

26. See, for example, *Auto Workers v. Russell*, 356 U.S. 634 (1958) (mass picketing); *Southern Steamship Co. v. NLRB*, 316 U.S. 31 (1942) (strike contravening federal maritime law); *NLRB v. Fansteel Metallurgical Corp.*, 306 U.S. 240 (1939) (sit-down strikes in violation of state trespass law); *Cambro Mfg. Co.*, 312 N.L.R.B. 634 (1993) (holding that in-plant work stoppage resulted in forfeiture of the act's protection when employees "failed to return to work or to leave the plant after . . . [a] second directive [to do so]").

27. Craig Becker, "'Better than a Strike': Protecting New Forms of Collective Work Stoppages under the National Labor Relations Act," *U. Chi. L. Rev.* 61, no. 2 (1994): 351, 354.

28. See, for example, *Yale University*, 330 N.L.R.B. 246 (1999) (refusal by graduate teaching fellows to submit final student grades while willing to perform all other duties an unprotected "partial strike").

29. *C.G. Conn, Ltd. v. NLRB*, 108 F.2d 390, 397 (7th Cir 1939) (refusal to work overtime is unprotected); *Omni Int'l Hotel*, 242 N.L.R.B. 248, 254–255 (1979) (refusal to work weekends is unprotected); *Honolulu Rapid Transit Co.*, 110 N.L.R.B. 1806, 1807 (1954). (same).

30. The NLRB has stated that to be protected, "the strike or stoppage must be complete, that is, the employees must withhold all their services from their employer." *Audubon Health Care Center*, 268 N.L.R.B. 135, 137 (1983).

31. Becker, "Better than a Strike," 376.

32. 9 N.L.R.B. 676, 686 (1938).

33. 91 N.L.R.B. 333 (1950).

34. 108 F.2d 390, 397 (7th Cir 1939).

35. Becker, "Better than a Strike," 387.

36. James B. Atleson, *Values and Assumptions in American Labor Law* (Amherst: University of Massachusetts Press, 1983), 57–66 (also explaining the long history of workers informally setting their pace and other conditions of employment, and that it is questionable whether there exists "social condemnation" of the slowdown and refusal to work overtime, especially since expanding overtime negates the little free time that many workers have available to them).

37. *NLRB v. Insurance Agents Intl. Union*, 361 US 477, 491, 495 (1960).

38. *Lodge 76, International Ass'n of Machinists v Wisconsin Employment Relations Commission*, 427 US 132 (1976).

39. 336 US 245 (1949).

40. *International Union, U.A.W.A., A.F.L., Local 232 v Wisconsin Employment Relations Board (Briggs-Stratton)*, 336 US at 256.

41. This is the approach adopted in the PRO Act, § 110.

42. But see *Darling & Co.*, 171 N.L.R.B. 801 (1968) (preimpasse offensive lockout lawful, assuming no proven motive to discourage union activity or to evade bargaining obligation).

43. See *Ancor Concepts*, 323 N.L.R.B. 742 (1997) (a lawful lockout initiated when an employer communicated to striking workers that the employer would refuse to offer reinstatement until a new agreement was reached).

44. See, for example, *Harter Equip.*, 280 N.L.R.B. 597 (1986) (absent anti-union motivation, no violation of the NLRA to use temporary replacements during an offensive lockout). Cf. *Ancor Concepts, Inc.*, 323 N.L.R.B. 742 (1997) (unlawful to use permanent replacements during an offensive lockout).

45. *Inland Trucking Co., v. NLRB*, 440 F.2d 562, 564 (7th Cir. 1971).

46. See *Midwest Generation EME*, 343 N.L.R.B. 69 (2004).

47. This is the compromise adopted by the PRO Act, § 104(b). A common form of defensive lockout occurs when employers that bargain on a multiemployer basis lock out employees in response to a union striking one, but not all, of the employer members of the multiemployer association. In *NLRB v. Truck Drivers, Local 449, International Brotherhood of Teamsters [Buffalo Linen Case]*, 353 U.S. 87 (1957), the Court held that this was a lawful defensive lockout needed to preserve the multiemployer bargaining structure from disintegration threatened by the union's one-employer-at-a time "whipsaw" strike strategy. See also *NLRB v. Brown*, 380 U.S. 278 (1965) (lawful for employers who initiate a "*Buffalo Linen*" defensive lockout to maintain operations during the lockout by hiring temporary replacements); *NLRB v. Martin A. Gleason, Inc.*, 534 F.2d 466 (2d Cir. 1976) (it is lawful for an employer who has initiated a *Buffalo*

Linen lockout to tell employees who have asked to work during the strike that they may do so if they resign from the union).

48. See, for example, the PRO Act, § 104(d).

49. Paul C. Weiler, *Governing the Workplace: The Future of Labor and Employment Law* (Cambridge, MA: Harvard University Press, 1990), 263.

50. See NLRA § 8(b)(4), 29 U.S.C. § 158(b)(4); *United Brotherhood of Carpenters and Joiners, Local 1976 v. NLRB (Sand Door)*, 357 U.S. 93 (1958) (holding that any direct appeal to employees not to handle goods produced by an employer with whom the union has a dispute constitutes an unlawful secondary boycott).

51. See *Burlington Northern v. Brotherhood of Maintenance Employees*, 481 U.S. 429, 430, 447n13 (1987).

52. Richard White, *The Republic for Which It Stands: The United States during Reconstruction and the Gilded Age, 1865–1896* (New York: Oxford University Press, 2017), 818–819. See also Francis Bowes Sayre, "Labor and the Courts," *Yale L.J.* 39 (1930): 682.

53. See Felix Frankfurter and Nathan Greene, *The Labor Injunction* (New York: Macmillan, 1930), 43.

54. *Bossert v. Dhuy*, 221 N.Y. 342, 117 N.E. 582, 587 (1917). See also *Goldfinger v. Feintuch*, 276 N.Y. 281, 11N.E.2d 910 (1937) ("picketing may be carried on not only against the manufacturer [with whom a union has a primary dispute], but against a non-union product sold by [a retailer] in unity of interest with the manufacturer who is in the same business for profit" by the union picketing a retail store and asking customers not to purchase products manufactured by a primary employer). See Jerome R. Hellerstein, "Secondary Boycotts in Labor Disputes," *Yale L.J.* 47 (1938): 341, 352.

55. 312 U.S. 219 (1941).

56. See, for example, *Edward J. DeBartolo v. Building & Const. Trades Council (Florida Gulf Coast) (DeBartolo II)*, 485 U.S. 568 (1988) (peaceful handbilling, unaccompanied by picketing or coercive conduct, is lawful even though handbills seek a complete consumer boycott of the neutral employer); *Fruit and Vegetable Packers Local 760 (Tree Fruits Labor Relations Comm.)* 377 U.S. 58 (1964) (picketing at a secondary employer's retail store directed at consumers, requesting consumers not to purchase products produced by a primary employer lawful).

57. *Carpenters v. NLRB*, 357 U.S. 93, 98 (1958).

58. See *International Rice Milling Co.*, 341 U.S.665, 670–671 (1951) (1947 Taft-Hartley ban on secondary boycotts a bar on inducement of a "concerted" refusal to strike or perform services directed at two or more employees, and not a bar on inducement of one employee, or several employees induced one at a time, to strike or refuse to perform services).

59. *Burlington Northern v. Brotherhood of Maintenance Employees*, 481 U.S. at 430, 446–447 (holding that the RLA does not expressly limit the scope of self-help available to a union once its resolution provisions have been exhausted. The RLA's silence in this regard read by the Court to "signify an intent to allow the parties to resort to whatever self-help is legally available at the time a dispute arises").

60. Reginald Alleyne, "Boycott Ban Prolongs Eastern Strike: Secondary Picketing Could Force Bush or Congress to Act," *Los Angeles Times*, March 24, 1989, https://www.latimes.com/archives/la-xpm-1989-03-24-me-92-story.html.

61. Megan Stater Shaw, "'Connote No Evil': Judicial Treatment of the Secondary Boycott before Taft-Hartley," 96 *N.Y.U. L. Rev.* 96 (2021): 334, 339n29 (2021) (collecting authority).

62. Catherine L. Fisk, "A Progressive Labor Vision of the First Amendment: Past as Prologue," *Colum. L. Rev.* 118, no. 7 (2018): 2057, 2081–2082.

63. See General Counsel's Statement of Position to the Board on Remand from the Ninth Circuit Court of Appeals, Preferred Building Services, Inc. (Case No. 20-CA-149353) (Dec. 7, 2021), available in Ian Kullgren, "Punching In: NLRB Memo Explores Expanding Union Picketing Rights," *Bloomberg Law*, December 20, 2021, https://news.bloomberglaw.com/daily-labor-report/punching-in-nlrb-memo-explores-expanding-union-picketing-rights.

64. *Lodge 76, Int'l Ass'n of Machinists v. Wis. Emp't Rel. Comm'n*, 427 U.S. 132 (1976).

65. *Machinists*, 427 U.S. at 146 (quoting *Garner v. Teamsters Union*, 346 U.S. 485, 500 (1953)).

66. *Golden State Transit Corp.*, 475 U.S. at 619 (Golden State I) (quoting *Machinists*, 427 U.S. at 149, 150).

67. Shaw, "'Connote No Evil,'" 373.

68. Section 201 of the PRO Act is a technical addition. It repeals § 303s of the NLRA, a provision that provides employers with a private right of action to sue unions that conduct secondary strikes and other activity. Because the PRO Act would permit such secondary activity, the bill repeals this private right of action as extraneous.

69. 138 S. Ct. 1612 (2018).

70. This is the position adopted by § 104(i) of the PRO Act.

71. 29 U.S.C. §§ 201–219.

72. 42 U.S.C. §§ 2000a-2000h-6.

73. See. for example, *Murphy Oil, USA, Inc.*, 361 N.L.R.B. 774 (2014) (employees brought a collective action pursuant to the FLSA on behalf of themselves and other employees similarly situated, alleging that the employer failed to compensate the

plaintiffs for overtime and for various required work-related activities performed off the clock, including driving to the fuel stations of the employer's competitors to monitor fuel prices and the accuracy of their signage).

74. See the discussion in Simon Jacobs, "Arbitration and Title VII Pattern-or-Practice Claims after *Epic Systems*," *U. Chi. L. Rev.* 88, no. 5 (2021): 1157, 1165–1168.

75. See, for example, *Mozee v. Am. Com. Marine Serv. Co.*, 940 F.2d 1036, 1038 (7th Cir. 1991), *aff'd and reh'g denied*, 963 F.2d 929 (7th Cir. 1992).

76. See *Jock v. Sterling Jewelers Inc.*, 942 F.3d 617 (2d Cir. 2019).

77. Jacobs, "Arbitration and Title VII Pattern-or-Practice Claims," 1160.

78. 563 U.S. 333, 352 (2011).

79. Jacobs, "Arbitration and Title VII Pattern-or-Practice Claims," 1161–1162.

80. See Cynthia Estlund, "The Black Hole of Mandatory Arbitration," *N.C. L. Rev.* 96, no. 3 (2018): 679, 688, 696. But see Samuel Estreicher, Michael Heise, and David S. Sherwyn, "Evaluating Employment Arbitration: A Call for Better Empirical Research," *Rutgers U. L. Rev.* 70 (2018): 375 (challenging Estlund's methodology and conclusions).

81. Jacobs, "Arbitration and Title VII Pattern-or-Practice Claims," 1162 (quoting Linda Hamilton Krieger, "Message in a Bottle," *Berkeley J. Emp. & Lab. L.* 39 (2018): 53, 75–78).

82. 361 N.L.R.B. 774 (2014) (reaffirming *D. R. Horton, Inc.*, 357 N.L.R.B. 277 (2012)).

83. 138 S. Ct. 1612 (2018) (in *Epic Systems*, the Court consolidated an employer's request for review in *Murphy Oil* with two FLSA cases that raised the issue of whether a mandatory arbitration agreement in employees' contracts precluded their bringing FLSA judicial claims).

84. *Epic Systems*, 138 S. Ct. at 1625 (quoting *NLRB v. Alternative Entertainment, Inc.*, 858 F.3d 393, 414–415 (6th Cir. 2017) (Sutton, J., concurring in part and dissenting in part).

85. See this adoption in the PRO Act, § 104(i).

86. *Vaca v. Sipes*, 386 U.S. 171 (1967); *Syres v. Oil Workers, Local 23*, 350 U.S. 892 (1955).

87. *NLRB v. General Motors Corp.*, 373U.S. 734 (1963).

88. *NLRB v. General Motors Corp.*, at 742.

89. 487 U.S. 735, 745 (1988).

90. In *Janus v. American Federation of State, City, & Municipal Employees, Council* 31, 138 S. Ct. 2448, 2460 (2018), the Court held that it was a violation of First Amendment

rights for a public employer to agree with a union to condition a public employee's employment on payment of even the "financial core" referred to in the *General Motors* decision. *Janus* has no direct applicability to private-sector union security agreements because of the absence of government action when a private-sector employer voluntarily agrees to a union security agreement in a collective bargaining agreement with a private-sector union. But see Michelle Quach, "The *Janus* Decision and the Future of Private Sector Unionism," *Hastings Bus. L.J.* 16, no. 1 (2020): 119, 129–130 (arguing that the Court in *Janus* explicitly left unanswered the question of extending the *Janus* decision to private-sector unions and stating that courts could conclude that government action is implicated from the exclusive bargaining representation status that the NLRA grants to unions).

91. Workplace Fairness, "Right to Work Laws," https://www.workplacefairness.org/unions-right-to-work-laws.

92. See, for example, the PRO Act § 111.

Epilogue

1. Terri Gerstein, "State and Local Workers' Rights' Innovations: New Players, New Laws, New Methods of Enforcement," *St. Louis U. L.J.* 65, no. 1 (2020): 45, 47.

2. See the discussion in Benjamin I. Sachs, "Labor Law Renewal," *Harv. L. & Pol'y Rev.* 1 (2007): 375, 375–376.

3. Sachs, "Labor Law Renewal," 378.

4. See Roger C. Hartley, "Non-Legislative Labor Law Reform and Pre-recognition Labor Neutrality Agreements: The Newest Civil Rights Movement," *Berkeley J. Emp. & Lab. L.* 22 (2001): 369.

5. Adrienne E. Eaton and Jill Kriesky, "Union Organizing under Neutrality and Card Check Agreements," *Indus. and Lab. Rel. Rev.* 55, no. 1 (2001): 42, 47–48 (giving as examples an employer agreement of "neither helping nor hindering the union's organizing effort" and "the employer will not communicate opposition," and that the employer could communicate "facts" (sometimes only in response to inquiries) or provide that "management will tell employees that it actually welcomes their choice of a representative").

6. Hartley, "Non-Legislative Labor Law Reform," 365–366.

7. Eaton and Kriesky, "Union Organizing under Neutrality and Card Check Agreements," 48.

8. See Hartley, "Non-Legislative Labor Law Reform," 386–387.

9. Sachs, "Labor Law Renewal," 382.

10. The union may obtain leverage from its ability to provide employers some benefit, such as securing business for the employer. See, for example, Benjamin I. Sachs, "Despite Preemption: Making Labor Law in Cities and States," *Harv. L. Rev.* 124 (2011): 1153, 1171n90. See also Hartley, "Non-Legislative Labor Law Reform," 387–396 (summarizing various ways in which organizing agreements are reached, including a union leveraging state and local political power).

11. University of Wisconsin-Madison, Public Health Institute, County Health Rankings and Roadmaps, "Living Wage Laws," https://www.countyhealthrankings.org/take-action-to-improve-health/what-works-for-health/strategies/living-wage-laws.

12. See, for example, Cynthia L. Estlund, "The Ossification of American Labor Law," *Colum L. Rev* 102, no. 6 (2002): 1527, 1569–1577; Michael H. Gottesman, "In Despair, Starting Over: Imagining a Labor Law for Unorganized Workers," *Chi.-Kent L. Rev.* 69, no. 1 (1993): 59.

13. See, for example, San Diego Building Trades Council v. Garmon, 359 U.S. 236 (1959); Lodge 76, Machinists v. *Wisconsin Empl. Rel. Comm'n*, 427 U.S. 132, 140, 146 (1976).

14. Terri Gerstein, "State and Local Workers' Rights' Innovations: Labor and Technology in the 21st Century," *St. Louis U. L.J.* 65, no. 1 (2020): 45.

15. See Gerstein, "State and Local Workers' Rights' Innovations," 50–54; Terri Gerstein, "Workers' Rights Protection and Enforcement by State Attorneys General," *Econ. Pol'y Inst.*, August 27, 2020, https://www.epi.org/publication/state-ag-labor-rights-activities-2018-to-2020/.

16. 475 U.S. 608, 618 (1986).

17. 554 U.S. 60, 68 (2008).

18. See *Metro. Milwaukee Ass'n of Commerce v. Milwaukee County*, 431 F.3d 277 (7th Cir. 2005) (the ordinance also required the employer to agree not to compel employees to attend captive audience meetings and to limited access to the workplace during nonwork time).

19. *California Grocers Assn. v. City of Los Angeles*, 52 Cal.4th 177, 197 (2011) (emphasis added).

20. See *Metropolitan Life Ins. Co. v. Massachusetts*, 471 U.S. 724, 753 (1985).

21. *Fort Halifax Packing Co. v. Coyne*, 482 U.S. 1, 20 (1987).

22. See Partnership for Working Families, *Policy & Tools: Worker Retention Policies*, http://www.forworkingfamilies.org/resources/policy-tools-worker-retention-policies (discussing several varieties of worker retention policies and their increasing use).

23. See *Washington Service Contractors Coalition v. District of Columbia*, 54 F.3d 811, 813–814 (1995).

24. 41 D.C. Reg. 1011 (codified at D.C. Code Ann. 361501 to 1503).

25. As is true of most worker retention statutes, the DWPA also provides that those so retained may be terminated only for "cause," and at the end of the transition period, the contractor is to prepare a written performance evaluation for each employee retained. For those employees whose performance is found to be satisfactory, the contractor "shall offer the employee continued employment under the terms and conditions established by the new contractor." The DWPA provides a private right of action for back pay, costs, and attorney's fees for employees who are discharged in violation of the Act.

26. See, for example, *Rhode Island Hospitality Association v. Providence*, 667 F.3d 17 (1st Cir. 2011) (Providence, Rhode Island Worker Retention Ordinance); *Washington Service Contractors Coalition v. District of Columbia*, 54 F.3d 811 (1995) (D.C. DWPA); *Paulsen v. GVS Properties, LLC*, 904 F.Supp.2d 282 (E.D.N.Y. 2012) (New York City Displaced Building Service Workers Protection Act (DBSWPA)); *Alcantara v. Allied Properties*, LLC, 334 F.Supp.2d 336 (E.D.N.Y. 2004) (New York Displaced Building Service Workers Protection Act (DBSWPA); *California Grocers Association v. City of Los Angeles*, 52 Cal.4th 177, 254 P.2d 1019 (2011) (Los Angeles Worker Retention Ordinance).

27. See, for example, *Rhode Island Hospitality Association v. Providence*, 667 F.3d 17 (1st Cir. 2011).

28. See the discussion in Gerstein, "State and Local Workers' Rights' Innovations," 71–74.

29. See Sachs, "Despite Preemption," 1155–1156 (giving as one example a case of "the City of New Haven, the Yale–New Haven Hospital, and the New Haven hospital workers' union engag[ing] in three-way negotiations over the construction of a cancer facility. The union wanted new rules for organizing. The hospital needed zoning and development permits from the City. Following a series of meetings mediated by the New Haven mayor, a package deal was reached: the City issued the permits in exchange for the hospital's agreement to reorder contractually the rules of organizing").

30. Gerstein, "State and Local Workers' Rights' Innovations," 83–88.

31. Gerstein, "State and Local Workers' Rights' Innovations," 83–84.

32. See, for example, Sachs, "Labor Law Renewal," 391 (discussing a worker center in Bushwick, Brooklyn—called Make the Road by Walking—that is "dedicated to facilitating Bushwick workers' efforts to collectively secure rights at work").

33. Gerstein, "State and Local Workers' Rights' Innovations," 86–87.

Bibliography

Aaron, Benjamin. "Amending the Taft-Hartley Act: A Decade of Frustration." *Indus. & Lab. Rel. Rev.* 11, no. 3 (1958): 327.

Adams, Roy. "Union Certification as an Instrument of Labor Policy: A Comparative Perspective." In *Restoring the Promise of American Labor Law*, 265, edited by Sheldon Friedman et al. Ithaca, NY: ILR Press, 1994.

Andrias, Kate. "The New Labor Law." *Yale L.J.* 126, no. 1 (2016): 2.

Andrias, Kate. "Peril and Possibility: Strikes, Rights, and Legal Change in the Age of Trump." *Berkeley J. Emp. & Lab. L.* 40, no. 1 (2019): 135.

Atleson, James B. *Values and Assumptions in American Labor Law*. Amherst: University of Massachusetts Press, 1983.

Barbash, Jack. "Labor Movement Theory and the Institutional Setting." *Monthly Lab. Rev.* 104, no. 9 (1981): 34.

Barbash, Jack. "Union Response to the 'Hard Line'." *Indus. Rel.* 1, no. 1 (1961): 25.

Becker, Craig. "'Better than a Strike': Protecting New Forms of Collective Work Stoppages under the National Labor Relations Act." *U. Chi. L. Rev.* 61, no. 2: 351.

Becker, Craig, and Diana Orantes Ceresi. "Toward a Rational Interpretation of the Term 'Supervisor' after Kentucky River." *Lab. Law.* 18 (2003): 385.

Befort, Stephen F. "Revisiting the Black Hole of Workplace Regulation: A Historical and Comparative Perspective of Contingent Work." *J. Emp. & Lab. L.* 24 (2003): 153.

Bell, Daniel. *The End of Ideology: On the Exhaustion of Political Ideas in the Fifties*. Cambridge, MA: Harvard University Press, 1960.

Bernstein, Irving. *The Lean Years: A History of the American Worker, 1920–1933*. Boston: Houghton Mifflin, 1969.

Bernstein, Irving. *Turbulent Years: A History of the American Worker, 1933–1941*. Boston: Houghton Mifflin, 1970.

Black, Charles L., Jr. "He Cannot Choose but Hear: The Plight of the Captive Auditor." *Colum. L. Rev.* 53, no. 7 (1953): 960.

Block, Sharon. "Go Big or Go Home: The Case for Clean Slate Labor Law Reform." *Berkeley J. Emp. & Lab. L.* 41, no. 1 (2020): 168.

Blumrosen, Alfred W. "Group Interests in Labor Law." *Rutgers L. Rev.* 13 (1959): 432.

Bok, Derek C., and John T. Dunlop. *Labor and the American Community*. New York: Simon and Schuster, 1970.

Bonnett, Clarence E. "The Origin of the Labor Injunction." *S. Cal. L. Rev.* 5 (1931): 105.

Bronfenbrenner, Kate. "Employer Behavior in Certification Elections and First-Contract Campaigns: Implications for Labor Law Reform." In *Restoring the Promise of American Labor Law*, edited by Sheldon Friedman et al. Ithaca, NY: ILR Press, 1994: 78.

Bronfenbrenner, Kate. *Uneasy Terrain: The Impact of Capital Mobility on Workers, Wages, and Union Organizing: Report Submitted to the U.S. Trade Deficit Review Commission: Causes, Consequences, and Recommendations for Action*. Washington, DC: US Trade Deficit Review Commission, 2000.

Bronfenbrenner, Kate, Sheldon Friedman, Richard W. Hurd, Rudolph A. Oswals, and Ronald L. Seeber. "Introduction." In *Organizing to Win: New Research in Union Strategies*, edited by Kate Bronfenbrenner et al. Ithaca, NY: Cornell/ILR Press, 1998: 6.

Bronfenbrenner, Kate, and Robert Hickey. "Changing to Organize: A National Assessment of Union Strategies." In *Rebuilding Labor: Organizing and Organizers in the New Union Movement*, edited by Ruth Milkman and Kim Voss. Ithaca, NY: Cornell University Press, 2004: 25.

Bruce, Peter G. "On the Status of Workers' Rights to Organize in the United States and Canada." In *Restoring the Promise of American Labor Law*, edited by Sheldon Friedman et al. Ithaca, NY: ILR Press, 1994: 273.

Chaison, Gary N., and Joseph B. Rose. "The Canadian Perspective on Workers' Rights to Form a Union and Bargain Collectively." In *Restoring the Promise of American Labor Law*, edited by Sheldon Friedman et al. Ithaca, NY: ILR Press, 1994: 222.

Chamberlain, Neal W. *Labor*. New York: McGraw-Hill, 1958.

Cohen, Larry, and Richard W. Hurd. "Fear, Conflict, and Union Organizing." In *Organizing to Win*, edited by Kate Bronfenbrenner et al. Ithaca, NY: Cornell/ILR Press, 1998: 182.

Commons, John Rogers, and Eugene A. Gilmore. *A Documentary History of American Industrial Society*, vols. 1 and 3. Norman, OK: Arthur H. Clark Co., 1910.

Compa, Lance. *Unfair Advantage: Workers' Freedom of Association in the United States under International Human Rights Standards*. Ithaca, NY: Cornell University Press, 2000.

Comstock, Phil, and Maier B. Fox. "Employer Tactics and Labor Law Reform." In *Restoring the Promise of American Labor Law*, edited by Sheldon Friedman et al. Ithaca, NY: ILR Press, 1994: 93.

Conway, Jack T. "New Challenges to Union Leadership." *Monthly Lab. Rev.* 92 (1969): 56.

Cox, Archibald. "The Role of Law in Preserving Union Democracy." *Harv. L. Rev.* 72, no. 4 (1959): 609–610.

Daniel, Cletus E. *The ACLU and the Wagner Act: An Inquiry into the Depression-Era Crisis of American Liberalism*. Ithaca, NY: Cornell/ILR Press, 1980.

Dannin, Ellen. "At Age Seventy, Should the National Labor Relations Act Be Retired?" In *Proceedings of the 2005 Annual Meeting, Association of American Law Schools Section on Labor Relations and Employment Law*, edited by Katherine Stone et al. *Emp. Rts. & Emp. Pol'y. J.* 9 (2005): 121.

Dannin, Ellen. "From Dictator Game to Ultimatum Game . . . and Back Again: The Judicial Impasse Amendments." *U. Pa. J. Lab. & Emp. L.* 6, no. 2 (2004): 241.

Delchamps, Alfred F., III. "The Employment at Will Rule." *Ala. L. Rev.* 31 (1980): 421.

DeMaria, Alfred. *How Management Wins Union Organizing Campaigns*. Hoboken, NJ: Prentice-Hall, 1980.

Denice, Patrick, and Jake Rosenfeld. "Unions and Nonunion Pay in the United States, 1977–2015." *Soc. Sci.* 5 (2018): 541.

Derber, Milton. *The American Idea of Industrial Democracy, 1865–1965*. Champaign: University of Illinois Press, 1970.

Dey, Matthew, Susan N. Houseman, and Anne Elise Polivka. "What Do We Know about Contracting Out in the United States? Evidence from Household and Establishment Surveys." In *Labor in the New Economy*, edited by Katharine Abraham, James Spletzer, and Michael Harper. Chicago: University of Chicago Press, 2010: 267.

Dickens, William T. "The Effect of Company Campaigns on Certification Elections: Law and Reality Once Again." *Indus. & Lab. Rel. Rev.* 36, no. 4 (1983): 560.

DiNardo, John, Nicole M. Fortin, and Thomas Lemieux. "Labor Market Institutions and the Distribution of Wages, 1973–1992: A Semiparametric Approach." *Econometrica*, 64, no. 5 (1996): 1001.

Doorey, David J. "The Medium and the 'Anti-Union' Message: 'Forced Listening' and Captive Audience Meetings in Canadian Labor Law." *Comp. Lab. L. & Pol'y J.* 29, no. 2 (2008): 79.

Dulles, Foster Rhea. *Labor in America*. New York: Thomas Y. Crowell Company, 1963.

Eaton, Adrienne E., and Jill Kriesky. "Union Organizing under Neutrality and Card Check Agreements." *Indus. and Lab. Rel. Rev.* 55, no. 1 (2001): 42.

Edsall, Thomas Byrne. *The New Politics of Inequality*. New York: W. W. Norton, 1984.

Estlund, Cynthia. "The Black Hole of Mandatory Arbitration." *N.C. L. Rev.* 96, no. 3 (2018): 679.

Estlund, Cynthia L. "The Ossification of American Labor Law." *Colum. L. Rev.* 102, no. 6 (2002): 1527.

Estreicher, Samuel, Michael Heise, and David S. Sherwyn. "Evaluating Employment Arbitration: A Call for Better Empirical Research." *Rutgers U. L. Rev.* 70 (2018): 375.

Farber, Henry S. "Union Success in Representation Elections: Why Does Unit Size Matter?" *Ind. & Lab. Rel. Rev.* 54 (2001): 329.

Ferguson, John-Paul. "The Eyes of the Needles: A Sequential Model of Union Organizing Drives, 1999–2004." *Ind. & Lab. Rel. Rev.* 62, no. 1 (2008): 3.

Fisk, Catherine L. "A Progressive Labor Vision of the First Amendment: Past as Prologue." *Colum. L. Rev.* 118, no. 7 (2018): 2057.

Fisk, Catherine L., and Deborah C. Malamud. "The NLRB in Administrative Law Exile: Problems with Its Structure and Function and Suggestions for Reform." *Duke L.J.* 58 (2009): 2013.

Fletcher, Bill, Jr., and Richard Hurd. "Beyond the Organizing Mode: The Transformation Model in Local Unions." In *Organizing to Win: New Research in Union Strategies*, edited by Kate Bronfenbrenner et al. Ithaca, NY: Cornell/ILR Press, 1998: 37.

Fortin, Nicole M. et al. "Labor Market Institutions and the Distribution of Wages: The Role of Spillover Effects," NBER Working Paper 28375 (2021), 42, https://www.nber.org/papers/w28375.

Frankfurter, Felix, and Nathan Greene. *The Labor Injunction*. New York: Macmillan, 1930.

Freeman, Richard. "How Much Has De-unionization Contributed to the Rise in Male Earnings Inequality?" In *Uneven Tides: Rising Inequality in America*, edited by Sheldon Danziger and Peter Gottschalk. New York: Russell Sage Foundation, 1993: 133.

Freeman, Richard B., and Joel Rogers. *What Workers Want*. Ithaca, NY: Cornell/ILR Press, 1999.

Friedman, Sheldon, Richard W. Hurd, Rudolph A. Oswald, and Ronald L. Seeber. "Introduction: the Context of Reform of Labor Law." In *Restoring the Promise of American Labor Law*, edited by Sheldon Friedman et al. Ithaca, NY: ILR Press, 1994: 4.

Galenson, Walter. "Communists and Trade Union Democracy." *Indus. Rel.* 13, no. 3: 228.

Galenson, Walter, and Robert S. Smith. "The United States." In *Labor in the Twentieth Century*, edited by John T. Dunlop and Walter Galenson. Amsterdam: Elsevier, 1978: 50.

Gerstein, Terri. "State and Local Workers' Rights' Innovations: New Players, New Laws, New Methods of Enforcement." *St. Louis U. L.J.* 65, no. 1 (2020): 45.

Getman, Julius G. *The Supreme Court on Unions: Why Labor Law Is Failing American Workers*. Ithaca, NY: Cornell/ILR Press, 2016.

Getman, Julius G., Stephen Goldberg, and Jeanne B. Herman. *Union Representation Elections: Law and Reality*. New York: Russell Sage Foundation, 1976.

Ginsburg, Matthew. "Nothing New under the Sun: 'The New Labor Law' Must Still Grapple with the Traditional Challenges of Firm-based Organizing and Building Self-sustainable Worker Organizations." *Yale L.J. Forum* 126 (2017): 488.

Goldfield, Michael. *The Decline of Organized Labor in the United States*. Chicago: University of Chicago Press, 1987.

Goldfield, Michael, and Amy Bromsen. "The Changing Landscape of U.S. Unions in Historical and Theoretical Perspective." *Annual Rev. of Pol. Sci.* 16 (2013): 231.

Goldman, Tanya, and David Weil. "Who's Responsible Here? Establishing Legal Responsibility in the Fissured Workplace." *Berkeley J. Emp. & Lab. L.* 42 (2021): 55.

Goldstein, J. *The Government of British Trade Unions*. London: Allen & Unwin, 1952.

Gomberg, William. "Government Participation in Union Regulation and Collective Bargaining." *Lab. L.J.* 13 (1962): 941.

Gottesman, Michael H. "In Despair, Starting Over: Imagining a Labor Law for Unorganized Workers." *Chi.-Kent L. Rev.* 69, no. 1 (1993): 59.

Gould, William B., IV. *Agenda for Reform: The Future of Employment Relationships and the Law*. Cambridge, MA: MIT Press, 1996.

Gross, James A. *Broken Promises: The Subversion of U.S. Labor Relations Policy, 1947–1994*. Philadelphia: Temple University Press, 1995.

Gross, James A. "The Demise of National Labor Policy: A Question of Social Justice." In *Restoring the Promise of American Labor Law*, edited by Sheldon Friedman et al. Ithaca, NY: ILR Press, 1994: 56.

Hafiza, Hiba. "Structural Labor Rights." *Mich. L. Rev.* 119, no. 4 (2021): 651.

Hartley, Roger C. "Non-legislative Labor Law Reform and Pre-recognition Labor Neutrality Agreements: The Newest Civil Rights Movement." *Berkeley J. Emp. & Lab. L.* 22 (2001): 369.

Hatton, Erin Elizabeth. *The Temp Economy: From Kelly Girls to Permatemps in Postwar America*. Philadelphia: Temple University Press, 2011.

Hays, Paul R. "The Union and Its Members." *N.Y.U. Ann. Conf. on Lab.* 11 (1958): 35.

Hellerstein, Jerome R. "Secondary Boycotts I Labor Disputes." *Yale L.J.* 47, no. 3 (1938): 341.

Hertel-Fernandez, Alexander, William Kimball, and Thomas Kochan. "What Forms of Representation Do American Workers Want? Implications for Theory, Policy, and Practice." *Indus. & Lab. Rel. Rev.* 75, no. 2 (2020): 1.

Hiatt, Jonathan. "At Age Seventy, Should the National Labor Relations Act Be Retired?" In *Proceedings of the 2005 Annual Meeting, Association of American Law Schools Section on Labor Relations and Employment Law*, edited by Katherine Stone et al. *Emp. Rts. & Empl. Pol'y. J.* 9 (2005): 121.

Hiatt, Jonathan P. "Policy Issues Concerning the Contingent Work Force." *Wash. & Lee L. Rev.* 52, no. 3 (1995): 739.

Hirsch, Barry T. "Sluggish Institutions in a Dynamic World: Can Unions and Industrial Competition Coexist?" *J. of Econ. Perspectives* 22, no. 1 (2008): 153.

Hirsch, Jeffrey M. "NLRB Elections: Ambush or Anticlimax?" *Emory L. J.* 64 (2015): 1647.

Hurd, Richard, and Joseph B. Uehlein, "Patterned Responses to Organizing: Case Studies of the Union-Busting Convention." In *Restoring the Promise of American Labor Law*, edited by Sheldon Friedman et al. Ithaca, NY: ILR Press, 1994: 62.

Igoe, Hunter. "I Know It When I See It." *Hofstra Lab. & Empl. L. J.* 38 (2021): 285.

Jacobs, Simon. "Arbitration and Title VII Pattern-or-Practice Claims after *Epic Systems*." *U. Chi. L. Rev.* 88, no. 5 (2021): 1157.

Kalleberg, Arne L. *Good Jobs, Bad Jobs: The Rise of Polarized and Precarious Employment Systems in the United States, 1970s to 2000s*. New York: Russel Sage Foundation, 2011.

Kasper, Hirschel. "The Size of the Bargaining Unit and the Locus of Union Power." *Q. Rev. Econ. & Bus.* 6 (1966): 59.

Katznelson, Ira. *Fear Itself: The New Deal and the Origins of Our Time*. New York: Liveright, 2014.

Kemble, Penn. "Rediscovering American Labor." *Commentary* 51, no. 4 (April 1, 1971): 45.

Kistler, Alan. "Union Organizing: New Challenges and Prospects." *Annals Am. Acad. of Pol. & Soc. Sci.* 473 (1984): 96.

Kleiner, Morris M. "What Will It Take? Establishing the Economic Costs to Management of Noncompliance with the NLRA." In *Restoring the Promise of American Labor Law*, edited by Sheldon Friedman et al. Ithaca, NY: ILR Press, 1994: 139.

Kochan, Thomas A. *Contemporary Views of American Workers toward Trade Unions*. Alexandria, VA: National Technical Information Service (US Department of Commerce), 1978.

Kochan, Thomas A. "How American Workers View Labor Unions." *Monthly Lab. Rev.* 102, no. 4 (1979): 23.

Kochan, Thomas A., Duanyi Yang, William T. Kimball, and Erin L. Kelly. "Worker Voice in America: Is There a Gap between What Workers Expect and What They Experience?" *Indus. & Lab. Rel. Rev.* 72, no. 1 (2019): 3.

Krieger, Linda Hamilton. "Message in a Bottle." *Berkeley J. Emp. & Lab. L.* 39 (2018): 53.

Lebowitz, Todd. "Who Is My Employee? Exploring Issues of Independent Contractor Misclassification & Joint Employment Issues." December 27, 2022, https://whoismyemployee.com/.

Leiserson, William Morris. *American Trade Union Democracy*. New York: Columbia University Press, 1959.

Lieberman, Elias. *Unions before the Bar*. Rev. ed. New York: Harper & Bros., 1960.

Lipset, Seymour Martin, Martin Trow, and James S. Coleman. *Union Democracy: The Internal Politics of the International Typographical Union*. New York: Doubleday Anchor, 1956.

Lopez, Steven H. "Overcoming Legacies of Business Unionism." In *Rebuilding Labor: Organizing and Organizers in the New Union Movement*, edited by Ruth Milkman and Kim Voss. Ithaca, NY: Cornell/ILR Press, 2004: 124.

Macdonald, David. "How Labor Unions Increase Political Knowledge: Evidence from the United States." *Political Behavior* 43 (2019): 1.

Magrath, Peter. "Democracy in Overalls: The Futile Quest for Union Democracy." *Indus. & Lab. Rel. Rev.* 12, no. 4 (1959): 503.

Milkman, Ruth, and Kim Voss. "Introduction." In *Rebuilding Labor: Organizing and Organizers in the New Union Movement*, edited by Ruth Milkman and Kim Voss. Ithaca, NY: Cornell University Press, 2004: 1.

Mishel, Lawrence, Joshua Bivens, and Heidi Shierholz. *The State of Working America, 2012–2013*. Ithaca, NY: Cornell University Press, 2012.

Moore, Wilbert Ellis. *Industrial Relations and the Social Order*. New York: Macmillan Company, 1946.

Morris, Richard B. *Government and Labor in Early America*. New York: Columbia University Press, 1946.

Nace, Ted. *Gangs of America: The Rise of Corporate Power and the Disabling of Democracy*. San Francisco: Berrett-Koehler, 2002.

Nelles, Walter. "The First American Labor Case." *Yale L.J.* 41, no. 2 (1931): 165.

Paul, Sanjukta. "Fissuring and the Firm Exemption." *Law & Contemp. Probs.* 82, no. 2 (2019): 65.

Pavy, Gordan R. "Winning NLRB Elections and Establishing Collective Bargaining Relationships." In *Restoring the Promise of American Labor Law*, edited by Sheldon Friedman et al. Ithaca, NY: ILR Press, 1994: 110.

Penney, Robert A. "Workers against Unions: Union Organizing and Anti-union Countermobilizations." In *Rebuilding Labor: Organizing and Organizers in the New Union Movement*, edited by Ruth Milkman and Kim Voss. Ithaca, NY: Cornell University Press, 2004: 92.

Petruska, Brian J. "Adding Joy Silk to Labor's Reform Agenda." *Santa Clara L. Rev.* 57, no. 1 (2017): 97.

Piketty, Thomas, and Emmanuel Saez. "Income Inequality in the United States, 1913–1998." *Q. J. Econ.* 118, no. 1 (2003): 1.

Podgursky, Michael. "Unions, Establishment Size, and Intraindustry Threat Effects." *Indus & Lab. Rel. Rev.* 39, no. 2 (1986): 277.

Pomper, Gerald. "Labor Legislation: The Revision of Taft-Hartley in 1953–1954." *Lab. Hist.* 6, no. 2 (1965): 143.

Pope, James Gray. "How American Workers Lost the Right to Strike, and Other Tales." *Mich. L. Rev.* 103, no. 3 (2004): 518.

Quach, Michelle. "The *Janus* Decision and the Future of Private Sector Unionism." *Hastings Bus. L.J.* 16, no. 1 (2020): 119.

Raskin, A. H. "Management's Hard Line: 'Class War' or Labor's Chance to Reform?" *Monthly Lab. Rev.* 102, no. 2 (1979): 34–36.

Reder, M. W. "Job Scarcity and the Nature of Union Power." *Indus. & Lab. Rel. Rev.* 13, no. 3 (1960): 361.

Reinhardt, Stephen R. "The Demise of Habeas Corpus and the Rise of Qualified Immunity." *Mich. L. Rev.* 113, no. 7 (2015): 1219.

Reuther, Walter. "The United Automobile Workers: Past, Present, and Future." *Va. L. Rev.* 50, no. 1 (1964): 58.

Richardson, Charley. "The Role of Technology in Undermining Union Strength." In *Restoring the Promise of American Labor Law*, edited by Sheldon Friedman et al. Ithaca, NY: ILR Press, 1994: 233.

Rogers, Brishen. "Employment Rights in the Platform Economy: Getting Back to Basics." *Harv. L. & Pol'y Rev.* 10 (2016): 479.

Rogers, Joel. "Reforming U.S. Labor Relations." In *Restoring the Promise of American Labor Law*, edited by Sheldon Friedman et al. Ithaca, NY: ILR Press, 1994.

Rosenfarb, Joseph. *The National Labor Policy*. New York: Harper & Bros., 1940.

Rosenfeld, Jake. *What Unions No Longer Do*. Cambridge, MA: Harvard University Press, 2014.

Sachs, Benjamin I. "Despite Preemption: Making Labor Law in Cities and States." *Harv. L. Rev.* 124 (2011): 1153.

Sachs, Benjamin I. "Labor Law Renewal." *Harv. L. & Pol'y Rev.* 1 (2007): 375.

Sampson, William. *Trial of the Journeyman Cordwainers of the City of New York*. New York: L. Riley, 1810.

Sayles, Leonard R., and George Strauss. *The Local Union: Its Place in the Industrial Plant*. New York: Harper & Bros., 1953.

Sayre, Francis B. "Criminal Conspiracy." *Harv. L. Rev.* 35, no. 4 (1922): 393.

Shapiro, J. Peter, and James F. Tune. "Implied Contract Rights to Job Security." *Stan. L. Rev.* 26, no. 2 (1974): 335.

Shaw, Megan Stater. "'Connote No Evil': Judicial Treatment of the Secondary Boycott before Taft-Hartley." *N.Y.U. L. Rev.* 96 (2021): 334.

Silverman, Scott. "The Impact of Recent NLRB Decisions on Supervisory Status." *Lab. Law.* 23, no. 1 (2007): 11.

Smith, Hedrick. *Who Stole the American Dream?* New York: Random House, 2012.

Sprague, Robert "Updating Legal Norms for a Precarious Workforce." *ABA J. Lab. & Emp. L.* 35 (2020): 85.

Stone, Katherine V. W. *From Widgets to Digits: Employment Regulation for the Changing Workplace*. New York: Cambridge University Press, 2004.

Summers, Clyde. "American Legislation for Union Democracy." *Mod L. Rev.* 25, no. 3 (1962): 273.

Summers, Clyde. "Individual Protection against Unjust Dismissal: Time for a Statute." *Va. L Rev.* 62, no. 3 (1976): 481.

Summers, Clyde. "Industrial Democracy: America's Unfulfilled Promise." *Clev. St. L. Rev.* 28, no. 1 (1979): 29.

Summers, Clyde. "Internal Relations between Trade Unions and Their Members." *Intl. Lab. Rev.* 91 (1965): 175.

Summers, Clyde, and Harry H. Wellington. *Labor Law: Cases and Materials*. Washington, DC: Foundation Press, 1968.

Taft, Philip. "Internal Affairs of Union and the Taft-Hartley Act." *Indus. & Lab. Rel. Rev.* 11, no. 3 (1958): 352.

Taschereau-Dumouchel, Mathieu. "The Union Threat." *Rev. of Econ. Stud.* 87, no. 6 (2020): 2859.

Tyler, Gus. "The Role of Trade Unions in a Democratic Society." *N.Y.U. Ann. Conf. on Lab.* 14 (1961): 277.

Ulman, Lloyd. *The Rise of the National Trade Union*. Cambridge, MA: Harvard University Press, 1955.

US Bureau of Labor Statistics. "What Happened to Temps? Changes since the Great Recession." *Monthly Lab. Rev.* (February 2021). https://www.bls.gov/opub/mlr/2021/article/temp-help.htm#:~:text=Temps%20grew%20by%2075%20percent,employment%20change%20of%2019%20percent.

Van Wagtendonk, James. "Is There an Employer in the House? Evaluating the National Labor Relations Board's Joint-Employer Standard in the Fissured Health Care Workplace." *B. U. L. Rev.* 98, no. 4 (2018): 1105.

Vogel, David. *Fluctuating Fortunes: The Political Power of Business in America*. New York: Basic Books, 1989.

Warner, Savannah. "Employers Now Liable for Acts of Sub-contractors." *Corp. Couns. Rev.* 38 (2019): 161.

Weaver, Julia H. "Two Sides of the Same Coin: Examining the Misclassification of Workers as Independent Contractors." *Ga. L. Rev.* 55, no. 3 (2021): 1355.

Weil, David. *The Fissured Workplace: Why Work Became So Bad for So Many and What Can Be Done to Improve It*. Cambridge, MA: Harvard University Press, 2014.

Weil, David. "Understanding the Present and Future of Work in the Fissured Workplace Context." *RSF: The Russell Sage Foundation J. Soc. Sciences* 5, no. 5 (2019): 147.

Weiler, Paul C. *Governing the Workplace: The Future of Labor and Employment Law*. Cambridge, MA: Harvard University Press, 1990.

Weiler, Paul C. "A Principled Reshaping of Labor Law for the Twenty-First Century." *U. Pa. J. Lab. & Emp. L.* 3, no. 2 (2001): 177.

Weiler, Paul. "Promises to Keep: Securing Workers' Rights to Self-organization under the NLRA." *Harv. L. Rev.* 96, no. 8 (1983): 1769.

Wellington, Harry H. *Labor and the Legal Process*. New Haven, CT: Yale University Press, 1968.

Wellington, Harry H. "Union Democracy and Fair Representation: Federal Responsibility in a Federal System." *Yale L. J.* 67, no. 8 (1958): 1327.

White, Ahmed "Its Own Dubious Battle: The Impossible Defense of an Effective Right to Strike." *Wis. L. Rev.* 1261 (2018): 1065.

White, Richard. *The Republic for Which It Stands: The United States during Reconstruction and the Gilded Age, 1865–1896*. New York: Oxford University Press, 2017.

Windham, Lane. *Knocking on Labor's Door: Union Organizing in the 1970s and the Roots of a New Economic Divide*. Chapel Hill: University of North Carolina Press, 2017.

Witte, Edwin E. "Early American Labor Cases." *Yale L. J.* 35, no. 7 (1926): 825–837.

Index

Page numbers in **bold** refer to tables.